Care of the Canine Athlete

Lowri Davies BVSc Dip ACVSMR MRCVS CCRP

First published in 2018 by First Stone Publishing, an imprint of Westline Publishing Limited

The Old Hen House, St Martin's Farm, Zeals, Warminster BA12 6NZ, United Kingdom

ISBN 9781910488492

Cover and interior design: Stubbs Design

Printed by Printworks Global Ltd., London & Hong Kong

1 2 3 4 5 6 7 8 9 0

The publishers would like to thank Angharad Gwenter Photography and Anne-Marie Waugh.
With special thanks to Charlotte Harding and 'Scandal'.

Line drawings taken from *Hills Atlas of Clinical Anatomy* (C. Hills)

CONTENTS

Chapter One:

EVOLUTION OF THE CANINE ATHLETE

Over the millenia, today's dog has evolved from its common ancestor the wolf. The twin necessity of feeding and maintaining territory drove the wolf's movement or locomotion, neither of which are issues for the modern dog. Domestication has brought about numerous changes in both structure and behaviour.

THE DOMESTICATED DOG

Skull shape has changed as has the dental array. A reduction in the production of the stress hormone, cortisol, has occurred through domestication. At the same time, serotonin – the feel good hormone – has increased, potentially facilitating domestication and increasing trainability. The reproductive system has also changed significantly; the modern dog is on heat more often, produces more offspring and reaches sexual maturity earlier than its wild ancestors. The timing of heats has also lost any link with the seasons of the year.

The other major change is the lengthening of the sensitisation period; the time at which a dog becomes receptive to stimuli starts earlier and continues for longer *(M. Fischer, Dogs in Motion, 2011)*. As domestication progressed, the dog's ability to understand and respond to verbal cues and signals increased; it is estimated that today's Border Collie understands more than 500 commands.

DOG BREEDS

The term 'dog breed' was coined in the United Kingdom in the mid 19th century, reflecting the growing recognition of desirable traits within

The conformation and movement of wolves - distant ancestors of the domesticated dog - was dictated by the need to survive, and hold territory, in the wild.

The Greyhound: Built for speed.

The Mastiff: Built for strength.

a population of dogs and the practice of specifically breeding for those traits. In this way, dog breeds became definable not by their own characteristics but by human whimsy. Thus, dogs of the same breed can look very dissimilar whilst dogs of different breeds can look very similar. Consider the working Border Collie versus the show standard – they are very different in appearance, temperament and physical performance. As a result of genetic adaptations over the centuries, working Border Collies retain sufficient predatory behaviour to control livestock – but without the killer instinct. The trainability of a Border Collie is also dependent on the ability to stop this predatory behaviour on command *(C. Price, Collie Psychology, 2013)*.

Different types of dogs, used for different purposes, have been around for over 4000 years. Dogs were initially selected for the work that they undertook, with no regard for appearance. It was only in the 19th century when Breed Standards were formalised that form and function took a separate path. The majority of today's dogs are fairly young in genetic terms. Only two distinct groups exist alongside the 'young' breeds, namely a group of Asian breeds and the Basenji *(M. Fischer, Dogs in Motion, 2011)*.

In terms of body type, some dogs have retained the same ratio of wither height to limb length whilst others, such as the Poodle and the Dachshund, are completely morphologically different. Large dogs have certain advantages; their proportionally smaller surface area to bodyweight ratio means that they conserve energy and are more efficient in their movement pattern.

One of the most obvious evolutionary divides facilitated some dogs to be built for speed and others for strength. Speed and strength characteristics confer anatomical differences in the skull and pelvis and in the cross sectional area of the long bones. Dogs built for speed, such as the Greyhound, are generally long and thin in the body and tend to distribute their weight in a 60:40 ratio between the fore and hindlimbs. This allows the legs to pendulum freely, propelling the dog by using the maximum possible range of motion for their limb joints. Dogs built for strength such as the Mastiff have a completely different, more rounded outline, wider, thicker skulls, a barrel-like ribcage and much more rounded limb bones.

GAIT PATTERNS

The best athlete is the one who will cover the ground using the minimal amount of effort for the maximum amount of power. This requires an efficient gait pattern which, in turn, is determined by the orientation of the skeleton and the activation and adaptations of the muscles which move the bony levers. During movement, dogs adopt different patterns or gaits: walk, trot, canter and gallop.

A gait is defined as a regularly repeating sequence of limb movement and each gait will have its own pattern of limb sequencing. This is composed of a stance phase when the foot is on the ground and a swing phase when the limb is in the air.

Stride Length: This is the distance covered by the dog between 2 consecutive touchdowns of the same limb.

Stance Phase: This is the weight-bearing component of the stride. During early stance, the dog's body is behind the limb and the forces are directed towards slowing the movement down or braking. As the body moves over the limb into caudal stance, the forces become propulsive and serve to accelerate the body forward.

Swing phase: This is the flight phase of the stride.

The walk, trot and pace are symmetrical gaits, with limbs on both sides of the body following the same rhythm and pattern of movement. The canter and gallop are asymmetric gaits.

THE WALK

The walk is the slowest canine gait and as such requires significant muscle effort to stabilise the joints. In the walk, the gait starts with the hindlimb and is followed by a forelimb on the same side. Normally, the hind paw should fall just in front of where the front paw was during its recent stance phase. The hind paw falls just in front of the front paw on the same side. The walk is the only gait where three feet are on the ground at once.

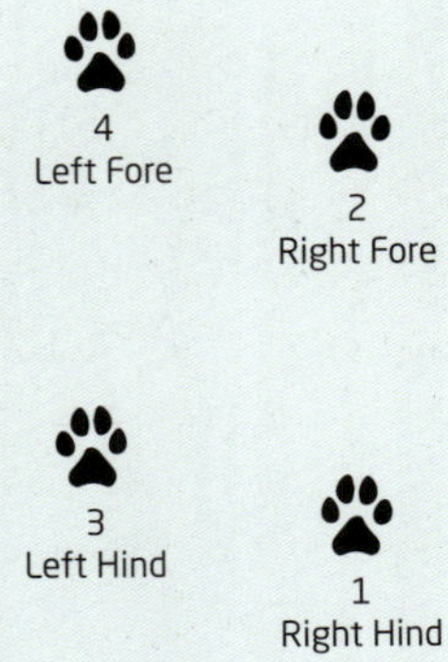

The walk.

THE TROT

The trot is again a symmetrical gait with a diagonal footfall pattern. The diagonal pairs will move alternatively: right front/left hind (RF/LH) and left hind/ right front (LF/RH). There is a brief period of time when the dog is suspended after each diagonal pair lifts off and before the other pair makes contact. The hindleg should naturally fall into the footfall of the front leg on the same side.

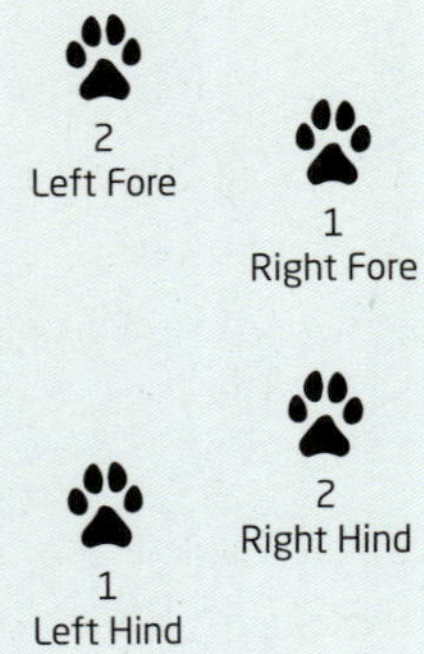

The trot.

The trot is an extremely efficient gait in a sound dog with the diagonal limb pairs swinging freely from under the body in such a way that the front leg comes forward well in front of the body and the rear limb swings all the way back with the hip fully extended.

Dogs trot with a symmetrical gait.

THE CANTER

Dogs have two movement options in the canter: the rotary or the transverse canter In general they adopt the rotary canter.

In the canter, the leading leg is always the last forelimb and hindlimb to strike the ground as it lands furthest forward. In the rotary canter, a different lead leg is adopted in the forelimbs and hind limbs. The rotary canter results in a rolling gait as the pair of limbs on one side of the body swing out to propel the dog forward.

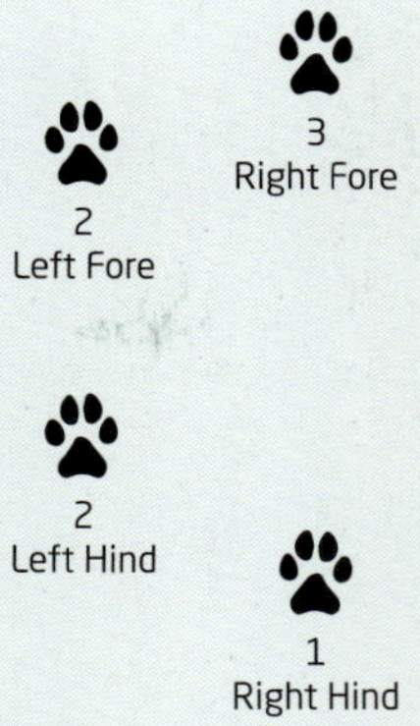

Rotary canter.

In the transverse canter, the dog will use the same lead leg in the front and rear limbs. The transverse canter is also the canter pattern adopted by the horse.

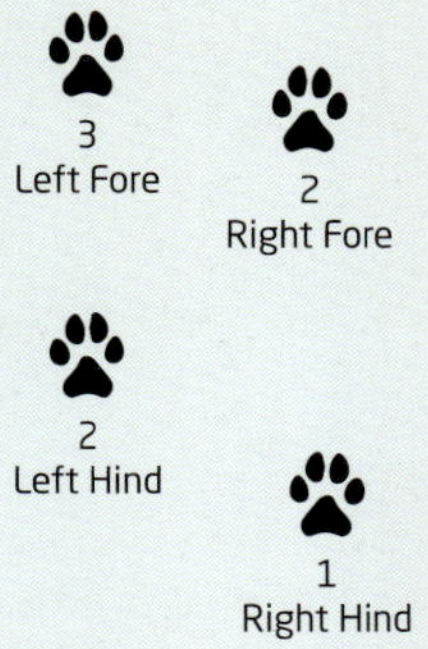

Transverse canter.

When turning – regardless of whether the rotary or transverse canter has been adopted – the lead leg will always be placed in the direction of the turn, i.e. when turning right, it will be the right fore as lead, and when turning left, it will be the left fore as lead. This allows the dog to swing the lead leg out of the turn and pull himself through the turn.

THE GALLOP

The gallop is an asymmetrical gait with the two forelimb pair and hindlimb pairs touching down one after the other. The gallop has two flight phases where no limbs are in contact with the ground. This allows the back to contribute to the stride.

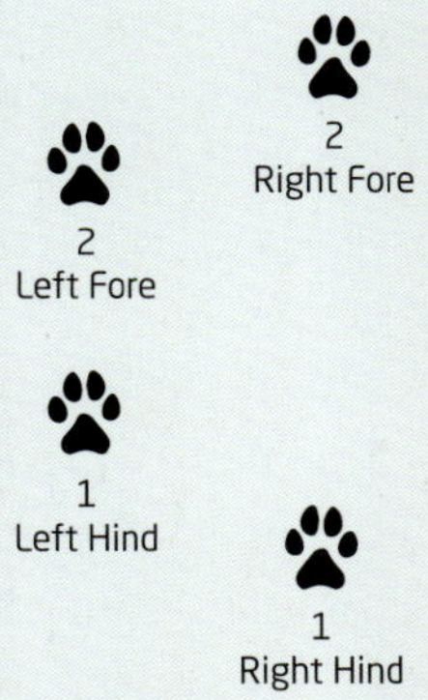

The gallop.

The first flight phase happens after the front legs have left the ground, at this point the spine flexes, bringing the back legs forward in front of the front legs. After the hind legs have struck the ground and pushed off again, there is a second flight phase where the dog extends through the back. In general, the dog uses different lead legs in the front and back when galloping.

THE PACE

Some dogs adopt the pace when walking or trotting. In the pace the pairs of limbs on the same side of the body are moved forward together, i.e. left hind and left fore and then right hind and right fore. Since the dog's centre of gravity moves from side to side, the dog appears to roll forwards when adopting the pace.

The pace is very inefficient in terms of energy of movement as more effort is required to stabilise the body. It makes turning very difficult and also reduces the dog's ability to move smoothly between different gaits. Often the pace is associated with an underlying problem in the musculoskeletal system such as back or joint pain.

In the gallop, there is a phase when there is no contact with the ground.

When standing, the German Shepherd bears more weight on the forelimbs.

HOW DOGS MOVE

Movement depends on an interaction between the body's neural, muscular and skeletal system. It is a balance between stability and movement which is dependent on feedback from the environment. This occurs through sensory receptors in the limbs and trunk, input from the eyes and from the vestibular system of the ear.

The system is completely dynamic with continuous adjustments of posture, balance, centre of mass and gravity and alternating levels of stiffness allowing the dog to remain upright in the face of external environmental forces. Pain or stiffness, in even a small part of the locomotor system, can affect this balance and result in an inability to move efficiently.

Irrespective of breed, when the dog is standing or walking, there is an unequal distribution of bodyweight between fore and hindlimbs. For example when a German Shepherd Dog is at rest, each forelimb bears 38 per cent of body weight and each hindlimb bears 19 per cent. At the walk, forelimb weight distribution is approximately 60:40 front to back. These forces increase with the speed of travel in order to accelerate the body forwards and are approximately 80 per cent higher at the trot than at the walk. At certain points in the stride, more than the total bodyweight is borne by each forelimb. This increases to more than twice the bodyweight at the gallop, so it is no wonder that high levels of athletic activity result in a tremendous amount of strain on body tissues.

In most breeds the forelimbs exert the most force (50 per cent higher than the hindlimbs); the faster the speed of travel, the shorter the stance time and therefore the greater the peak vertical force placed through each limb as the bodyweight stays the same.

Moving uphill shifts the dog's centre of gravity back while moving downhill moves it forward. Under normal circumstances this unequal weight distribution results in the forelimbs being primarily used for braking and the hindlimbs for propulsion.

A movement cycle in the dog starts with a backwards movement of the limb during the stance phase, then its protraction during the flight phase. Through various neural pathways, dogs must coordinate movement of the fore and hindlimbs, and of the right and left side of the body.

Young dogs have a very loose or rolling gait and often struggle to sequence their fore and hindlimbs, particularly in novel situations such as stair climbing or when encountering different surfaces for the first time. This can generate significant fear in the face of new challenges and should not be misinterpreted as the dog being difficult. Under some circumstances, this lack of body control can lead to fear aggression.

We often assume that dogs are born knowing how to walk, but this is not true. Movement is a learnt behaviour and develops in response to training. The gait starts to mature at around six months of age, but this is largely dependent on the challenges that the young dog encounters. Puppies that are exposed to many different terrains will develop quicker than those limited to walking on flat, uniform surfaces.

The linking of muscles and joints into a movement pattern is known as a kinetic chain. Each activity will have its own kinetic chain, e.g. trotting, jumping, weaving. One of the aspects of training is to establish connections between the nervous system and the muscles. This allows the correct muscle to be activated in order to move the joints in the correct sequence and at the correct speed.

This type of training requires frequent repetitions at low intensity, preferably on a daily basis. In general it takes 4-6 weeks to teach a young dog to trot consistently. This can be achieved through placing 8-10 poles on the ground in a parallel array and spaced approximately one body length apart. The poles will encourage the dog to pick up his limbs in a rhythmical fashion. The dog should be moved over the poles for short repeating sessions (1-2 minutes) at a time. Once this exercise is easily achieved, different height and width configurations can be introduced to intensify the challenge.

CONFORMATION

Joint angulation and muscle fibre type play a significant role in a dog's athletic potential and in determining the sport that will suit them best. Conformation describes the symmetry, size and shape of various body regions relative to each

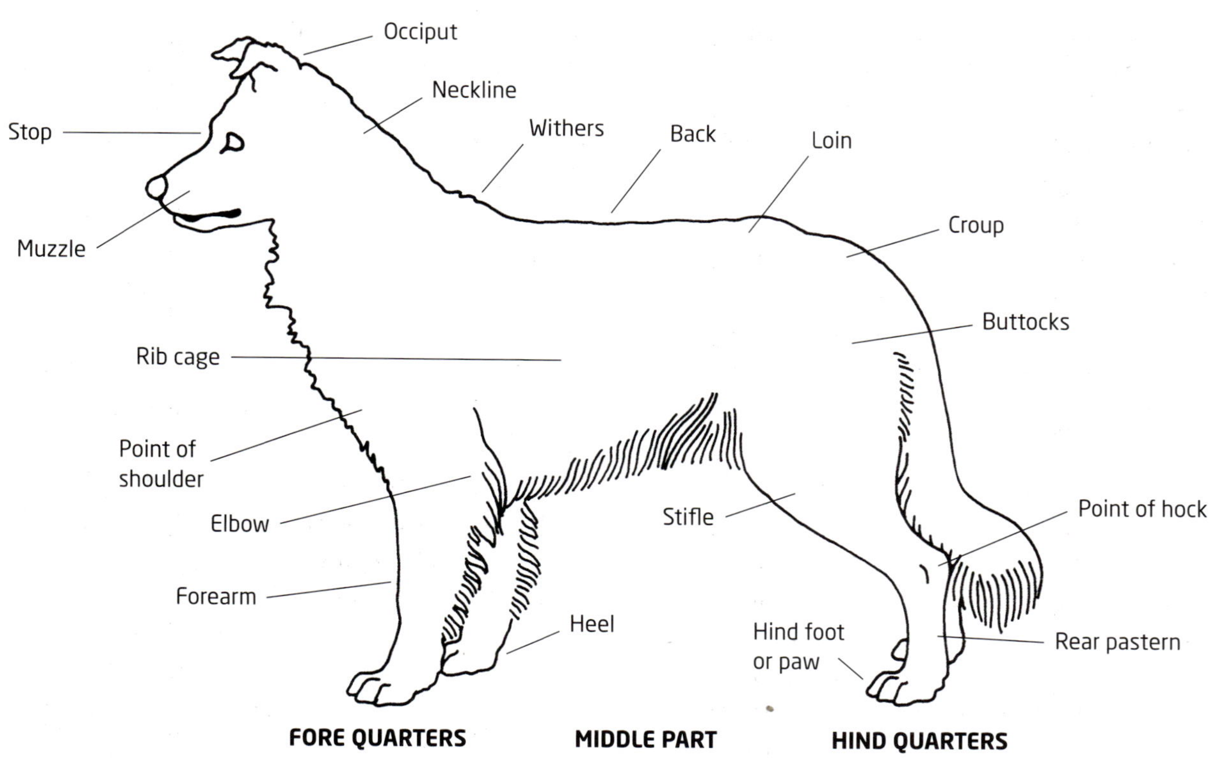

Points of Anatomy.

The skeleton

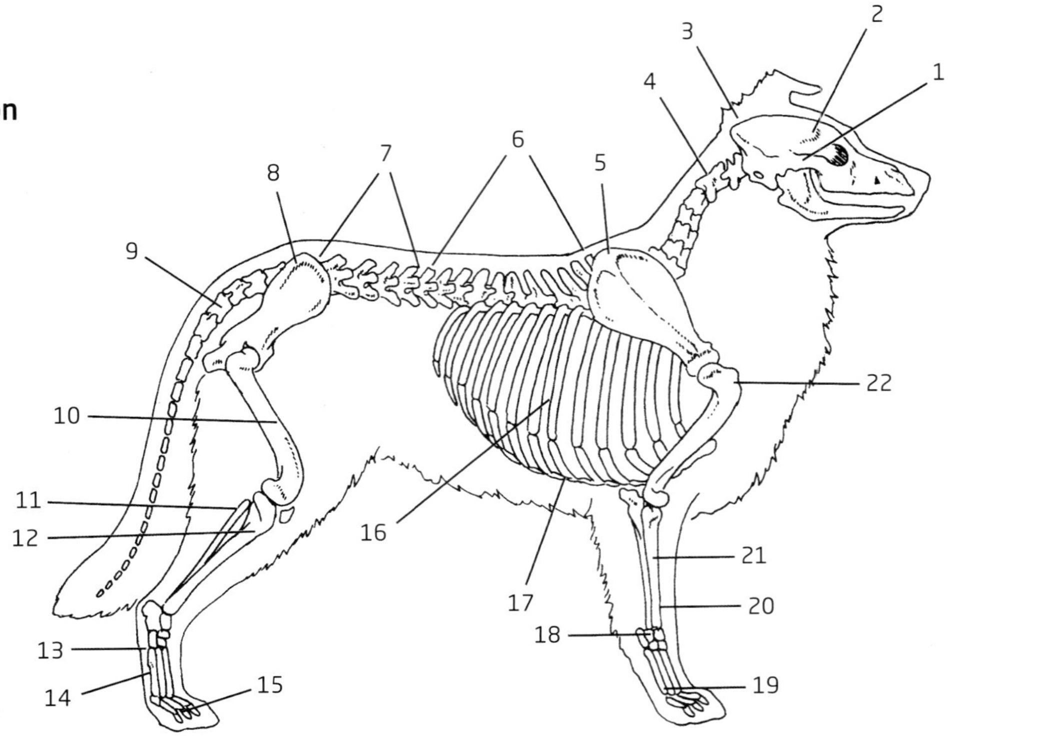

1. Zygomatic arch
2. Cranium
3. Occipital bone
4. Cervical vertebrae
5. Scapula
6. Thoracic vertebrae
7. Lumbar vertebrae
8. Illium (pelvis)
9. Coccygeal vertebrae
10. Femur
11. Fibula
12. Tibia
13. Tarsal bones (hock)
14. Metatarsal bones (hind pastern)
15. Phalanges
16. Ribs
17. Sternum
18. Carpal bones
19. Metacarpal bones (pastern)
20. Radius
21. Ulna
22. Humerus

other. Poor conformation or design can predispose to injury and often results in an abnormal gait.

Forelimb conformation is generally assessed in terms of the scapula angle from the vertical and the length of the humerus. The angle of the scapula can be assessed with the dog standing and the forearm perpendicular to the ground and the head and neck elevated as demonstrated.

Scapula angulation is determined by the bisection of a line drawn from the top of the scapula (shoulder blade) to the greater tubercle of humerus, and a second line drawn from the ground to the greater tubercle of bony landmark on humerus – the humerus. This angle should ideally be around 30 degrees. A good scapula angle allows the dog to extend the forelimb and take longer steps with each stride, thus conserving energy. It also reduces the concussion of the shoulder joint when jumping.

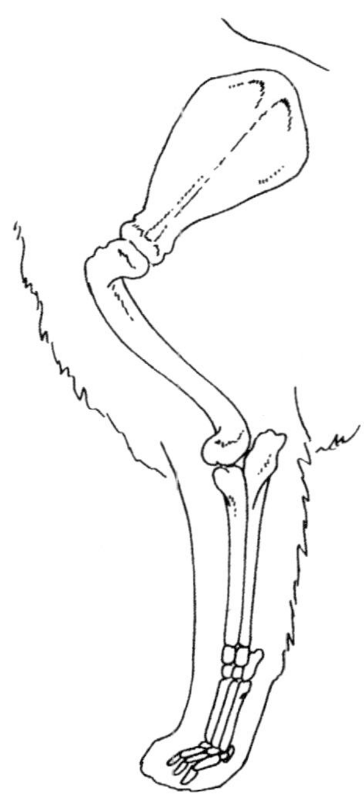

Correct angle of shoulder and upper arm.

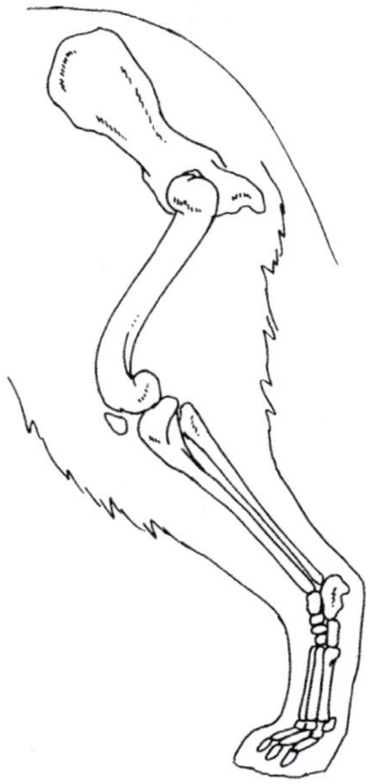

Correct rear angulation.

The second forelimb variable is the length of the humerus. A short humerus results in the forearm being positioned forward and as a consequence the whole forelimb becomes more upright in nature. Ideally the humerus should be of sufficient length to position the forearm under the body, allowing the shoulder to flex a little and maintaining the biceps muscle and triceps muscle at the optimum resting length. This, in turn, reduces the concussive forces on the legs.

In the hindlimb, differences in conformation contribute to different rear angulation angles. Some individuals will have a very upright hindlimb profile, with the hock placed in line with the back of the pelvis. In others, with plenty of hindlimb angulation, the hock is placed well back from the rear of the pelvis.

It is postulated that less angulation allows the dog to be more accurate with hindlimb placement, thus enabling tight, sharp turns. More angulation, on the other hand, allows for a longer stride length and more efficient movement. However, it also increases the challenge for the nervous system and the hindlimb musculature to control the hind legs.

MUSCLE FUNCTION

During movement, muscles have one of two functions: they can either facilitate or prevent movement, i.e. provide stability. Prevention of movement is essential to keep the body upright against the force of gravity as happens during the stance phase of the stride. At the end of the stance phase muscles must then bend or flex the limb in order to move it forward. A muscle can either actively contract or be passively stretched. Injury will impair both of these abilities.

Movement is not just dependent on the muscles of the fore and hindlimbs, but also on the muscles of the back. At slower gaits, the back muscles are involved in bending and stabilising the back – creating a strong core. At faster gaits, the back muscles are actively involved in flexing and extending the spine in synchrony with the distal limb movement. Back pain inhibits core muscle function and leads to loss of stability. This, in turn, prevents the legs from moving freely and leads to loss of balance and flexibility.

Forelimb muscles

The main forelimb muscles involved in stabilisation and movement can be divided into three groups:

1. The first group are active during the stance phase of the stride, i.e., during weight-bearing and are concerned with stabilising the limb and therefore the dog against the force of gravity. These muscles are:

Infraspinatus
Triceps
Extensor carpi ulnaris
Flexor Carpi ulnaris

Collectively they extend the limb and keep it relatively straight. They are also known as anti-gravity muscles and play an important role in stabilising the joint. They are influential in proprioception (an awareness of where the limbs are placed, and the strength required for movement) and continuously adjust in tension when the dog moves over uneven terrain.

2. As the body travels forward over the limbs, a second group of muscles are activated, these are:

Pectoral muscle
Teres major muscle
Deltoid muscle
Flexor carpi radialis

The primary role of these muscles is to start bringing the leg backwards, and to start the process

The muscle groups

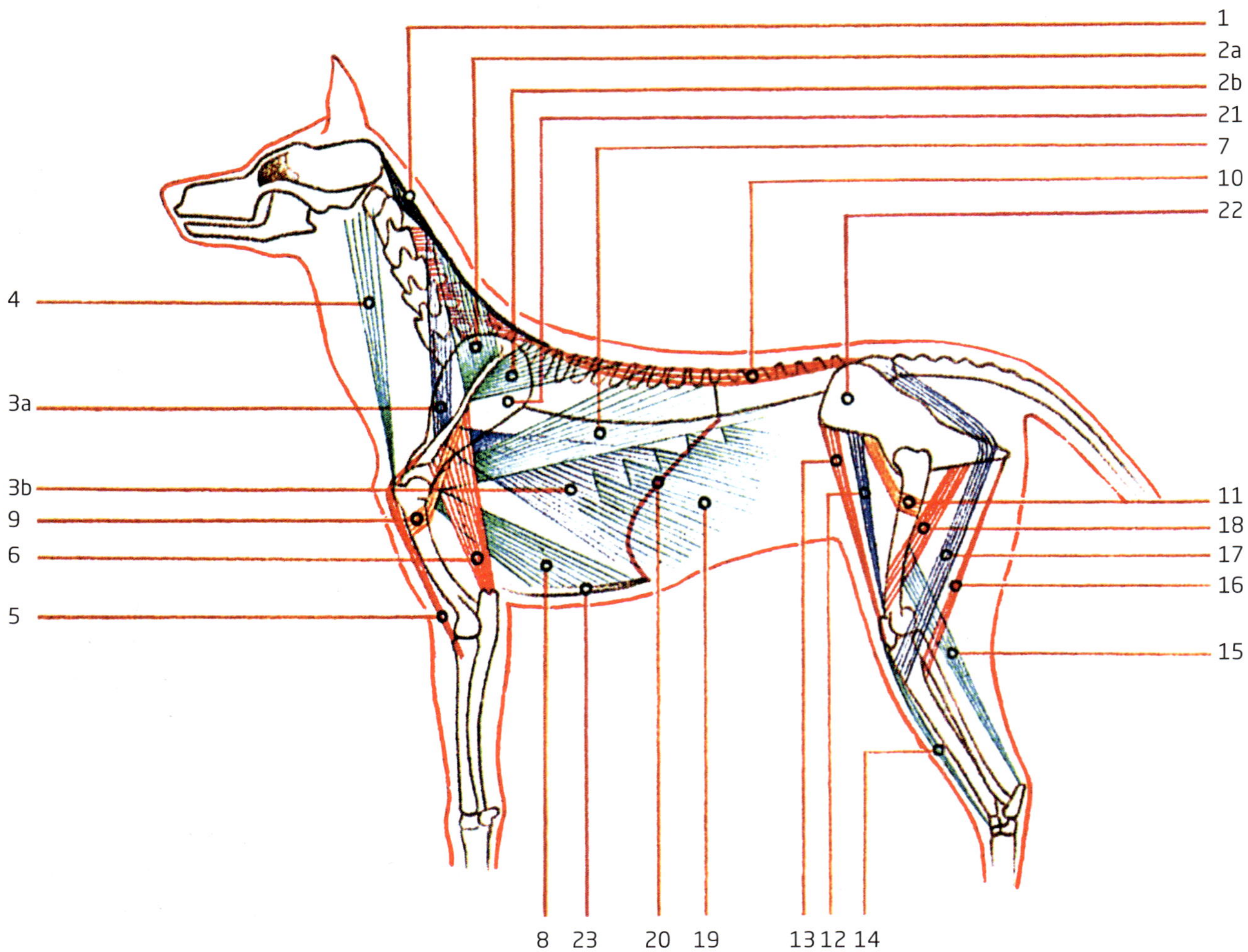

1. Nuchal ligament (Ligamentum nuchae)
2. Top shoulder muscle, trapezius muscle (musculus trapezius) [in green]
3. Undermost shoulder muscle (musculus serratus) [in blue]
4. Head-neck-arm muscle (musculus brachiocephalicus) [in green]
5. Flexors of the elbow joint (musculus biceps brachii) [in red]
6. Extensors of the elbow joint (musculus triceps brachii) [in red]
7. Wide back muscle, (musculus latissimus dorsi) [in green]
8. Breast muscle (musculus pectoralis) [in green]
9. Deltoid muscle (musculus deltoideus) [in orange]
10. Long back muscle (musculus longissimus) [in orange]
11. Flexors of the hip joint [in orange]
12. Extensors of the thigh [in blue]
13. Extensors of the knee joint [in red]
14. Flexors of the ankle joint [in green]
15. Extensors of the ankle joint musculus gastrocnemius) [in green]
16. Flexors of the knee joint (musculus biceps femoris) [in red]

17-18. Sprint muscles, musculus semitendinosus

19. Slant abdominal muscle [in green]
20. Diaphragm
21. Shoulder blade (scapula)
22. Hip bone (pelvis)
23. Breast bone (sternum)

of bending or flexing the limb in preparation for the forward swing of the forelimb.

3. The third group of muscles are active throughout stance and are again primarily involved in stabilising the limb. These include:

Serratus ventralis
Supraspinatus
Deltoid
Biceps brachi
Digital flexors

The biceps brachi plays a crucial role in moving the limb forward. It flexes the elbow, extends the shoulders and facilitates the forward swing of the forelimb. The brachiocephalicus is another important shoulder flexor while the brachialis assists with shoulder flexion. During the trot and the gallop, these muscles have to work at a much higher level.

Hindlimb muscles

In the hindlimb, three muscle groups are again responsible for protraction and retraction of the limb:

1. Hindlimb retraction, and therefore propulsion, is primarily dominated by the hamstring. Thus any shortening or discomfort in this muscle group will significantly affect athletic activity.

2. The hamstrings are assisted in this role by the gluteal muscles:

Biceps femoris
Semitendinosus
Semimembranosus
Superficial, middle and deep gluteal

Running uphill significantly increases the work of these muscles – a 10 per cent gradient can increase the workload by 20 per cent.

3. Hindlimb retraction is largely dependent on hip joint extension. Muscles which extend the stifle also contribute to retraction of the hindlimb. These include the:

Gracillis
Semitendinous
Semimembranosus
Biceps femoris

The most important muscles during the swing phase include the:

Quadriceps – rectus femoris, vastus
Illiopsoas
Tensor fascia lata
Sartorius

WHAT HAPPENS WHEN A DOG JUMPS?

Jumping can be separated into three distinct components: the take off, the suspended phase and the landing. During take off, the hindlimb muscles provide the propulsive forces, in suspension the back muscles, pelvic floor muscles and abdominals stabilise the trunk. The suspensory muscles of the trunk assist with lifting the forequarters and, together with the forelimbs, absorb the forces on landing.

Regardless of breed or size, all dogs jump using the same sequence of movements:

- As a dog approaches a jump, the front feet are placed, one slightly ahead of the other, at a take off spot. A number of factors interact to determine the take off point, including: speed, height of jump, weight/height ratio of dog, ground conditions, fitness and conditioning, experience and athletic ability.
- As the front feet come into position, the forelimbs flex and the head is lowered. At the same time, the spine is flexed as the hindlegs move forward under the body to a position slightly in front of the front feet.
- During propulsion, both front and hind legs extend to lift the body up and at the same time, the head lifts and the neck extends. The fore and hindlimbs should now be fully stretched.
- Once suspended, increased activation of the back, trunk, chest and pelvic muscles help to keep the body in a relatively flat, neutral alignment without excessive upward or downward arching of the back. This also allows the legs to move through their full range of movement. Lack of stability in the back will lead to premature flexing of the limbs and less efficient aerodynamics. This, in turn, predisposes to injury.
- At the top of the arc, the dog should lower his head and lift his tail to help rotate the body forward and downward.

Jumping involves three distinct components: take off, suspended phase, and landing.

- During the landing phase, the forelimbs stretch out towards the ground.
- Dogs land with one front foot after the other. The main braking force occurs in the second limb whilst most of the weight is taken through the first limb to contact the ground. The rear legs are then pulled forward under the body and help absorb some of the impact of landing. They then push the dog forward into the next stride.

To jump successfully, a dog needs to raise his centre of gravity high enough in order that limbs and trunk clear the jump. The ability to raise the centre of gravity is influenced again by conformation, training, athletic ability and injury. Movement is made easier by the ability of muscles and tendons to stretch and store energy as potential energy before releasing it as elastic energy when they contract or actively stretch. In this way, the muscle and tendons behave like springs. Without this ability the energy cost of movement would be much, much higher.

During ground impact, the body stores energy and then releases it back during propulsion. The heel hits the ground first and the fatty-fibrous configuration of the pads help absorb the impact. The dog then rolls over the toes which provide an important contribution to the flight phase as they help spring the dog forwards. Although the extensor muscles (the muscles which straighten the legs out) activate as the fore and hind limbs hit the ground, the force of gravity – and all the forces of movement – are so great as to cause the hip, stifle and hock to flex or bend in early stance. This action helps to cushion the impact from landing.

The forelimb performs slightly differently, particularly at the level of the carpal joint which, on impact, can undergo extreme extension and in rare cases will contact the ground before propelling the limb forwards.

The first forelimb to contact the ground on landing sustains the greatest peak vertical force. The second forelimb is predominantly involved with braking. Both are dependent on appropriate muscle recruitment and efficiency of the muscle tendon unit. The angulation of the forelimb will, in part, determine the efficiency of the shock absorbing properties of the regional musculature.

A dog with greater angulation can absorb the impact of landing better than a dog with a straighter front assembly. This is because greater angulation allows the dog an imperceptibly longer period of time for the muscles to slow the impact, while the bones and tendons behave like springs, folding up then straightening out again. *(Lanting F. Front and Rear Angulation in the Working Dog, 2008).*

Vertebrate animals exploit the elastic properties of their tendons in several different ways.

Firstly, metabolic energy can be saved in locomotion if tendons stretch and then recoil, storing and returning elastic strain energy, as the animal loses and regains kinetic energy. Leg tendons save energy in this way when birds and mammals run, and an aponeurosis (layers of flat, broad tendons) in the back is also important in galloping mammals.

Secondly, tendons can recoil elastically much faster than muscles can shorten, enabling animals to jump further than they otherwise could.

Thirdly, tendon elasticity affects the control of muscles, enhancing force control at the expense of position control. *(R.M. Alexander; Tendon Elasticity and Muscle Function, 2002).*

Height to weight ratio can have a significant impact on a dog's suitability for agility. Proportionally, heavier dogs in relation to their height require more effort during movement. This, in turn, increases the stress on their body tissues and energy sources. In a table of weight:height ratios by breed, Zink and Daniels, (Jumping from A to Z, 2005) showed that weight increases at a faster rate than height therefore making it difficult to find parity between jumping height and wither height in dogs. This data would suggest that proportionately, larger dogs should jump smaller heights to reduce the risk of injury.

Zink and Daniels conclude that dogs with a weight/height ratio of greater than 4 are in the danger zone for jumping and should be trained very carefully. Those in the 2.5 to 4 range are more efficient and less injury prone while those with a ratio of less than 2.5 are likely to be the most successful.

Another structural factor is body length in relation to height. Dogs that are significantly

Ratio of weight to height

Breed (typical measurements)	Weight (lbs)	Height (ins)	Ratio
Australian Shepherd	42	20	2.1
Basset Hound	45	11	4.1
Border Collie	37	20	1.9
Doberman	78	26	3.0
GSD	74	25	3.0
Golden Retriever	74	24	3.1
Great Dane	150	31	4.8
Labrador	64	23	2.8
Papillon	7	11	0.6
Pembroke Corgi	30	12	2.5
Sheltie	22	15	1.5

The Basset Hound's weight to height ratio puts him at an obvious disadvantage when it comes to jumping.

longer than they are tall bear more weight on their front legs and are therefore disadvantaged.

Finally we must consider leg length: the longer the forearm, the higher the centre of gravity. Flexion of the shoulder and elbow are critical in allowing the dog to clear the jump. Successful jumping depends on dynamic stability, i.e., the dog's ability to move through the air like a gymnast. It relies on core strength, flexibility, full range of motion of the limb joints, efficient aerodynamics and a high level of muscle function in terms of aerobic and anaerobic activity, as well as its shock absorbing capacity. Premature lifting of the head and neck will force the centre of gravity back and result in early ground contact with the hindlimbs. This can have a knock on effect on the dog's ability to move off quickly after landing.

As with any sport, participation predisposes to injury. There is a very narrow margin between peak performance and injury. As will be discussed later, sporting injuries fall into one of two main categories, acute trauma and repeated strain, with the latter being the most common cause of injury in agility dogs. Lack of fitness or conditioning, weight management issues as well as sports specific issues such as two-on/two-off contacts, vertical forelimb landing posture, overextension and repetitive maneuvers such as tight turning all predispose to injury.

Peak vertical forces in the forelimb can be as great as four times the bodyweight when landing. Although body tissues adapt to the strain placed upon them, they only do so if the rate of damage is balanced by the rate of repair. Over-focusing on jumping at the expense of conditioning can therefore lead to common injuries such as biceps tendonitis and medial compartment disease of the elbow. The peak vertical forces increase significantly with jump height and speed. The dog's bodyweight and breed also influences the vertical ground reaction forces. Statistical analysis of the effect of weight on force shows that heavier dogs impact with greater force at each jump height.

ALL IN THE MIND

The desire to win or succeed is an essential component of any athlete; it is what pushes them to train in all weathers, to repeat the same manoeuvre time after time, even when it hurts, and to try and perform better or faster than any other competitor. Without this mental toughness, no athlete can succeed. The same is true for our canine athletes. Border Collies were born to chase and just like humans, high levels of exercise release endorphins.

As a consequence, dogs get addicted to exercise in exactly the same way that humans do. While this can be harnessed in sports such as agility and flyball, unrestrained it can lead to the chasing of vehicles, people or other livestock and may include nipping and herding behaviour. Not all dogs – including Collies – are born with this high drive, however, and these individuals can provide a significant challenge in terms of motivation and trainability.

A good athlete will generally demonstrate obsessive behaviour to a greater or lesser degree. They are prepared to work or train for long periods of time, often in the face of injury to achieve their goal. This obsessive behavior, in moderation, is a desirable trait in the canine athlete. Without it, dogs may tire of training or sour very quickly. Inappropriately handled, however, it can quickly spiral out of control and contribute to other issues such as fear or aggression.

Over-stimulation on the part of the handler can lead to an escalating cycle of manic behaviour and self-stimulation in high drive dogs and should be avoided. It takes away a dog's ability to think clearly or rest. In the same way as walking must be taught to the young puppy, a balanced state of mind must also be trained for. A calm dog requires a calm handler.

Dogs respond as much to our body language as they do to our voice. Therefore, the handler should aim to move slowly and calmly at all times whilst trying to give clear signals. When a dog does not respond to the question, the handler should always ask themselves what they have done wrong – rather than just immediately blaming the dog.

Often the handler's tone of voice and body language has given out mixed messages and the dog is confused and uncertain how to respond most appropriately, rather than choosing to ignore or failing to co-operate. Many training issues and progression to injury have their roots in poor communication between athlete and trainer. This may be a failure to spot when the athlete has either not been trained appropriately, been pushed too hard, or is simply not suitable for the sport.

References

Price C., *Collie Psychology*, 2013, www.performancedog.co.uk

Alexander R.M., *Tendon Elasticity and Muscle Function*, 2002

Lanting F., *Front and Rear Angulation in the Working Dog*, 2008, www.fredlanting.org

Zink & Daniels, *Jumping from A to Z*, 2005, Canine Sports Productions, Ellicott City, MD.

Fischer M., *Dogs in Motion*, 2011, www.performancedog.co.uk

Chapter Two:

HOW TO MAKE AN ATHLETE

The early stages of a puppy's development, both mentally and physically, are hugely influential in later life. This chapter will consider the pup's development from birth to maturity, looking at how emotional and physical development are linked, and how to provide an environment that will be most likely to produce a confident, well-adjusted juvenile.

PRE-CONCEPTION AND GENETIC COUNSELLING

Genetic counselling, which enables people to explore the possibility of passing on potential genetic defects is now widely available, most particularly in the USA. Compared with the research carried out on valuable racehorses or syndicated bulls, this is a relatively recent phenomenon, and in less valuable animals, such as dogs, it is in its infancy.

It is estimated that in the USA, 1 in 4 domestic dogs has a serious genetic disease. It is often a moral question as to whether breeding should take place between affected individuals. This is most relevant in dogs with a known genetic problem which may influence their soundness or their potential to breed.

Predisposition to joint dysplasias, for example, is a significant problem that can be passed on by defective genes. Diseases of this type are often influenced by multiple genes, which makes it difficult to develop specific genetic tests. Developmental anomalies such as elbow dysplasia and hip dysplasia are also influenced by the dog's

Despite rigorous safeguards, there can never be total certainty as to how a puppy will turn out.

environment. It is much easier to trace the genetic origins of diseases such as progressive retinal atrophy (PRA) and haemophilia because a low number of genes are involved.

At this time, we do not have a wide network of canine genetics counsellors. However, by analysing the available information we can start to make more ethical choices for future generations of dog. The ideal situation would be for vets and breeders to work together to develop breeding programmes. One way of approaching mate selection is to base it exclusively on conformation and appearance, which fails to give consideration to the temperament or health status of puppies. The other extreme is to set culling levels for traits, for example excluding all animals with less than perfect hips from a breeding programme. However, this gives very little room for flexibility and is not always practical when there are so many factors to consider when breeding.

There is a misconception that mixed breed animals are immune to genetic defects. It is also worth acknowledging that the 'perfect dog' does not exist, so there is an element of chance and magic as to how each and every puppy will develop.

INDEX SCHEMES FOR BREEDING

The application of selection index schemes is considered to be the best means of gaining a reasonably objective measure of an individual dog's suitability for breeding. Schemes may vary, but the same scheme must be applied to the same group of dogs for this to be effective. For example, in working stock, 50 points may be assigned for health, 30 for conformation and 20 for behaviour. There would be specific detailed criteria for scoring and the highest scored individuals would be selected for breeding.

HIP SCORING AND ELBOW SCORING

A study of American assistance dogs showed that those who had decent joint health throughout life were more likely to have a high proportion of littermates with joints in a similar condition. Therefore, littermate joint health is more of a determinant for long-term quality mobility than the joint health of parents, grandparents and great-grandparents. However in practical terms, we do not have a crystal ball so cannot access this information before we select a puppy and take it home. That is why we rely on hip and elbow scoring.

The more heritable a trait, the easier it is to breed out the defective gene. It takes longer and is more challenging in polygenic traits such as hip dysplasia and elbow dysplasia. It is also interesting to note that when we are breeding for genetic superiority, the average pup will improve – but this does not apply to every pup in the litter. That is why a dog may have hip dysplasia even though the parents had low hip scores.

Historically, there has always been a lot of secrecy surrounding genetics and breeding. For a better future, it is essential to provide open registers where both positive and negative genetic information is available.

KEY EMBRYOLOGY

There are key components to look for as the embryo develops which could have long-term influence on the canine athlete.

BONE DEVELOPMENT

Bones lengthen from specific areas of growth known as growth plates which are located at either end of the limb bones. Growth also develops in the very end of the bones, known as the epiphysis. The growth plates in young dogs are very fragile and can be damaged by high impact injury which compresses the growth plate and stops the growth. They are also common areas of fracture in young dogs.

In the canine foetus the developing bones are soft and made of cartilage. After birth, the soft cartilage becomes calcified apart from at the growth plates which makes them prone to injury. The bones do not continue to grow indefinitely; at predetermined times the growth plates close and no further change in bone length can occur. Early growth plate closure can predispose the dog to orthopaedic disease, such as joint disease and twisting of the limbs otherwise known as angular limb deformities. It is therefore extremely important to make sure that when the growth plates are open, a pup does not engage in repetitive high impact work, such as jumping, which could cause serious damage.

Growth plate closure of the long bones

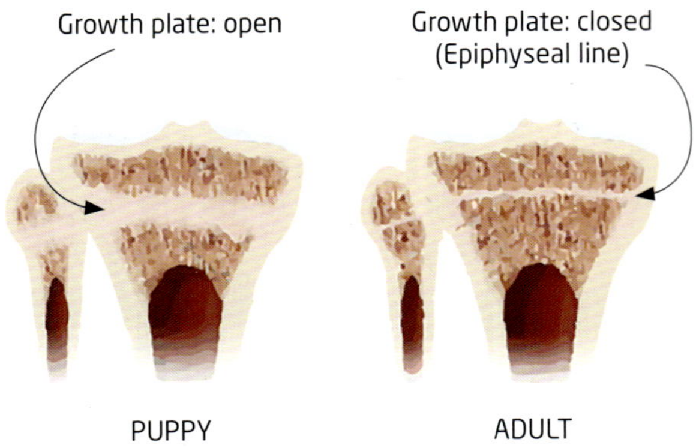

Growth plates.

completes in most dogs between 12 and 14 months. However, this may take up to 18 months in giant breed dogs.

EFFECTS OF FOETAL POSITION ON LATER LIFE

People often question as to why certain dogs develop subtle imbalances with their mobility. Perhaps their back is less flexible in one direction, or perhaps they are prone to injury in one particular limb. Since function governs form, the activities and possible impacts that these dogs undertake from birth will also have an effect.

There is also a hypothesis that the position that the pup adopts in the uterus may be influential in the development of musculoskeletal anomalies. It is thought that this is governed by the bio-electrical (or piezo-electric current or charge within the bone) qualities of developing bone and muscle.

THE BIRTHING PROCESS

The birthing process may also affect the puppy's musculoskeletal system. Normal presentation is either cranial (with both front feet and head coming together), or caudal (with both hind feet coming together). Cranial presentation takes place in 60 per cent of births and leads to a quicker birth due to engagement of the pup's head in the cervix which stimulates the birth canal.

Dystocia means there is a problem with birthing. The most common cause is uterine inertia of the bitch when the uterus does not contract with sufficient frequency or strength to expel the puppies. The other cause is puppy mal-presentation when a puppy is incorrectly positioned so is not able to pass through the birth canal.

If mal-presentation is found to be the cause there are several different abnormal foetal positions:

- **Transverse:** The puppy lies on his flank with all 4 feet presenting simultaneously.
- **Breach:** The tail and backside present first.
- **Lateral or ventral deviation of the head**

As you can imagine, in the case of a mal-presentation, repetitive straining against the entrance of the birth canal will cause significant compressive forces to musculoskeletal systems that are already incorrectly aligned.

Manual correction of incorrect birthing position should only be attempted by a vet, and should only be attempted if the dystocia is mild and the puppy is a normal size. Huge quantities of sterile water-based lubricant are required and small fingers are beneficial. The use of excessive force, or tools such as forceps, should be avoided as this will lead to trauma to limbs, the spine and the skull.

It is recognised in human osteopathy that those babies presenting in the breach position (bottom first) often have sacral (lower back) pain. There is also a theory that this backwards presentation produces a milking effect of fluid back towards the head end. This, in turn, has compressive effects on the neck and skull.

OUR INFLUENCE

There are a number of medical interventions that we routinely undertake which, again, may affect a dog's ability to reach his full potential as an athlete.

VACCINATION

In recent years, evidence based medicine has become an important concept in both human medical and veterinary fields. It is an ethos of making clinical decisions based on the evidence available. Accordingly, the Vaccination Guidelines Group of the World Small Animal Veterinary Association has developed a set of guidelines concerning the use of core vaccines.

The three life-threatening diseases implicated are distemper, adenovirus and parvovirus. The recommendation of the group is for puppies to receive multiple core vaccines with the final one being administered at 16 weeks or over. In

The timing of vaccination should tie in with key socialisation periods.

cases where economics do not allow for multiple vaccination, it is acceptable to have one single dose above the age of 16 weeks. A booster vaccination can be given between 6 and 12 months subsequently.

The best practice recommended by the group is to blood test the dog for antibody levels one month or more following the initial puppy vaccination programme. If the antibody test is positive (within reference range), core vaccines can be repeated no sooner than three years later. If the test is negative (below reference range), vaccination should be repeated as should serum testing. A small number of dogs are non-responders, but this is not within the scope of this chapter. It is possible that lifelong immunity is provided with the initial course of vaccines.

The time of puppy vaccination often corresponds to the key socialisation window (8 weeks to 4 months). Often pet owners are advised to avoid contact with the outside world until seven days after the second vaccination, which would mean missing out on a vital period of socialisation. A sensible approach is to wait until the pup has had his first injection and then allow him to interact with dogs who have been vaccinated, and to meet people in a variety of different situations. However areas such as parks, which are severely contaminated, should be avoided, as the disease challenge may be very high.

Non-core vaccines are those that pose a risk to groups of dogs in a certain geographical situations or in particular circumstances. Leptospirosis is classified as a non-core disease in the UK. Immunity following vaccination lasts for a matter of months and this will often be repeated yearly in the UK. Parainfluenza is another non-core vaccine.

Individual vaccination needs should always be discussed with your veterinarian.

NEUTERING

The issue of neutering dogs is becoming more and more contentious with on-going research in the field. Neutering has some obvious health benefits to the reproductive system, for example, it significantly reduces the likelihood of developing mammary tumours or pyometra (uterine infection) in the bitch. In the veterinary community, it is widely accepted that neutering (spaying) should take place before 2.5 years of age. In male dogs the chances of developing prostate disease and testicular cancer are reduced greatly by neutering (castrating). The most interesting question is: when should we neuter? There is a strong argument not to neuter early, i.e. before sexual maturity.

A research study carried out in 1991 showed that those bitches spayed at seven months grew a lot taller than those not spayed. Sex hormones communicate with growth hormones at the time of puberty to close growth plates. If the release of sex hormones is not possible because of the removal of the gonads (sex glands) when neutering, these dogs' limbs will be longer and lighter, with lower bone density. This may lead to increased probability of injuries such as cruciate rupture. Another study has shown that bitches spayed before 5 months of age were more likely to develop hip dysplasia. A further study found there was an increased chance of uterine incontinence in later life for those bitches spayed before their first season.

Obviously there are significant health benefits that come from neutering, but I would suggest that neutering should be delayed in sports dogs until 14 months or over when the growth plates have closed. Note that growth plate closure may be later in giant breeds.

From a performance perspective, male dogs have the benefit of testosterone which aids muscular development and strength. This is another reason to wait until maturity, particularly if there is a question over potential inherited musculoskeletal diseases.

Spay via laparoscopy

This is a relatively new procedure which is showing excellent results. A laparoscope, which is a fibre-optic imaging probe with a light-source, is placed into the abdomen of the bitch through a tiny incision in the mid-line of her abdomen. Instruments are inserted through another tiny incision. In this way, ligation and removal of the ovaries can take place while being watched on an enlarged screen in the operating theatre.

The equipment is expensive and surgeons performing this procedure are usually specialists in soft tissue surgery, so it is not widely available. However, veterinary medicine is a private system so this can be sought if desired.

The benefits are less post-operative pain in the long term (though some dogs can experience a lot of pain in the first 24 hours), faster recovery times and a smaller wound. Less interference with the abdominal wall means that abdominal and core function are less disrupted and the chance of developing soft tissue adhesions, which can affect flexibility for athletes, is reduced.

This technique is slightly more expensive than the traditional technique and cannot be carried out in obese patients, those who are very small, those with a septic abdomen or a diaphragmatic hernia.

EARLY PUPPY DEVELOPMENT

A newborn puppy is unable to look after itself. In the first few weeks of life, critical changes are occurring in the nervous system and brain growth is a significant part of this development. Over-stimulation or lack of stimulation in the first 6 to 8 weeks of life could have long term effects.

THE NERVOUS SYSTEM

The mental landscape of a dog is determined by genetics and development. Development has been found to occur in a succession of phases, although there is considerable overlap between these phases:

SENSITIVE PERIODS

Animal behaviourist, Dr Joel Dehasse has observed that during 'sensitive periods', a small number of experiences can have major effects on a dog's future behaviour. It is a time of emotional, sensory and social growth. Sensitive periods are preceded and followed by a period of lower sensitivity. A puppy's sensitive period is thought to be between 3 weeks and 3 months.

Pre-birth

The offspring of a mother who has been stroked and patted throughout pregnancy show a greater acceptance of touching than pups born of a mother who did not receive such attention.

Neonatal period

The first stage of development is the 'neonatal phase'. This lasts from birth to approximately 13 days of age. In this phase pups are completely dependent; their main behaviours are heat and milk seeking. Human interaction can have little influence on their long-term mental state at this time.

After this phase, gentle handling can have positive effects on relaxation and digestion and play an important role in the puppy's ability to form emotional attachments.

Identification phase

Following the neonatal phase, the identification phase is when a puppy learns to recognise himself and his counterparts as being canine. It takes place from 2.5-3.5 weeks until 11-17 weeks. This has the more global function of ensuring survival of the species by giving the pup the tools to build social, sexual and familial bonds throughout life. Play fighting is an important part of this phase. At 17 weeks, fighting behaviour becomes somewhat more serious.

During this process of play fighting, puppies learn to develop boundaries as their littermates respond to a painful bite by crying out and then inflicting a similar bite. These simple behaviours teach empathy and bite control. If owners allow pups to keep biting without helping to establish such boundaries, it may lay foundations for dominant behaviour. The play-fighting phase is much shorter in stressed animals, for example, feral canines. Encouraging a puppy to pull on objects with his mouth can reinforce the bite strength.

Neonatal: In the first days, human interaction has no lasting impact on a puppy's development.

Identification: Play fighting between littermates develops during this phase.

Socialisation-domestication: Interactions with people are crucial at 3-4 weeks.

Homeostasis: A stimulating environment is key to establishing emotional equilibrium.

Precocious learning condition: Puppies learn to relieve themselves away from the sleeping/eating area.

Weaning detachment: By 7 weeks, puppies have become emotionally detached from their mother and are eating independently.

If dogs are not exposed to their own species between 3 and 12 (+/– 5 weeks), they may imprint on another species. There is also the possibility that they may reject their own species later on.

Socialisation-domestication phase

During this phase the dog is able to form a relationship with another species, significantly human beings. The concurrent phase of species identification allows this to happen. At around 3 weeks, puppies display investigatory behaviours towards the unknown. This tendency decreases at 5 to 9 weeks. At 14 weeks, they show no interest in exploring another novel species.

If human interaction occurs at the correct juncture, it is easy to acquire canine-human social relationships but this needs to be repeated to avoid desocialisation. Without this, the development of predatory behaviour may become a possibility.

Puppies who are well socialised tend to leap forward to greet humans. This confident type of puppy is more likely to assert himself over other dogs later on in life.

Homeostasis phase

This is when a puppy establishes emotional equilibrium. The presence of a stimulating environment is key in this process. If lacking in stimuli, puppies will subsequently respond to new situations with fear and anxiety. A puppy that is under-stimulated may develop hyper-attachment to his owner and become prone to behavioural syndromes such as separation anxiety. Exposure to a varied stimulating environment for all the senses will also make the pup more adaptable to new situations in later life.

Think about the soundscape as well as the tactile and visual environment for a puppy. Exposure to children, male and female humans, dogs of different shapes and sizes, and a variety of different species if possible, will be very beneficial.

Tactile stimulus can come in the form of walking on a wide variety of surfaces, stroking and tickling the belly and limbs and altering body position, e.g. turning the puppy upside down.

Lack of environmental stimulation in early life can lead to abnormally high activity levels in the adult due to over-excitement. Learning new skills may also be very challenging.

The key time for this phase is from 2.5-3.5 weeks until 10-14 weeks.

The precocious learning-conditioning phase

This phase relates to elimination, it starts at 2.5-3.5 weeks and lasts until 10-14 weeks. This is the stage when defecation, eating and vocalisation behaviours develop. In the first 2 weeks of life, elimination is facilitated by the dam licking the perineal area. At 2-3 weeks this becomes spontaneous. After 3 weeks the puppy leaves the sleeping area to defecate and by 8.5 weeks the puppy is defecating in specific spots away from the sleeping and eating area.

For young pups acquired at 7-9 weeks, a suitable defecation medium (e.g. paper towelling), environment or area should be provided 2-3 metres away from the sleep and eat area. It may be worth varying this so the pup does not become too attached to one defecation medium.

It is possible that puppies develop food preferences and aversions during this phase according to choices made by their mother or carer. To avoid this it is a good idea to expose the puppies to different foods.

A key mistake, made by many owners, is to respond to vocalisation when a pup is left alone at night for the first time. If a puppy is first left at around 7 weeks, this behaviour will subside after a few days. If vocalisation triggers a response from his human family, such as contact to comfort or even to shout at the puppy, the behaviour has been positively reinforced by attention, and is likely to continue.

Weaning-detachment and food hierarchical phase

Pups are highly attached to their mother at 3 weeks. At 5 weeks the mother starts to growl at attempted nursing and the puppy tends to roll away in a submissive posture. The presence of the mother at this age is useful for the development of appeasement rituals and helps with the development of, and ability to establish, social hierarchy.

At 7 weeks the bitch has detached from puppy feeding behaviour and is passive in allowing puppies access to solid food. There is a possibility

Salter Harris classification of growth plate fractures in juvenile dogs.

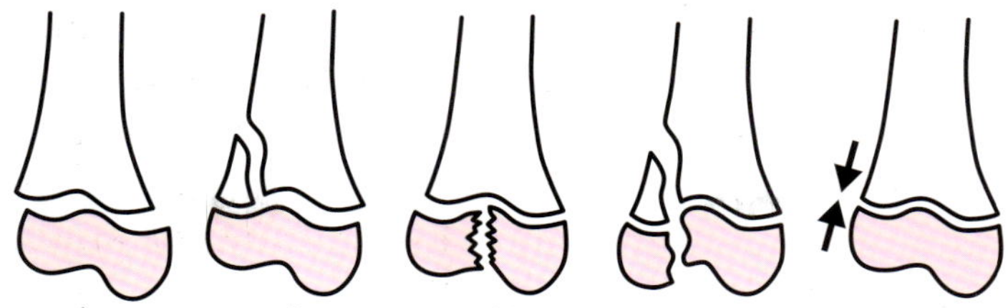

that the human need to give and receive attention can create a hyper-attached state around feeding.

At 16 weeks, the puppy will normally be in his new human family. He is now ready to establish and recognise a pecking order so it is important that a sensible feeding ritual is developed.

This section has focused on emotional development from 3 weeks up to 17 weeks of age. In most cases, cognitive development is in its most sensitive from 5-18 months. During this time further awareness of hierarchy and territory takes place, and more rational thought processes develop.

In order to integrate with the human family or multi-species environment, and to maintain mental wellbeing, a puppy needs to be exposed to environmental enrichment. This comes in the form of handling, inter-canine relationships, human-canine relationships and novel circumstances from birth well into adolescence.

PHYSICAL CONSIDERATIONS

Puppies are not small dogs. Up to 12 months of age, their body systems – muscles, heart, lungs, nervous, digestive – are continuously evolving. A pup can be compared to a blank canvas and the experiences of life are the brushstrokes on the canvas. Each encounter is a different brush stroke and determines whether a good or a bad picture is painted.

Some experiences are positive, for example, short periods of controlled exercise on an interesting surface will help develop normal joints, strong bones and muscles. In contrast, repetitive ball play can lead to focused wear and tear, pain and abnormal development of the joints, muscles and bones. Obviously, this must be considered when designing an exercise programme for a puppy.

GROWTH PLATES

As already discussed, growth plates do not close until 14 months of age on average. It is extremely important to avoid intense training until the growth plates have closed to avoid trauma and even potential fracture. If the growth plate is damaged, it may close early leading to a malformed or shortened limb.

Because the growth plates are so soft while growing, an impact that would cause a ligament strain in an adult could cause a growth plate fracture in a younger dog. This can be caused by one single blow or from repeated strain. That is why jumping and weaving should be delayed until growth plates are closed. Such stresses on the joints from over-training too young may not become apparent in a young dog but may manifest as a career ending spinal problem at 6 to 7 years of age. If a young dog becomes lame, he needs to be checked by a vet immediately.

The larger the dog, the later the growth plates close. It would therefore be safer to avoid high impact work in a breed such as the Great Dane until 18 months of age.

CARDIOVASCULAR ABILITY

Efficient exercise depends on two main factors: the ability to deliver blood to the lungs for oxygenation, and the ability to bring oxygen in to the lungs. The former is dependent on the cardiovascular system and the latter on the respiratory system.

In young puppies, neither system is as well developed as in the adult and, therefore, their ability to exercise for either long periods of time or at high intensity is impaired.

In human adults, aerobic training (training in the presence of oxygen) aimed at improving cardiovascular function can bring about a 30 per cent improvement in endurance parameters. In comparison, only 10 per cent improvement is possible in children showing that a pre-pubescent individual is less well equipped to adapt to the challenge of long distance running.

This can be extrapolated to dogs. Long distance running puts excessive strain on young dogs and increases the rate of injury. It should therefore be undertaken with care and caution.

THERMOREGULATION

Another important factor in exercise is the ability to control body heat. Racing Greyhounds, for example, will increase their body temperature from a resting temperature of 38.5° C to 42° C in a 30-second race. Puppies are less able to regulate their body temperature. Therefore, they are more prone to overheating (hyperthermia) with activity, or losing body temperature very quickly (hypothermia). Their high surface area to body mass ratio means that their body temperature can drop very quickly in a cold environment, particularly if it is windy.

Muscles, tendons and ligaments are also prone to cold injury in immature dogs. In the cold they become stiffer and less elastic and thus more prone to injury. This can be easily prevented by a five-minute warm up.

COORDINATION

Young animals are less coordinated and body aware. Learning to walk and to place the limbs is a skill that has to be learnt. Technically this is known as motor control and proprioception. Think of three year old children who fall on their knees several times a day, and of the range of gaits we see in the pavement outside secondary schools.

Lack of control and awareness of limb placement can contribute to injury. A well thought out exercise regime can help with developing the skill of walking and should be considered an essential part of a pup's development.

THE POWER OF PLAY

Play is an important part of a puppy's development and will contribute to the fulfillment of an individual's full potential. The same is seen in humans and other species; 'burn-out' or chronic fatigue are possible outcomes for young athletes who

The canine brain

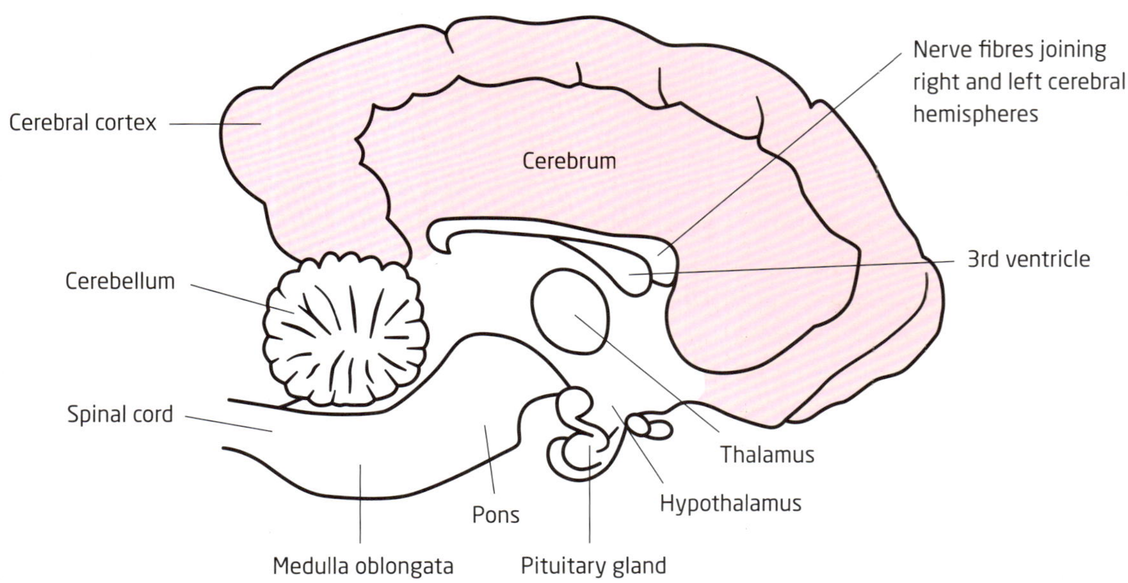

simply don't have enough fun. The old saying 'all work and no play makes Jack a dull boy' rings true.

To look into this in more depth, an understanding of the function of various parts of the brain is useful.

The cerebellum is the part of the brain that controls movement and cognitive function. Studies have shown a direct correlation between access to play in animals and growth of the cerebellum.

The pre-frontal cortex is the part of the brain which controls emotions and attention. It may also be referred to as the 'mind'. This may help with motivation and focus in agility training and competing, and in the ability to understand complicated tasks. The more animals play, the bigger the pre-frontal cortex.

In a study, young rats were deprived of play, and they responded as if their pre-frontal cortex was damaged. When presented with a cat smell, they went into hiding. Rather than starting to come out of hiding after a period of time, they remained in hiding and went into decline.

AVOIDING BRAIN OVERLOAD

Training is most effective when performed 'little and often'. It is also important to include plenty of play – it is well documented that play forms the foundation of learning skills in both children and animals.

Electroencephalograms, which measure electrical activity in the brain, are comparable in seven-week-old puppies and adult dogs. This shows us that the amount of information processed in pups of this age, and above, is similar to adults. However, puppies are energy rich but experience poor. Their young brains are unaware of which pieces of information they need to respond to for survival, and which pieces of information can be ignored. This is why 'brain overload' can happen so easily. It's often useful to take a step back with your puppy and to remember that with age comes experience. It's a skill to balance the eagerness of the puppy to participate with the possibility of getting brain and body overload.

THE POWER OF TOUCH

There is so much written about the power of touch; nurturing contact is important for mental and emotional development and for wellbeing. It also has a beneficial effect on general health, including improved sleep quality and enhanced immune function.

With a puppy, touch could be in the form of stroking, tummy tickling, grooming or massage. It also helps with body awareness and reinforces the bond between puppy and owner. Being accustomed to touch will also make him more accepting of handling and veterinary examinations in later life. It is a good idea to have a gentle look into your dog's ears, eyes and teeth (perhaps even brushing the teeth) to reduce stress levels during these, and similar procedures in later life. If possible, foot touching and stroking should be also be included, as this will make nail clipping easier.

TRAINING PROGRAMMES FOR YOUNG DOGS

In young dogs, training must be undertaken with extreme care; their growth plates are open, their muscles are weak, their endurance is poor and their mental capacity for concentration is short. All of these factors make it extremely easy to over train and ruin a young dog very quickly. Perhaps the easiest mistake to make is to assume that the hyperactive pup remains full of energy and needs more exercise when, actually, the opposite is true.

Hyperactivity in a young dog is often a sign of tiredness, both physical and mental. When he does not have the ability to control his movement and emotions, he can become stressed with a potential increase in adrenalin release which 'hypes' him further. This type of behaviour can form a vicious cycle, with the pup never relaxing properly. This pattern can become a habit that continues into adulthood.

There is a strong correlation between body balance and control. If the pup is in pain or unable to control his movements, e.g. when meeting a slippery surface for the first time, he will naturally be a little scared. This often leads to a stiffening of the body which, in turn, makes him less balanced and stable. This situation can be approached in two ways:

- The pup can be forced to walk over the surface, in which case he will learn very little and be even more fearful next time.

- The handler can take time to teach the pup how to approach a difficult surface, breaking it down to small challenges, e.g. encouraging the pup to stand on the slippery surface and giving him a treat, then performing a head turn on the surface, and then moving forward for one or two steps. At this point, the pup is likely to be tired and should be taken away from the challenge. The next time it meets the surface, the first experience can be built upon and 5 or 6 steps can be accomplished with the pup gaining confidence at each stride. Pups learn quickly, and generally by the third encounter he will handle the surface confidently.

When designing an exercise programme for puppies it is essential that it is balanced in terms of:

- Body awareness/proprioception.
- Balance and flexibility.
- Endurance.
- Strength.
- Power.

The programme should result in:

- Skilled walking.
- Balanced development of the musculoskeletal and neurological system.

In addition it should:

- Prevent wear and tear of joints.
- Train focus and concentration.

For comprehensive fitness training, it is useful to break it down into different categories: strength, endurance, proprioception, core training and skills training.

STRENGTH

Strength is defined as the ability of a structure to withstand force. In a sports sense, this refers to the body's capacity to support and stabilise its own mass under the influence of gravity. It also refers to the ability of the body to cope with external forces. In the human field, strength training often utilises resistance techniques.

In the case of dogs, we are not asking them to carry weight – as would be the case with a weightlifter – but we are asking them to tolerate the forces on their body that are created by gravity and speed. The direction, speed and intensity of these forces are constantly changing on the

Strength training, such as running uphill, should be conducted on a limited timescale, depending on the pup's age.

agility field. So when looking at exercises that can strengthen the dog, we have to rely on external forces, such as the terrain, to increase resistance to movement in the dog's body.

There is a subtle difference between strength and power training. Strength is the body's ability to withstand or move a load, whereas power is the rate at which this can be done. In essence it represents the dog's explosive capacity.

$$\textbf{Power} = \frac{\textbf{Force x Acceleration}}{\textbf{Time}}$$

Therefore we could say that the two main components of power are strength and speed, as power brings in the concept of movement over distance in time.

The body often uses more than its available oxygen during power tasks. This type of training is known as anaerobic (without oxygen). In a strength or power based conditioning programme there is an increase in the density of muscle fibres within a muscle, as a result both the size and strength of the muscles increase. The anaerobic ability of the individual also improves.

In the human field, power training would be seen as activities such as power lifting, weights training, or rock climbing. Agility is seen as both an anaerobic and aerobic event. Strength or power tasks within agility include jumping and accelerating towards jumps, as well as going up the dog-walk. Greyhound racing is another dog sport which is more strength or power based.

Strength and power training should be undertaken with care in the young dog as his muscles are weak and his bones are soft. It's good to let a youngster run both on the flat and uphill, but sessions should be kept short, ranging from 1-2 minutes up to 15 minutes depending on the pup's age. As the muscle gets tired, it can no longer cushion the joint. The soft nature of the developing bone/joint in a young dog can therefore be easily damaged if too much strength work is undertaken early on. For this reason, jumping either up or down should be avoided in a young dog until his growth plates have closed.

Beware: There is plenty of footage on-line of people standing their young dog on a peanut ball for minutes on end and introducing complicated routines with pods. Practices like this may well over fatigue muscles and place more strain over young joints.

Any exercise undertaken should promote the best possible alignment of bones and muscles so that all forces placed upon them are in the correct direction. This ensures that tissues develop accordingly. Exercises such as standing a dog with feet close-coupled, e.g. in a shoe-box, is not recommended as this is an abnormal posture and works the muscles and joints in an abnormal position, encouraging the tissues to remodel inappropriately.

There is a world of advice out there on exercises for your puppy. But you should always ask yourself the question: 'does this prepare my pup for the tasks he will be doing in his daily life?' If the question is 'no', then exercise caution. If you are unsure ask a vet who specialises in rehabilitation or sports medicine, or a fully qualified animal physiotherapist.

Flexibility exercises, such as head turns following a treat, can be carried out. However, care should be taken as young dogs are more flexible naturally and we do not want to over-stretch soft tissue structures or take joints through an abnormally extreme range of motion.

ENDURANCE

Endurance training develops the ability to perform at a moderately higher intensity than the physiological baseline for sustained periods of time. Long distance events are associated with endurance programmes. Events that require significant endurance or stamina include herding, field trials, canicross and husky sled events. In the human field, marathon running is an example of an endurance sport.

Endurance training may also be known as aerobic training. The activity mostly takes place within the body's ability to obtain oxygen from the atmosphere. The oxygen supplied is used in the generation of energy for muscle contraction and movement. Cardiovascular and respiratory function are important for endurance.

A puppy's endurance is poor, therefore even

5 minutes of sustained activity can represent endurance training. In the early stages, endurance training should focus on periods of controlled walking on lead with incremental increases being undertaken every week. This type of exercise is excellent for strengthening bones, muscles ligaments and tendons. It also promotes healthy joint development and the production of good quality joint fluid which nourishes and lubricates the joints.

As the pup gets older, short periods of jogging can be introduced in an interval pattern, e.g. 5 minutes walking, 2 minutes jogging, 5 minutes walking.

More strenuous endurance regimes should not be undertaken until growth plates are closed and the dog is physiologically mature at around 12-14 months of age.

PROPRIOCEPTIVE

Proprioception is a term that describes our ability to control our movement and know where we are in space. It relies on a combination of information from joint sensors, muscle sensors, visual cues and information from our vestibular system in the middle and inner ear.

Proprioceptive exercises tend to require lots of concentration, but not too much in the way of strength and endurance. Simply put, they should help brain to foot communication. Examples of suitable exercises to develop proprioception in puppies will be dealt with in more detail in Chapter 11, but examples include, learning to walk slowly over lots of different surfaces in close succession, or stepping over a series of obstacles placed on the ground in a novel pattern.

Proprioceptive exercises are designed to make you think and are therefore good for developing the nervous system and helping the pup develop concentration.

CORE

The core function comes into play in all aspects of movement. By the very nature of his shape, a tiny pup has no core strength – he just looks like a ball. However, exercises to develop the core should be instigated between 8 and 12 weeks, as he becomes leggier and leaner.

Think of the core as a box: back muscles at the top, stomach muscles at the bottom, diaphragm and chest muscles at the front, and the pelvic floor at the back. Core function is critical for efficient movement and injury prevention and is multi-factorial.

Functions performed by the core include:

- Absorbing environmental resistance.
- Spinal alignment.
- Protecting the spine (and other joints).
- Providing a foundation for correct posture.
- Stability.
- Providing intra-abdominal pressure (to support organs and assist in evacuation of bowels and bladder).
- Movement.

Teaching your puppy to sit square is an important first step in building core strength.

Teaching a youngster to walk on a narrow plank encourages balance and co-ordination which will be needed when he attempts obstacles on the agility course.

Teaching your puppy to sit square is an early and safe way to train the core. To make it harder, tap the pup over the ribcage, alternating side to side. You can progress by getting him to sit on a balance cushion. Other examples of early core training include, standing square, balance work, slow lead walking and pole stepping.

Keep it short and sweet

The key for youngsters is not to over-do it. A young dog would, generally benefit from walking up and down a ladder placed on the floor or a course of poles (approximately 5 cm high) somewhere between 5 and 10 times per day, equating to 1 minute, 2-3 times a day.

SKILLS

Skill training in youngsters should be directed at maturing or improving the quality of their walking and running and their natural balance and co-ordination. Only once this has been achieved should skill training be progressed to include sports specific tasks.

Exposure to many different textures is really useful as this sensory input to the brain will improve awareness of limb position in space. In turn this will affect the quality of the messages travelling from the brain to muscles via motor neurones. With this focus, movements can be more accurately controlled. Optimum control contributes to injury prevention.

You can be as creative as you wish with the range of surfaces. Ideally you should encourage the dog to take a few strides on each surface which can range in texture from towelling to raffia matting to rubber matting to cardboard. Slow walking over these textures for a few minutes, twice a day, is beneficial. A 20 cm wide plank on the ground can provide an interesting balance challenge.

Similarly an obstacle course is a more glamorous version of the proprioceptive road insert photo of walkway with different surfaces. Obstacles such as a tarpaulin, a puddle, a hosepipe on the ground, and a tunnel made from a cardboard box can be negotiated to further improve awareness and coordination.

Practice makes perfect

The saying 'practice makes perfect' is very apt when developing skills. Every time a new task is performed, a particular pathway of neurones is activated in the nervous system. If this action is repeated, this pathway becomes more efficient and 'programmed', and less deliberate effort is required to complete the particular task.

The most effective way to learn, keep and develop a skill is by practising that particular pattern for around 5 minutes per day. This way the molecules responsible for transmitting these messages are maintained within the nervous system. However, it is important to remember that it is just as easy to perfect an abnormal pattern of movement that can have life long consequences. Perhaps the simplest task to get wrong is walking your pup on the lead and allowing him to pull. This underuses the hind legs and increases the strain on the back and forelimbs. If this is not corrected it can result in a lifetime of abnormal movement patterns, impair hindlimb development and overload the forelimbs.

Treat each pup as an individual

Some of us are designed to be gymnasts, others sprinters and some marathon runners and, in exactly the same way, each pup is different. One size does not fit all, and exercise regimes should be tailored to the pup's physical and mental development.

TRAINING ASSESSMENT

Sometimes, despite our best efforts, puppies do not develop in a balanced, functional way. This is why assessing your dog's movement, balance and co-ordination early on is critically important. The gold standard is to have your pup professionally assessed by a vet specialising in sports medicine and rehabilitation, a qualified physiotherapist, or a veterinary physiotherapist.

If your pup's function is properly assessed, exercises can be introduced to develop essential skills or to correct imbalances. It is much easier to do this at an early stage, rather than later on when the patterns are fixed in an adult dog.

Chiropractice can also be a useful tool in ensuring that your pup is as balanced, vital and biomechanically efficient as possible. The key to seeking advice from professionals in physical therapy is to do your research so you receive the most appropriate information. Expert input can be beneficial from day one and can carry on through life. The ideal is to approach health from a holistic point of view, seeking on-going overall wellbeing and disease prevention, rather than addressing injury or illness when they occur.

References

Zink M.C., *Peak Performance. Coaching the Canine Athlete*, 2004 (ISBN 1-888119-02-0), p.61

Davidson A.P., *Genetic diseases: Diagnosis, Counselling and Control in Small Animal Medicine*, Scientific proceedings: Companion Animal Programme, European Veterinary Conference, 2007, pp.112-113

Ackerman L., *Genetic Counselling for Veterinarians*, Proceedings of the World Small Animal Veterinary Association, 2005

Day M.J., Horzinek M.C., Schultz R.D., Squires R.A., *Guidelines for Vaccination of Dogs and Cats*, 2015, World Small Animal Veterinary Association, Vaccination Guidelines Group

Zink M.C., *The Agility Advantage*, 2008 (ISBN 978-1-892694-18-8), pp.12-14, 39, 44-51

Salmeri K.L., Bloomberg M.S., Scruggs S.L., Shille V., *Gonadectomy in immature dogs: effects on skeletal, physical, and behavioural development*, JAVMA 1991, 198, pp.1193-1203

Dehasse, J. ,Sensory, *Emotional and Social Development of the Young Dog*, The Bulletin for Veterinary Clinical Ethology 1994, Vol. 2, No. 1-2, pp. 6-29

Related reading

Golden I., *Vaccination and Homoeoprophylaxis? A review of risks and alternatives*, 7th Edition, 2010 (ISBN 9780957872677)

And many thanks to...

Dr Nick Thompson BSc (Vet Sci) Hons, BVM&S, VetMFHom, Holisticvet, Bath, UK (holisticvet.co.uk)

Chapter Three:

FEEDING FOR PERFORMANCE

Peak performance can only be attained through close attention to both training and nutrition. Achieving an optimal nutritional balance ensures that the correct amount of fuel reaches the musculoskeletal system at the correct rate to sustain exercise. It appears that scant attention is paid to what we feed our athletes, with many owners failing to achieve a correct body condition score, let alone a proper nutritional balance for their dogs. The cost of getting it wrong can be very high – not only can it hinder performance, it can also lead to:

- Musculoskeletal injury.
- Immunosuppression.
- Digestive issues.
- Poor recovery from training and a failure to adapt to training.
- Poor performance.
- Poor thermoregulation.
- Dehydration.

Ideally energy demand is matched to expenditure, thus minimising large fluctuations in bodyweight. According to this principle an athlete's diet should change throughout the year depending on the amount of exercise being undertaken, which is likely to have a degree of seasonable variability.

This chapter will review the nutritional needs of the agility dog and how we can manipulate the diet in order to maximise performance and prevent injury. It will also consider how nutritional needs alter during intense training, rest and at different stages of life. The current range of neutraceutical therapy and ergogenic products will also be reviewed.

WHAT DO WE WANT FROM A DIET?

Apart from the basic requirement to meet the metabolic needs of the dog, a well-formulated ration should include the following components:

- Highly digestible and palatable.
- Low in residue.
- Enhance performance.
- Minimise injury.
- Include an Omega 3:6 balance which minimises inflammation.
- Promote a healthy gastro-intestinal tract.
- Balanced in terms of vitamins and minerals in order to sustain growth and repair all body tissues.
- Practical or easy to feed.
- Provide no risk of disease.

The type of exercise that is undertaken underpins energy requirements. The racing Greyhound will have completely different nutritional requirements to the agility dog who will have different needs to a racing sled dog.

Racing Greyhounds undertake intense anaerobic exercise for very short periods of time (30-40 seconds) and therefore mainly burn

A Greyhound races at high intensity over a short period of time.

Sled racing requires stamina and endurance.

carbohydrate during exercise (up to 70 per cent). Because their period of intense work is so short, they do not need many more calories than a normal active dog that is not involved in racing activity. On average, a Greyhound will burn around 2000 calories per day in a thermoneutral environment, i.e. one which is neither too hot nor too cold.

The racing sled dog is at the other end of the spectrum. He may cover 100 miles a day at 20 miles an hour for 10 days in a row. Such sustained aerobic exercise can only be achieved through feeding a diet that is largely composed of fat (70-80 per cent) in order to meet the energy demands of exercise which can increase to 10,000 calories a day.

In terms of exercise undertaken, the agility dog lies somewhere towards the middle of the spectrum. During an agility round, ideally the dog will be deriving energy aerobically while converting to anaerobic exercise during times of increased demand, such as jumping and powering up the A-frame. He therefore needs an efficient aerobic and anaerobic pathway, using both fat and carbohydrate, as an energy source.

Although an agility round is short, many dogs will undertake multiple runs during the day and may compete over several consecutive days. As a result their calorific demand will rise to around 3000 calories a day during intense competition, with the added difficulty of timing their feeding so as not to interfere with exercise. In general a diet that is composed of 45 per cent fat, 30 per cent protein and 25 per cent carbohydrate works well for an agility dog during intense competition.

THE ENERGY UNIT

The energy released when protein, fat and carbohydrate is metabolised is known as the calorie or joule. Gross energy is the energy released when one gram of substrate is burnt inside a scientific piece of equipment, known as a bomb calorimeter, and does not take into account the energy lost in faeces due to incomplete digestion. Digestible

The agility dog lies in the middle of the spectrum, needing speed and power, plus the ability to keep going over a number of rounds.

Metabolising energy

Substrate	Gross Energy	Metabolisable Energy
Protein	5.24kcal/g	3.5kcal/g
Fat	9.16kcal/g	8.5kcal/g
Carbohydrate	4.26kcal/g	3.5kcal/g

energy gives a slightly lower value to account for this loss. Commercial dog foods use metabolisable energy values which take into account energy lost in urine, faeces and through fermentation.

Various formulas can be used to work out a dog's energy requirements. The most accurate appears to be the exponential equation: 70(Kg body wt). In this equation, the multiplication factor of 70 is considered to be the resting energy requirement. Various multiplication factors can be inserted depending on the individual's age and activity levels.

Inactive – 132
Active – 145
Very Active – 200
Endurance – 300

This equation factors in the increased metabolic rate of a well conditioned athlete that has a much higher lean muscle mass compared to the sedentary dog. However, feeding should always be geared to body condition score; the above equation acts only as a guideline.

BODY CONDITION SCORE AND LEAN BODY MASS

In order to perform at their peak, it is essential that the canine athlete maintains a body condition score somewhere between 2-2.5/5. Any extra weight will increase the load on the distal limbs and adds to the weight that the dog has to carry around the ring – a little like the handicapping system in a horse race.

With regard to the canine athlete, body condition scoring is far more effective than absolute weight measurements, as muscle weighs more than fat and an individual can lose weight and increase body condition score by exchanging muscle for fat.

A grading system based on 1-5 or 1-9 is used to identify body condition scores:

1. Ribs, lumbar vertebrae, pelvic bones and all bony prominences evident from a distance. No discernible body fat. Obvious loss of muscle mass.
2. Ribs, lumbar vertebrae and pelvic bones easily visible. No palpable fat. Some evidence of other bony prominences. Minimal loss of muscle mass.
3. Ribs easily palpated and may be visible with no palpable fat. Tops of lumbar vertebrae visible. Pelvic bones becoming prominent. Obvious waist and abdominal tuck.
4. Ribs easily palpable, with minimal fat covering. Waist easily noted, viewed from above. Abdominal tuck evident.
5. Ribs palpable without excess fat covering. Waist observed behind ribs when viewed from above. Abdomen tucked up when viewed from side.
6. Ribs palpable with slight excess fat covering. Waist is discernible viewed from above but is not prominent. Abdominal tuck apparent.
7. Ribs palpable with difficulty; heavy fat cover. Noticeable fat deposits over lumbar area and base of tail. Waist absent or barely visible. Abdominal tuck may be present.
8. Ribs not palpable under very heavy fat cover, or palpable only with significant pressure. Heavy fat deposits over lumbar area and base of tail. Waist absent. No abdominal tuck. Obvious abdominal distention may be present.
9. Massive fat deposits over thorax, spine and base of tail. Waist and abdominal tuck absent. Fat deposits on neck and limbs. Obvious abdominal distention.

It is unlikely that an athlete will require the same calorie intake throughout the year. At times of intense training and competition calorific demands will go up while in the rest period the athlete will burn less energy and therefore require less food or a different balance of protein: carbohydrate: fat.

Dogs should be conditioned scored on a weekly basis and their ration adjusted accordingly. Often inappropriate nutrition can underlie performance and concentration issues.

DIETARY FAT

Fat in the diet provides a source of concentrated, readily available energy, generally in the form of triglycerides. Triglycerides are composed of three fatty acid molecules attached to one molecule of glycerol. Triglycerides are broken down by enzymes in the gastro-intestinal tract and are then transported around the body where they can be converted into glycogen for energy or resynthesised into triglycerides for storage. For prolonged periods of exercise, i.e. greater than 30 minutes, fat becomes the main energy source.

Some studies suggest that dogs derive 90 per cent of their energy for muscle contraction from fatty acids *(Theriault D.G. et al,1973)*. Fat contains twice the number of calories of metabolisable energy per gram than either carbohydrate or protein: 8.5kcal as opposed to 3.5kcal. Increasing the fat content of the diet increases its energy density and palatability. Since the total dry matter content of the diet should not exceed 3.5 per cent of bodyweight, increasing the fat content is often the only way of getting more calories into a dog that is training hard without overloading the gastro-intestinal tract.

Not only is fat a valuable source of calories, it is an essential component of improving aerobic fitness. Increasing the amount of fat in the diet can:

- Increase mitochondrial numbers within muscle (25 per cent).
- Increase the concentration of enzymes involved in aerobic metabolism.
- Preserve muscle glycogen and reduce fatigue.
- Increase VO2max (genetically determined maximum level of oxygen delivery) by 20-30 per cent in a well-trained dog *(Reynolds et al, 1995)*.

Therefore increasing the amount of fat in the diet should be considered an integral part of training in the agility dog. This increase has to be undertaken slowly so that the body can adapt by producing more lipase (fat digesting enzyme) and by increasing blood flow though the fat stores within the body and releasing fatty acids into the circulation.

A higher dependency on fat in the diet also reduces resting insulin concentrations which facilitate fat uptake and use by the body.

During the off-season where exercise intensity is reduced, the quantity of fat in the diet can be reduced to prevent weight gain. As it can take up to six weeks for the body to adapt to a higher level of fat in the diet, dietary changes should be made up to six weeks before the onset of intense training.

DIETARY CARBOHYDRATE

Dietary carbohydrate is a critical component of a sprint athlete's diet (e.g. racing Greyhound), but is of less importance to the agility dog. Red blood cells, brain tissue and nerves rely on glucose as their primary source of energy. Even during extreme exercise glucose will be conserved for these tissues.

During pregnancy and in the very young (neonates), carbohydrate is also an essential part of the diet. However at all other stages of life, dogs can survive with no carbohydrate at all in their diet, provided there is enough substrate to synthesise glycogen from other sources such as fat *(Reinhart, 1998)*.

At the start of exercise when dogs are working anaerobically and at very high levels of exercise (heart rate of 80-90 per cent maximum), carbohydrate is the primary source of energy. Carbohydrate is stored in the body as liver or muscle glycogen. During intense exercise, these energy stores are mobilised to produce fuel for muscle work. While increasing muscle glycogen can improve sprint performance, in agility dogs excess carbohydrate in the diet can often be counterproductive.

Although in human exercise physiology carbohydrate loading in the two hours prior to exercise is an appropriate strategy, this is not the case in dogs. In fact, it can have the very opposite effect. The rapid release of large amounts of sugar in to the blood stream results in a sharp rise in blood insulin which, in some circumstances, can excessively lower blood glucose.

High insulin levels also inhibit fat metabolism within the body, thereby hampering the release of energy from fat stores. Muscle glycogen can thus become rapidly depleted and the dog will tire very quickly. This is in stark contrast to dogs fed a high fat diet which allows muscle glycogen to be spared *(Reynolds et al, 1995)*.

However, post exercise evidence suggests that feeding simple carbohydrates within 30 minutes of stopping exercise reduces muscle damage and helps restore muscle glycogen stores very quickly *(Kronfeld, 1973)*. Glucose fed in this 2-hour window post exercise is 4 times as efficient at replacing muscle glycogen stores as glucose fed outside this window. Supplements containing maltodextrin can be a useful source of carbohydrate replenishment in dogs at 15gm/Kg bodyweight *(Hinchcliff et al, Effect of racing on serum sodium and potassium concentrations and acid-base status of Alaskan sled dogs,1997)*.

It is important that the carbohydrate fraction of the diet is easily digestible in order to limit faecal production. Too much undigested carbohydrate can reduce performance by pulling water out of the body and into the colon. It also adds to the animal's weight and can increase body temperature due to fermentation. Excessive carbohydrate in the diet can also predispose the dog to a condition known as exertional rhabdomyolysis where severe muscle damage occurs with exercise.

Higher protein levels are required during the growing period.

PROTEIN IN THE DIET

Protein in the diet is primarily required for structural repair and for synthesis of hormones and enzymes. It should generally provide no more than 5-10 per cent of energy requirements of exercise. The basic unit of protein is the amino acid. Some amino acids can be synthesised within the body; 10 are essential and can only be supplied through dietary intake.

During certain periods, such as growth and development and early training, an individual's protein requirements are significantly higher. Amino acids are used to produce new muscle tissue and repair the damage to muscle tissue that occurs as part of training. Amino acids are also essential to facilitate the increase in circulating plasma volume. This is a critical component to adaptation during training.

The endocrine system has a strong influence on the body's ability to synthesise protein. Insulin, for example, promotes protein uptake and synthesis by the body and thus helps in muscle development. Cortisol, a stress hormone, has the opposite effect and inhibits protein synthesis and promotes protein breakdown. Dietary protein helps maintain muscle structure and is essential in the synthesis of red blood cells, globulins and albumin within the body.

Sled dog studies have demonstrated that approximately 30 per cent of energy intake should be derived from protein in order to prevent injury and maintain high concentrations of red blood cells, haemoglobin and albumin *(Kronfeld et al, 1989)*.

WATER

Water is often ignored as an essential part of the diet when, in reality, it is the single most important nutrient for survival. Performance can be severely impaired by as little as a two per cent depletion in body water. In an athlete, water makes up approximately 70 per cent of lean bodyweight; the figure is even higher in overweight dogs.

Water is essential for all cell activities and acts as a shock absorber within the body and lubricates internal structures. It also absorbs heat generated by metabolic reactions – 80 per cent of muscle work is released as heat. In this way it prevents a catastrophic rise in body temperature. Water is also an essential component of blood; the ability to increase blood volume and transport heat away from the core of the body to the skin for dissipation is an extremely important training adaptation. This process is hampered if the athlete is dehydrated and is therefore likely to overheat very quickly.

Water is lost from the body through urinary loss, faecal loss and evaporation from the lungs. During exercise, respiratory rate increases dramatically. Under normal circumstances, 1ml/Kcal of metabolisable energy consumed per day is required, which equates to approximately 2L under temperate conditions for most dogs.

ANTIOXIDANTS

As we exercise, the demand for oxygen increases; the harder we exercise, the greater the demand. Even at a moderate level of exercise, an increase is seen in the production of very reactive oxygen free radicals which can damage tissue. At the same time various factors such as tissue ischaemia (lack of oxygen), and a drop in tissue pH associated with acidosis, causes further damage to body cells. This damage can be mitigated by the release of antioxidants within the body.

With increasing amounts of exercise, the body's innate antioxidant system can be overrun leading to the development of oxidative stress. If this is left unchecked, it is thought to contribute to chronic muscle fatigue and overtraining *(Finaud et al, Oxidative stress: Relationship with exercise and training, 2006)*.

However, there is much controversy regarding the benefit of supplementing with antioxidants, particularly in relation to the correct dose and composition which is undergoing clinical trials. It is also known that excessive dose of antioxidants can interfere with muscle contraction force *(Stone and Yang, Hydrogen peroxide: A signaling messenger. Antioxidants and Redox Signaling, 2006)*.

Commonly used antioxidants include vitamin C, vitamin E and selenium:

Vitamin C: Synthethised in the liver, it is a powerful reducing agent and re-synthesises vitamin E. Dogs appear to be less efficient at synthesising vitamin C than other species and levels can fall by as much as 50 per cent after exercise.

Vitamin E and selenium: These are important in stabilising cell membranes as well as protecting the body from free radical damage

Training enhances the body's innate antioxidant system *(Gomez-Cabrera et al, 2006)*, but whether it is beneficial to supplement with antioxidants remains open to debate. If supplementation is to take place, it is essential that a balanced supplement is used; if vitamin C or vitamin E is used singly, it appears to increase oxidative stress and leads to more tissue damage.

VITAMINS, MINERALS AND ELECTROLYTES

Vitamins, minerals and electrolytes have an important role in maintaining a stable environment (homeostasis) within the body during exercise. Commercial diets are well balanced in terms of all of the above, however issues can arise with home cooked diets. Minerals are classified as major and trace minerals.

Major minerals such as calcium, phosphorus, sodium, chloride, potassium and magnesium are vital to growth and development. The ratio of calcium:potassium are critically important in growing dogs, and a meat based diet without bone can lead to imbalances.

Calcium should be fed at between 0.6-1.2 per cent dry matter on a 1:1 ratio with phosphorus. Magnesium levels can also be affected on a meat based diet where bone is not added. Magnesium deficiency has been implicated in carpal hyperextension. Occasionally with intense exercise, sodium levels can fall but dietary supplementation has not been considered necessary as levels are quickly restored post exercise. Zinc deficiency may also occur on an occasional basis, characterised by hair loss, altered immune function and poor wound healing.

WHEN AND HOW TO FEED

Timing of feeding is critical: feed to soon and the dog might have insufficient energy to sustain performance, feed to late and the dog will have to move a large volume of undigested food and faeces around the agility ring and will be at risk of vomiting, regurgitating and diarrhoea. Feeding the correct diet, at the wrong time, can result in the dog failing to extract the nutrients he needs from that diet.

In addition, feeding too close to exercise will raise body temperature and affect the dog's ability to lose body heat through the skin and respiratory tract. This, in turn, will compromise athletic performance. Feeding too close to exercise also affects what substrates dogs use for exercise. Dogs fed within 6 hours of work are more dependent on carbohydrate and therefore more likely to deplete muscle glycogen stores. Conversely if insufficient nutrients are fed, blood glucose levels can fall resulting in poor performance and even collapse. This can be prevented by feeding small amounts of high energy snacks during the active period.

Ideally, athletes should be fed four hours before competing. Some studies do show a benefit from moderate food restriction (20 per cent) the day before competition in order to minimise faecal bulk and promote fat digestion *(Hill et al, 1999)*. However, this is not always practical.

Wherever possible soluble carbohydrate, such as malodextrine, should be fed within two hours of completing an intense bout of exercise to restore muscle glycogen. In order to minimise the risk of gastric dilation and torsion care should be taken not to feed large meals too soon after exercise. This is particularly important with deep chested dogs. Water should be offered as soon as possible after exercise. Under hot, humid conditions, dogs can become moderately dehydrated. They should be encouraged to drink little and often; ideally their body temperature should be monitored as their ability to control their temperature is reduced when dehydrated.

The exact ratio of fat:carbohydrate:protein remains open to debate. In terms of exercise physiology, when undertaking low levels of exercise – 30-40 per cent VO2max – fat is the main energy source. At moderate activity – 40-50 per cent VO2max – a combination of carbohydrate and fat will act as fuel for exercises. At intense exercise – over 70 per cent VO2max – carbohydrate becomes the sole energy source. The table below provides nutritional guidelines for low and high levels of intermediate (sprint and endurance combination) type exercise.

FEEDING FOR HEALTHY JOINTS

Due to the increased strain placed on the musculoskeletal system of the canine athlete, every effort should be made to prevent injury from occurring in the first place. There are many supplements and diets commercially available

Nutritional guidelines

Nutrient	Recommended levels for intermediate activity (low/moderate duration and frequency)	Recommended levels for intermediate activity (high duration and frequency)
Fat %	15-30 (>60%unsaturated)	25-40 (>60% unsaturated)
Carbohydrate %	30-55	30-35
Protein %	22-32	22-32
Vitamin E(IU/Kg)	>500	>500
Vitamin C (IU/Kg)	150-250	150-250
Selenium (mg/Kg)	0.5-1.3	0.5-1.3

Nutritional guidelines for low and high levels of intermediate (sprint and endurance combination) type exercise.

Adapted from a table Feeding Working and Sporting Dogs In Small Animal Clinical Nutrition, 5th edition ch. 18, p. 348, Mark Morris Institute

that purport to maintain joint health, but many of these claims are unsubstantiated. Two classes of compounds exist, namely neutraceuticals and functional foods.

NEUTRACEUTICALS

A neutraceutical is defined as any non-drug substance that is a food, or part of a food, that provides medical or health benefits, including the prevention and treatment of disease. In Europe, no specific indications can be legally recognised for neutraceuticals as no official evidence of efficacy is required to market them. In addition, manufacturers do not have to conduct the extensive studies that are necessary to obtain official approval for marketing medicinal products, such as antibiotics or anti-inflammatories, so many of their claims regarding potential health benefits are not always substantiated.

Neutraceuticals include:

Glucosamine sulphate/Hydrochloride
Chondroitin sulphate
Omega 3 fatty Acids
Antioxidants
MSM

FUNCTIONAL FOODS

These are foods into which neutraceuticals are incorporated; they provide a complete diet which has disease modifying potential.

Omega 3

The best body of evidence surrounds feeding the correct balance of omega 3:omega 6 fatty acids in the diet. Collectively, omega 3 and 6 are known as essential fatty acids; they are both polyunsaturated fatty acids. Omega 3 and 6 are crucial components of cell membranes, but they are also the precursors of inflammatory products.

Most dog foods combine saturated and polyunsaturated fatty acids from plant, animal or marine sources. Plant sources can supply linoleic acid (omega 6) or alpha linoleic acid (omega 3). The dog can process these compounds into longer fatty acids, known as eicosanopentanoic acid and arachindonic acid. Arachindonic acid acts as a precursor for a number of products involved in inflammation and joint damage; the breakdown products of eicosanopentanoic acid are less inflammatory.

Research has demonstrated that a higher level of omega 6 fatty acids within the body can lead to increased joint damage, mainly through the increase in levels of arachindonic acid. Most modern anti-inflammatories, such as metacam and rimadyl, work by preventing one or more steps in the pathway of arachindonic acid breakdown. In contrast, higher levels of omega 3 fatty acids in the diet reduces the concentration of arachindonic acid in cell membranes and, ultimately, reduces the level of inflammation and damage within the joint.

It is important that the correct type of omega 3 is used in the diet. Short chain omega 3 – those found in plant based oils, e.g. flax seed oil – are not as effective at reducing inflammation as the longer chain omega 3 compounds found in marine based oils. A total dose of 1g of EPA (eicosapentanoic acid) per 10Kg bodyweight has been found to be effective *(Fritsch et al 2010)*. Practically, this equates to 1 teaspoon of fish oil per 10Kg of bodyweight. This will add 45kcal to the food and should be factored in to the daily nutrient intake.

Green lipped mussel

Freeze dried perna cannaliculus, or green lipped mussel extract, is another excellent source of omega 3. It also contains glucosamine and chondroitin sulphate. This should be fed at a dose of 75-100mg/Kg body weight.

Glucosamine and Chondroitin

There remains considerable debate over the efficacy of glucosamine and chondroitin in maintaining joint health. The largest human clinical trial failed to demonstrate any significant benefit in their ability to reduce joint pain or improve joint range of motion. Potentially, Chondroitin sulphate has a greater benefit than glucosamine.

Chondroitin and glucosamine are thought to work by reducing the production of inflammatory substances within the joint, and by stimulating the production of glycosaminoglycans and collagen which are important constituents of cartilage. When using complete, manufactured dog food, where glucosamine and chondroitin has been added, it is difficult to assess the availability and stability of these compounds, so whether they are being fed at the correct level, or at a level sufficient to have any potential benefit, is unclear.

Other compounds

Turmeric has been cited as having anti-inflammatory properties but no clinical data exists to support this claim. In my experience, it can, in some cases, improve mobility in cases of osteoarthritis.

MSM or methylsulfonylmethane is a sulphur containing compound which has, in human clinical trials, shown to be effective in reducing pain and improving function.

References

Hill R.C. et al, *Minimal food restriction increases the speed of racing greyhounds*, J. Vet Int Med 1999, 13, 281

Theriault D.G. et al, *Intramuscular energy sources in dogs during physical work*, J. Lipid. Research 1973, 14: 54-61

Reinhart G.A., *Nutrition for sporting dogs*, in Bloomberg M.S., Dee J.F., Taylor R.A. (eds), *Canine Sports Medicine and Surgery*, Philadelphia, Saunders-Elsevier, 1998, 348-356

Reynolds A.J.et al, *Effect of diet and training on muscle glycogen storage and utilisation in sled dogs*, J Appl Physiol, 1995 79: 1601-1607

Kronfeld D.S., Adkins T., Downey R.L., *Nutrition, anaerobic and aerobic exercise and stress*, in Burger, J.H. & Rivers J.P.W. (eds), *Nutrition of the Dog and Cat*, Waltham Symposium, New York, Cambridge University Press, 133-145

Hinchcliff K.W. et al, *Effect of racing on serum sodium and potassium concentrations and acid-base status of Alaskan sled dogs*, J Am Vet Med Asso, 1997 210 1615-1618

Gomez-Cabrera M.C., Martinez A., Santangelo G., et al, *Oxidative stress in marathon runners: Interest of antioxidant supplementation*, British Journal of Nutrition 2006; 96 (Suppl. 1): S31-S33

Finaud J., Lac G., Filaire E., *Oxidative stress: Relationship with exercise and training*, Sports Medicine, 2006; 36: 327-358

Stone J.R., Yang S., *Hydrogen peroxide: A signaling messenger*, Antioxidants and Redox Signaling 2006; 8: 243-270

Fritsch D. et al, *Dose titration effects of fish oil in osteoarthritic dogs*, J Vet Int Med, 24, 2010, 1020-1026

Chapter Four:

OPTIMISING ENERGY AND EXERCISE

In order for a performance dog to train and work, he needs energy. All living organisms need energy to function and when we exercise, the requirement for energy increases. This chapter looks at the requirements of exercise, and how the body adapts to meet these requirements and increase energy production. In addition, we will look at how the body adapts to long term exercise or training, and how this applies to our agility dogs.

ENERGY PRODUCTION

Energy is released by the breakdown of adenosine triphosphate (ATP), a high-energy molecule found in all cells of the body. ATP is essentially the currency of energy in all living organisms. It stores and supplies all the energy required for the processes to stay alive, such as metabolism, cell repair, nerve transmission, and muscle contraction.

Because ATP is the immediate source of energy in cells there needs to be a ready supply of it. This is met by the breakdown of carbohydrates and fats from the diet, converting them into a product called glycogen which is mainly stored in the muscles and liver, as well as being present in the circulating blood. Glycogen can then be converted to glucose on demand, thus ensuring a steady flow of glucose as and when it's required.

Fats are stored in the body as triglycerides, which can be broken down into fatty acids which circulate in the blood and can be used by exercising muscle. The muscles themselves also store fats as triglycerides, which can then be broken down within the muscle to produce free fatty acids. ATP is released when the glucose or fatty acids are broken down.

The production of ATP takes place in the cells of the body and depends on the availability of glucose or fatty acids, and the availability of oxygen from respiration. Oxygen helps to drive the reactions which break down the carbohydrates and fats. Energy production, which relies on oxygen in this way, is described as aerobic. Energy is predominantly produced aerobically at low to moderate intensity levels of exercise.

AEROBIC ENERGY

Through a series of reactions, the glucose is broken down into smaller molecules, resulting in the release of ATP. The energy generated from the metabolism of one glucose molecule is 38 molecules of ATP. The production of ATP from the breakdown of fatty acids from fats results in very high yields of energy – upwards of 100 ATP molecules, depending on the fatty acid broken down. Dogs are particularly well adapted to metabolising fat as an energy source, though this ability tends to be limited to low intensity levels of exercise, e.g. steady state jogging or trotting but not sprinting.

As energy production requires oxygen, the supply of oxygen to muscle during exercise is essential to the performance of the animal. The diagram on the following page shows the passage of oxygen from the air to muscle in the body to be used in energy production.

Influencing the carriage of oxygen at any point along this pathway will consequently influence performance during exercise. Essentially, when we exercise we need to take in more oxygen and increase its delivery – along with nutrients – to the exercising muscles. During a bout of exercise, the body makes a number of adaptations to allow this to happen.

Probably the most obvious change during exercise is that the rate of breathing increases which means that more oxygen is breathed into the lungs per minute. The muscles that are involved in breathing and expanding the thorax work harder to allow the chest to expand, and to allow more oxygen to be breathed in per breath. In this way, more oxygen is available in the lungs to be transferred to the blood and on to the heart and muscles.

The thorax

The heart also adapts to exercise, working harder to optimise the delivery of blood around the body. The heart rate increases, and as the number of heart beats per minute increases, more blood per minute can be pumped around the body, delivering more oxygen and nutrients to the muscles. The volume of blood pumped out of the heart per beat also increases, again resulting in more blood being pumped around the body to make oxygen available to the muscles. The result of this increase in heart rate and volume of blood passing through the heart is an increase in blood pressure, and more effective circulation of the blood to the exercising muscles.

Blood supply to the heart, lungs and muscles is prioritised during exercise, and delivery of blood to these organs is aided by dilation of the blood vessels supplying them. At the same time, blood is diverted away from systems that are less involved in exercise – such as digestion – by constriction of the blood vessels supplying these systems.

ANAEROBIC ENERGY

Despite the mechanisms described above, there can come a point during hard exercise at which insufficient oxygen is delivered to the muscles to meet their demands. At this point the muscles start producing energy anaerobically, i.e. breaking down glucose in the absence of oxygen. The overall use of oxygen by an animal is described as its oxygen uptake (VO2).

During exercise, this value increases up to a point at which it can increase no further, known as the maximal aerobic metabolic rate (VO2max). This is the limit of the aerobic contribution to energy production, and any further energy required is supplied by anaerobic energy production.

Anaerobic energy production takes place through a series of reactions in the cells of the body, resulting in the release of ATP, and the additional production of lactic acid. Excessive concentrations of lactic acid have a negative effect on muscle contraction and energy production. The energy produced from anaerobic energy production is considerably lower than that of aerobic energy production, with the release of up to three ATP molecules from the breakdown of glucose.

Energy is mainly produced anaerobically at the start of exercise before the body starts to adapt to take in more oxygen, and at high intensity levels of exercise when the requirement for energy exceeds the amount of energy being produced.

Supply of oxygen to muscle

OXYGEN IN THE AIR
Making up approximately 20% of the composition of the air

↓

RESPIRATORY TRACT
Oxygen is breathed in to travel to the lungs via the respiratory airways

↓

CARDIOVASCULAR SYSTEM
Oxygen is transferred to the blood from the lungs by binding to haemoglobin and distributed in the blood circulation by the heart

↓

TISSUE PERFUSION
Oxygen is taken up by the muscles for use in energy production within its cells

The Thorax

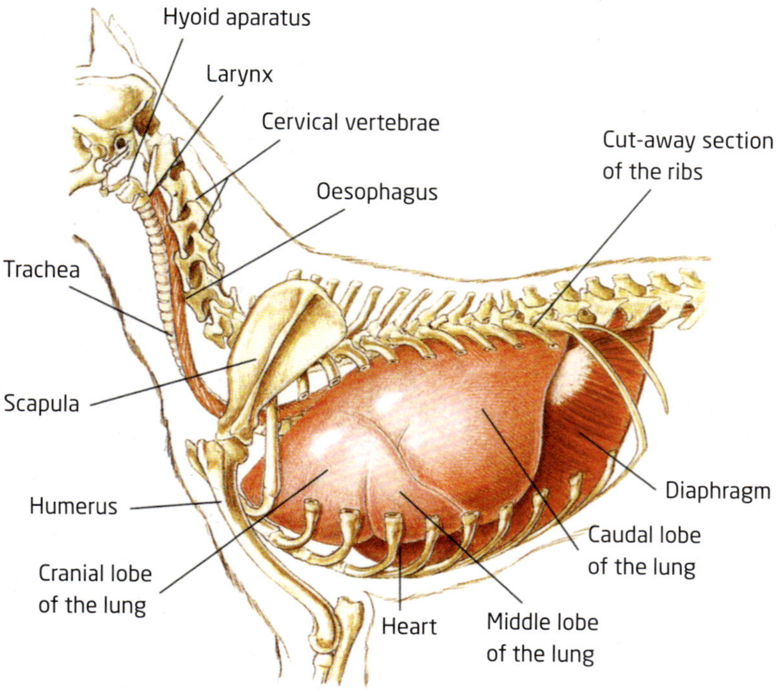

Although anaerobic energy production produces less ATP and thus smaller amounts of energy, it can occur at a greatly accelerated rate and is therefore particularly useful for sudden bursts of energy or the fast sprints required in racing Greyhounds. Given the difference in energy yield between aerobic and anaerobic energy production, combined with the effects of lactic acid, the ability to use aerobic energy sources during high intensity exercise is essential for maximising athletic performance and delaying fatigue. The dog's ability to do this is what makes him such a good athlete.

At any one time during exercise, there are aerobic and anaerobic contributions to energy production, depending on the species of animal and the job it is performing. Dog sledding, where the dog needs sustained energy supplies for endurance, is an aerobic sport, whereas Greyhound racing, where the dog needs short bursts of energy for sprinting, is anaerobic.

Dog agility has characteristics of both these sports; the distance run by agility dogs is relatively short and requires less energy, but the addition of acceleration, corners, jumping and climbing increases the energy that is needed for performance. The running element of agility can be considered as an aerobic activity, while the use of equipment – such as the A-frame, weaves etc. – is an anaerobic activity. The ability to switch between aerobic and anaerobic energy production is what makes a successful agility competitor.

MUSCLE STRUCTURE

Energy released from ATP drives the muscular reactions that allows animals to function, exercise and perform athletically. To understand muscle function and its dependence on ATP, basic muscle structure must be considered.

There are three types of muscle found in the canine body:

Cardiac muscle is found in the heart.

Smooth muscle is found within the walls of blood vessels, and within the walls of hollow organs and tracts.

Skeletal muscle is responsible for movement of the body and, as a whole, can account for up to half the bodyweight of a dog, depending on breed. A single skeletal muscle is made up of hundreds of muscle fibres which themselves consist of two protein types, actin and myosin. Bundles of muscle fibres are held together by, and enclosed within, layers of connective tissue to form the muscle.

In agility, running represents an aerobic activity.

Weaving and negotiating contact equipment is an anaerobic activity.

Blood vessels delivering oxygenated blood, and nerves delivering nervous impulses, which stimulate muscle contraction, run though the connective tissues of the muscle.

Muscle contraction depends on the arrangement and function of the actin and myosin filaments. Actin is a thin filament and myosin is a thick filament. The thick and thin filaments are arranged in alternating sets that overlap with each other and function as follows:

- The protein filaments slide against each other to create tension, propelled by cross bridges between the filaments acting as a kind of ratchet mechanism.
- When stimulated by nervous impulses, bridges on the thick filaments bond to sites on the thin filaments.
- Each bridge swings through an arc, effectively pulling the thin filaments past the thick ones.
- Once the movement of the bridge is complete, it detaches from the filament, swings back to its original position, and reattaches to the thin filament further along its length.
- When this happens to numerous fibres, the muscle shortens.

A single bridge will go through this cycle 50-100 times per second, and for each bridge to go through one cycle requires the energy released by one ATP molecule. It is therefore clear that the energy consumption of contracting muscle is incredibly high.

The way that skeletal muscle performs depends on the type of muscle fibres it consists of. There are two categories of muscle fibre, type I and type II:

Type I fibres are also known as slow twitch fibres as they are activated by the nervous system at a lower rate. They use energy produced aerobically and make up muscle groups that carry out low intensity or prolonged work, such as maintaining posture.

Type II fibres are also known as fast twitch fibres as they are activated by the nervous system at a higher rate. There are various types of fast twitch fibre, the most important being type IIa and type IIb.

Type IIa fibres use energy produced aerobically to carry out endurance work.

Type IIb fibres use energy produced anaerobically

Structure of skeletal muscle

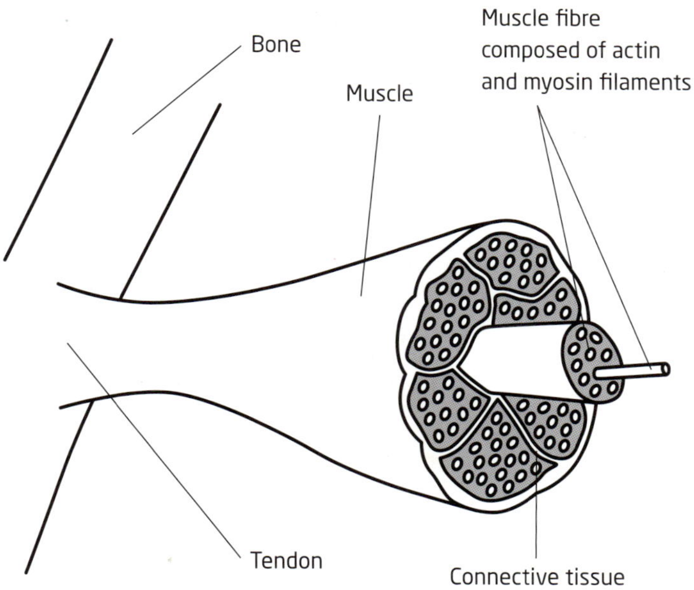

How muscle contracts

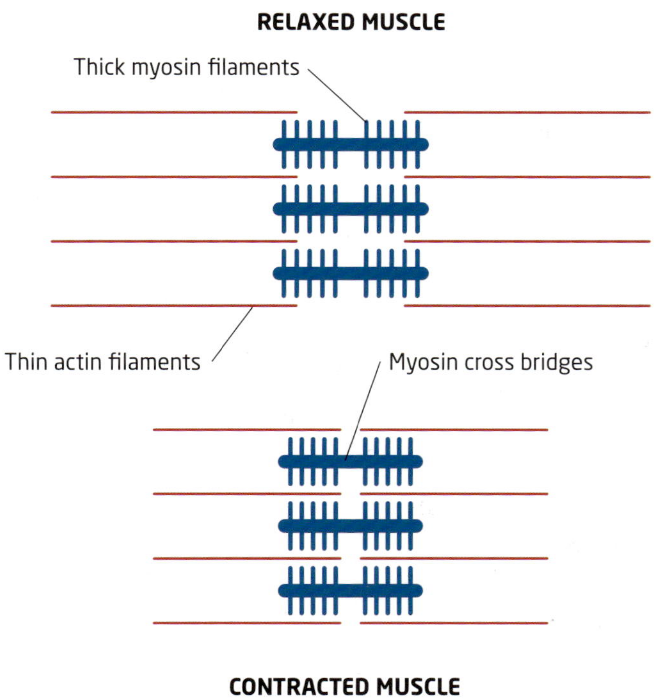

The sliding filament theory.

to carry out short bursts of work such as sprinting.

The proportions of the different type II fibres found in canine muscle depend on breed and activity. Sprinters such as Greyhounds, have a higher proportion of type IIb fibres, while endurance dogs such Huskies have more type IIa fibres. The representation of fibre types is also affected by exercise and training. Long distance or endurance training promotes type IIa fibres, while strength and interval training promote type IIb fibres.

FITNESS PROGRAMMES

For athletic dogs to perform effectively, they need to be able to optimise energy production, and promote the best muscle function appropriate to their sporting discipline. To do this, they need to undertake a training programme. Training can be described as regular exercise aimed at bringing about functional changes in the body, which in turn promote improved athletic performance.

To bring about change, the exercise must be specific and matched to the needs of the particular sporting discipline. Exercise must also be targeted at a level beyond which the body is usually accustomed, in order to appropriately overload the cardio-vascular and musculoskeletal system. This means that exercise for training purposes should increase in intensity, difficulty and duration.

Dogs that exercise maintain healthier weights, and have better cardiovascular function, than dogs that take less exercise. In the case of canine athletes, dogs that are appropriately conditioned perform better, are less likely to suffer injuries, and are better equipped to recover from injuries when they do occur. Training should be specific to the individual dog, the sport the dog is participating in, and based on a good understanding of the requirements of that sport.

Endurance training usually involves training aerobically and focuses on adapting the cardio-vascular and musculoskeletal systems. Strength training usually involves training anaerobically. Dogs should receive strength and endurance training in proportion to the activity the dog is required to perform in its sport. Agility requires both elements. There is an overlap between strength and endurance training and canine athletes can benefit from both forms of exercise.

EFFECTS OF TRAINING

Training has a variety of long term effects on the cardio-vascular, respiratory, and musculoskeletal system.

A major effect of training on the cardiovascular system is that the heart increases in size, with the walls of the heart becoming thicker and stronger. This, in turn, means that the heart can pump more blood per minute, allowing more effective delivery of blood to the muscles. The resting heart rate also decreases as a result of training, and is quicker to recover after working hard.

Respiratory function is also influenced by the effects of training. The diaphragm, and other muscles responsible for breathing, become stronger allowing the chest to expand so that bigger breaths can be taken. This means that more oxygen is breathed in per breath.

The lungs themselves adapt to training by increasing the number of air sacs within the lungs, which allow the movement of oxygen between the lungs and the bloodstream. In addition, more capillaries are formed in the lungs as a result of long term exercise so that more blood is flowing through the lungs, allowing increased oxygen uptake for delivery around the body and to the muscles.

These cardio-respiratory effects all improve the delivery of blood and nutrients to the muscles to make them more effective energy providers when needed for exercise. The muscles themselves also adapt to training to become more efficient energy providers.

Endurance/aerobic training brings about an increase in the number of capillaries surrounding the muscle fibres. The new capillaries result in increased blood flow to the muscle which, in turn, leads to a greater exchange of oxygen and improves aerobic energy production. Training also increases the diameter of the capillaries, again leading to increased blood flow to the muscle.

An obvious observable effect of training on muscle is that it increases in size and strength and becomes more able to resist fatigue. Long term exercise stimulates production of the proteins that make up the muscle fibres, enlargement of the fibres themselves, and production of molecules that maintain the fibres in an enlarged state. Muscle strength depends not only on muscle mass but also on the interaction between nerve and muscle that can be stimulated by training.

Exercise improves the ability of a single motor neuron, and the muscle fibres associated with it, to synchronise their action with multiple other motor neurones and their associated muscle fibres. In this way, more fibres can contract at the same time, increasing the strength with which the muscle contracts. Training also helps to develop more responsive and co-ordinated muscle contractions. It does this by promoting the activation of more motor neurones, and their associated muscle fibres, and increasing the rate at which muscle contractions are stimulated by the nervous system. In this way muscle contraction becomes more responsive and more co-ordinated.

Training muscle adapts it to the job it is expected to perform by promoting the appropriate fibre types. Endurance training promotes the growth of slow twitch fibres required for endurance work, while strengthening exercise promotes the growth of fast twitch fibres required for sprinting and strength work.

So the aim of owners and trainers of sporting dogs is to optimise the dog's capacity for exercise. Dogs need energy to exercise; long term training brings about adaptations in the body to make it a more efficient energy provider, allowing the dog to exercise more effectively. By making our dogs stronger, fitter, and better at producing energy, they have the ability to improve their athletic performance.

Chapter Five:

FOUNDATION TRAINING FOR THE YOUNG ATHLETE

The effectiveness of basic training in a young dog can determine whether an athlete is either made or damaged for life. If the handler gets it wrong at this stage, there is a risk of not only increasing strain on the joints, muscles, ligaments and tendons, but the dog may also develop abnormal movement patterns that can become fixed for life. In addition, a poor start and a failure to understand the needs of a young athlete can affect psychological wellbeing by increasing stress levels, allowing the dog to sour very quickly.

At the basic level in many canine sports there is less of an onus on the handler to be physically fit. As a consequence, there is no clear understanding of what is involved, both physically and mentally, in taking a pup from birth through to competition. Whereas, a handler that has regularly participated in sport should have a better understanding of how hard it is to develop the physical fitness and mental attitude that is required for training and competition.

Common mistakes include the absence of a conditioning programme and a failure to teach each step of a task in a systematic manner. For example, a handler will expect a dog to jump without first being taught the entry into the jump, the take off, flight, landing and the exit from the jump. Part and parcel of this approach is repeating sequences, over and over again, without realising how tiring it is for a dog to learn a new task. A failure to complete the task often sees the handler endlessly repeating the manoeuvre in an attempt to teach it, rather than giving the young dog some physical and mental time out. As a result, the dog becomes extremely stressed and is unable to focus in the agility ring.

The basic requirements for training a young dog can be outlined as follows:

- Teach the handler what it takes to be an athlete, especially if they are coming from a non-athletic background.
- Create a training programme that is more holistic and less end-skill focused.

This refers most particularly to the current trend of micromanaging details. This results in decreasing speed and confidence by over-training control and keeping skills out of context. An experienced trainer should be able to progress intuitively, establishing a solid baseline of movement patterns that make more advanced training easier to achieve. This develops the dog's natural athletic ability rather than stifling it.

WHAT DOES THE AGILITY DOG NEED?

Simply viewed, agility is the ability to successfully negotiate a series of obstacles in the shortest period of time. So what does it require to do this well? It is not just about speed, and it is not just about balance. Rather, it is the ability to combine physical and mental control with speed, flexibility and proprioception – while at the same time constantly speeding up and slowing down. No dog knows how to do this intuitively; each individual skill has to be taught in the correct way that allows the dog to realise his full athletic potential without hindrance from the handler.

Thus we have three fundamental skills:

- Acceleration (extension)
- Deceleration (collection)
- Turning (bending)

Acceleration: this is when the dog speeds up and runs in extension.

Deceleration: This is when the dog needs to slow down so he collects his pace.

Turning: This involves changing direction or bending around an obstacle, such as a jump wing.

Each of the above will have the following components to a lesser or greater degree:

- Balance
- Co-ordination
- Proprioception
- Power
- Strength
- Endurance

A suitable training programme should have elements that address all of these components individually. So, when the dog moves on to working on agility equipment, he has all the basic skills he requires; they just need to be developed in sequence to manage the challenge of each obstacle. Trying to develop skill over obstacles, without having perfected the individual components of the challenge, is likely to end in failure. For example, if a young dog persistently refuses to jump we can surmise:

He does not like jumping – *unlikely.*

He does not possess the necessary strength and balance to jump – *more likely.*

Jumping is painful – *possible, even in a young dog.*

The dog does not have the necessary decision making skills to tackle the jump and therefore runs out – *again possible; not every dog is a born athlete but most can be improved.*

Once the basics have been mastered, training will become so much easier. You will be able to train with purpose (optimise); applying what will become collection, extension, and bending. With a young dog, try to bring these skills or challenges into everyday situations, with or without equipment, but avoiding repetition. This puts movements rapidly into context and avoids drilling. If you then understand the movement behind the refined skills you are targeting, you are improving speed and precision. You are also improving both the dog and handler's decision-making skills on the course.

ATHLETE DEVELOPMENT STAGES

The table on page 54 should help identify the training needs of the young dog as well as providing a timeframe for progression. Remember, each dog is different and will progress at his own pace.

In this way, the three pillars of sporting performance are built upon, namely:

1. Sport movement: agility, quickness, multidirectional speed, external reaction skills, co-ordination, acceleration and deceleration.

2. Sport strength: muscular, whole body, multi-joint strength, muscular endurance, explosive power, power capacity, acidosis tolerance and recovery efficiency.

3. Sport balance: stability, kinesthetic awareness, proprioception, neuromuscular pathways, transitional balance and internal reactivity.

So how does this equate, in practice, to getting it right with our young dogs?

Currently, there is a trend for repeated training of young dogs on novel apparatus from a very young age, e.g. teaching them to stand for prolonged periods of time on pods or in very small boxes. At the same time, owners have become scared that exposing their puppies to the natural environment is likely to permanently damage their musculoskeletal system when, in fact, the converse is true. Provided the duration of the exercise is age appropriate, external environments, such as gardens, parks and woodlands, will challenge the young dog's sensory and motor system in a functional and physiological manner. They are an invaluable in the development of the musculo-skeletal system, and also help to establish functional and appropriate gait patterns without stressing or over-challenging the pup.

Obviously, walking a 12-week-old puppy for hours on end in such an environment would be detrimental to his development. At this age, the ideal scenario is to provide repeated short walks of 10-15 minutes duration interspersed with good quality rest and nutrition. This form of exercise introduces variability and combines moments of intense focus and balance requirements – such as negotiating a log – with moments of easy unchallenging movement opportunities, for example walking over short grass. In this way the challenge is gradual, not repetitive, and is on/off in nature, allowing both the mind and body to relax.

Simply exploring the environment encourages focus and balance.

Compare this with asking a pup to balance on a pod. Firstly, you are making the young pup retain a position for an extended period of – even 10 seconds can be too long at this stage. It uses the same muscle groups and is a constant 'on pressure' without scope for either mental or physical relaxation. It teaches the pup to stiffen when challenged and not to be relaxed and moving forwards. This can be a pattern that establishes for life, i.e. when challenged, the pup will stiffen rather than adapt fluidly. Over time this can lead to loss of flexibility, muscle stiffness and pain, and eventually, injury.

Once balance and flexibility have been established in the natural environment, these skills will transfer to more focused work on equipment. At all times when working with equipment, aim to keep the dog relaxed with his muscles in a neutral position. Any training circumstance that makes the dog hold an unnatural posture for a prolonged period of time, such as standing in a small box with all four legs drawn underneath, serves no purpose. Once again it teaches the dog to stiffen and fix rather than encouraging natural posture and balance.

However, climbing in and out of the box is a suitable proprioceptive challenge and teaches limb awareness and co-ordination. In this way it can be seen that there is rarely a bad tool, it's more a matter of whether we make the tool useful or inappropriate.

Again, the environment can be used to develop the normal movement patterns of acceleration and deceleration. It is far better to do this by allowing the pup to run around in the natural environment – accelerating up gentle gradients and decelerating down gentle inclines – rather than repeatedly throwing a ball. Remember, it is not the speeding up that is the problem but the slowing down.

Using the analogy of braking in a car, think about how warm the tyres get when we apply the brakes as the energy of movement is converted into heat. This also happens in the joints, muscles and tendons which, in the young dog, are much less resistant to wear and tear. Repeating challenges that cause the pup to come to a dead stop are likely to cause tissue injury and should therefore be avoided.

It is important to bear in mind that repetition does not equate to retention or learning. Repeating a bad movement over and over leads to damage and injury. The best strategy is to allow the pup to learn while out walking – both on and off lead – and while playing, without endlessly repeating the same challenge.

An athlete needs both physical and mental control. A level of physical control relies on the skeletal system, the cardiovascular system, and the respiratory system.

On a basic level an athlete needs:

- Bone, muscles, and ligaments to keep the body upright and moving.
- Blood flow to deliver nutrients and oxygen to bones, muscles, and ligaments, which keeps the body upright and moving.
- To breathe in order to generate oxygen and send it to the bones, muscles, and ligaments, which, again, keeps the body upright and moving.

Mental control is something that is rarely addressed in puppies. Often, signs of fatigue such as hyperactivity get misinterpreted as excess energy and the pup gets further stimulated. As a result, he does not learn to calm down and relax. Just like humans, some dogs find it more difficult to relax than others. If you have a high-drive dog and focus on fast, 'drivey' games, you will lose a lot of clear rounds trying to gain mental control later on – long after the dog has perfected physical control and has caught on to the game of agility.

There are a plethora of human based studies that demonstrate the strong connection between physical and mental development, and the same is seen in young dogs. When a young dog is not in control of his body, he is scared of the environment. This, in turn, makes him scared of every new encounter, whether it is in the form of meeting new people or dogs, or novel environmental challenges. When a dog has control of his body – through the development of proprioception, balance and co-ordination – he becomes confident in the environment and less daunted by new challenges. Such individuals need sympathetic handling and challenges should be introduced gradually:

- If your youngster is struggling to balance on the ground – don't make him balance on a wobble cushion.
- If he can't co-ordinate his legs on a flat, undemanding surface – don't make him walk upstairs.
- Take a step back and consider why your pup is reluctant or unable to complete the task rather then pushing him harder, increasing his stress levels and making him stiff, and therefore less able to cope with the exercise. Again, this is where it is so important to know when to turn the pressure up and when to turn it down.

A young dog is a blank canvas; with empathy and patience he will very quickly learn to balance and co-ordinate in response to basic challenges. You can then slowly start to increase the level of the challenge by introducing more demanding exercises, such as stepping on and off a small box to develop co-ordination, balance and strength. You should only repeat the exercise once or twice – a young dog gets tired very easily.

Similarly, balance can be trained by teaching the dog to walk along a broad plank. Once it can accomplish this without stress, make the plank a little narrower and finally lift it off the ground by a few centimetres. This gives the dog an opportunity to learn and perfect his balance rather than starting with a narrow plank, raised 10 cms from the ground. Make the basic challenge as easy as possible for the pup to complete to give him the confidence and skill to progress to harder challenges.

Once you understand basic athletic requirements, you can use this information to:

1. Increase the efficacy of your training in order maximise performance and retention.

2. Minimise impact and decrease the chance of injury.

If you have a young dog that is about to start agility training this is the best time in his career to take him to a veterinarian or a physiotherapist for a fitness assessment. This way, you can address any issues prior to starting training, as well as build a conditioning programme that is tailored to your dog. Issues that might be apparent at this early age include:

- Poor gait pattern.
- Poor proprioception.
- Over activation of certain muscle groups and under activation of others.
- Use of stiffness to cope with difficult challenges rather than having natural balance and flexibility.

As previously mentioned, there are three key movements in agility: acceleration, deceleration, and turning.

Can your puppy accelerate over a small hill on the first day he arrives in his new home? Probably not – he's more likely to fall on his head. But these are small movements you can naturally incorporate into your dog's life as you form a relationship with him.

Examples include:

- You are out in a field, and call your dog to you. You can recall him to the same side he started from, and reward him in a heel position. Eventually, you can ask for a small shoulder turn – this is the start of bending.
- You are walking your dog on-lead. Speed up and slow down your pace – can the dog react appropriately?
- You ask your dog to go into the down position, but he has to engage his rear end first. This is the key behaviour involved in a stopped contact.

Like any type of training: be fair, and set the dog up for success. Training for skilled movement patterns should mesh together balance, co-ordination, and proprioception. This is not only applicable to a puppy, but applicable to an older dog who is weak in one of these skills or has altogether missed out on learning the basics.

Can your dog keep his balance when his foot is picked up? Most dogs cannot perform this task.

Athlete development stages

Age	Proprioception	Endurance	Strength	Skill	Focus
Under 6 months	Play and exercise in the natural environment Backwards walking Walking over a proprioceptive road	Short repeating walks - start with 5-10min repeated 3-4 times a day Work up to 20min repeated 4 times a day	Play and exercise in a natural environment High 5	Square sit Square down Square stand Sit to stand to down transitions Playing chase - works on balance, flexibility, acceleration, deceleration	Maintain sit, down, stand for short periods of time Start with 1-2 seconds and increase Learn to relax
6 months to growth plate closure	As above Balance cushion under front or back legs alternately Stepping over poles Walking over a narrow plank Three legged stands with head turns Balance board	Gradually increase the length of walks Start low level interval training	Side stepping Walking up and down gradients Jogging up hills Stepping up and off boxes Dancing Cavaletti work on an incline and decline	Basic grid work Walking at heel with shoulder turns Delay jump work until growth plates have shut	Increase length of stays Stay and walk away
After growth plate closure	Balance cushion under all 4 feet Balance board Balance ball	Longer more challenging walks, e.g. on the beach, up steep gradients, for longer distances Longer periods of jogging	Sprinting in sand Sprinting up hill High five on balance cushion	Teach individual components of jumping, weaving, dog walk Keep sessions short and avoid over repetition	

Core strength and control are needed for the two-on, two-off position.

If he cannot balance on three legs when he is standing still, how can you expect him to weave which involves an essential skill, or to balance in the air with all four feet off the ground, as must also happen when jumping?

Balance can be trained in a puppy by exposing him to different challenges, such as subtle changes in incline, speed, and surface, so he learns to balance naturally as he grows and develops. This could be as simple as:

- Exercising on muddy pasture – and a dry field.
- Negotiating a small hill – and a few steps.
- Exploring a wooded area – and a beach.

Watch your pup as he changes week by week. He should grow from a rolling, uncoordinated ball of fluff at 6 weeks to a sleek, well-balanced smaller version of his adult self by 16 weeks. Yes, your puppy will look clumsy at times, but he should not look stiff or asymmetrical. Get to know what is normal for your pup and if things change, ask for advice. It could be that something is amiss with how the pup is developing. Bear in mind that too much training, or the wrong kind of training, may have adverse effects – learning an inappropriate gait pattern is just as easy as learning the correct one.

EXERCISES FOR DEVELOPMENT

In terms of preparing for agility, once the dog is around 6 months old, body awareness skills and end position training can be embarked upon.

TARGETING HINDLEGS

Train your dog to place his back legs on a target, starting on the floor with progression to a contact position where the hindlegs are higher than the front legs.

Positioning the hindlegs higher than the front legs requries a level of core strength and control, which is not possible in a very young pup; he will be unable to hold the contact position for very long. This is often misinterpreted as bad behaviour, or lack of focus, rather than physical inability.

RUNNING AT YOUR SIDE

During the early days of agility training, focus on getting the movement patterns right. Don't worry about introducing equipment; this will come naturally at a later date as the dog grows in confidence and skill.

One very important skill is to teach the pup to run at your side, focusing on you and nothing else. Start by running in a straight line, accelerate, decelerate, introduce wide turns to each side – and keep it fun.

You are training all the basics skills required for agility and, most importantly, you are teaching the dog to focus exclusively on you. This is an essential skill which every agility dog needs to learn before progressing. Remember to keep your sessions short, make them fun and always reward. Such flatwork exercises are an invaluable part of training and help establish communication between the handler and athlete right from the start. Remember to keep your turns soft and fluid; tight turns can damage tendons, ligaments, bones and joints in young dogs.

RUNNING IN A STRAIGHT LINE

We often forget that the Collie's natural instinct is to herd and keep wide. It can, therefore, be a challenge to keep your dog at your side and running in a straight line. Again, this should initially be taught on the ground, without the extra challenge of jumping or turning, as it is likely that the dog will find it very stressful to go against his natural instinct.

When your dog has mastered this skill, progress to running him at your side in-between the agility equipment, teaching him to focus on you, and then reward at the end of the 'course'.

PREPARATION FOR JUMPING

As your dog matures and the musculoskeletal system starts to stabilise at around 8 months of age, other skills can be developed.

At this stage, you can place some obstacles on the ground, such as guttering pipes cut in half, to start training the skills required for take off and landing, and to introduce the concept of striding and bouncing between jumps.

Open up clear channels of communication when handling your dog.

It must be emphasised that such obstacles should not stand off the ground. The impact on the dog's joints should be kept to a minimum as he is still growing and developing.

INTRODUCING AGILITY EQUIPMENT

Once the dog reaches 12 months, simple exercises involving agility equipment can be introduced. Again, the idea is to make it easy, so start with some very low jumps (25 cm) in a straight line and make your turns wide.

When introducing sequencing – jumps and a tunnel, for example – make it easy for the dog so he can be rewarded for a good performance. Don't make the entry and exit into the tunnel difficult, and keep the tunnel straight. After a while you can progress to some shallow curves in the line of the tunnel, but acute angles should be avoided until the dog has developed a good level of strength, balance and flexibility. A dog's confidence is easily damaged at this stage, and is difficult to restore.

LEARNING TO BALANCE

Working on a balance board can be an excellent way to prepare for the seesaw. A moving platform is scary, particularly if you are not balanced or have poor proprioception, and a narrow, moving plank is the worst of all worlds. A broad, wide board – even one that moves – is easier to cope with in the early stages. Once this has been negotiated, the dog will more easily accept the narrow plank.

COMMUNICATING WITH YOUR DOG

We expect a lot from our young dogs. They are not mini adults and, in just the same way as we would expect a toddler to tire quickly and behave badly when placed under pressure, the same is true of dogs. Teenagers are notoriously difficult – so are young dogs. They need patient, firm and careful handling where boundaries are set and respected, but empathy and sensitivity is maintained at all times.

It is very easy to confuse a young dog with commands/cues that are unclear or given at an inappropriate time. This is a particular problem in the novice handler, who is thinking things through rather than acting intuitively. Thinking takes time – that means a delay in relaying the command to the dog – by which time he has moved past the point where the cue should have been given. This can be very stressful and confusing for the dog.

The aim of every handler should be to keep things simple during training. Plan the manoeuvres in your head, and work out what you want to achieve before you put the sequence into practice. Be very clear, in your own mind, about what you need to tell the dog and when you should give the cue, to ensure you both react in time.

Verbal cues and signaling should also be very distinct so as not to confuse the young dog. There is a considerable difference between a wide and a tight turn. Make this clear in your handling, otherwise the dog will become confused and stressed. The need to keep things simple – and easy to reward – cannot be over-emphasised at this stage.

GOLDEN RULES

- **Keep the emphasis on play.**
- **Keep sessions very short: 1-2 minutes, 3 times a week is much better than a single 10-minute session.**
- **Quality not quantity.**
- **Use the environment and don't rely on equipment.**
- **Always ask yourself first: what did I do wrong?**
- **Video your performance and watch and learn.**
- **Don't rush.**
- **Each dog is an individual and will achieve results in his own time.**

Chapter Six:
CONDITIONING THE AGILITY DOG

Injury starts with poor conditioning. For the purpose of this chapter, the term 'conditioning' is used rather than 'training' so as not to cause confusion between conditioning for cardiovascular and muscle fitness and skill training.

Basic conditioning is fundamental to sustained athletic ability and performance. It should bring about purposeful adaptations within the musculoskeletal system and the cardiovascular system and thus provide firm foundations for skill training, which is different for each sporting activity.

In general, the principles of conditioning are applicable across every sporting field and do not differ greatly between agility, canicross, sledding or even obedience. Hand in hand with conditioning comes fatigue, and the skilled handler will recognise when a dog is becoming fatigued and how to manage or prevent this with appropriate conditioning. Nutrition is equally important. Nutrients provide the energy for work; a poorly balanced diet with inadequate calories, or a diet that may be balanced but does not allow the calories to be released when required, will hamper a conditioning programme.

Most athletic activity is seasonal, allowing dogs to have a rest period in winter. This is essential to prevent the athlete from becoming sour as it allows the tissues time to recover and takes away the mental pressure of sustained competitive activity. The dog is not idle but he does less, particularly with respect to skill training. Rapid detraining results in rapid loss of cardiovascular endurance and a slowed down regulation of skeletal muscle fitness, with loss of endurance and power generating capacity. It also results in stiffening of connective tissue, such as the fascia, and loss of elasticity within the ligaments and tendons.

This loss of flexibility will be even more marked if the tissues are inflamed. Loss of flexibility can manifest as either reduced range of motion at the level of a specific joint, or a general loss of flexibility such as in the vertebral column where a large number of individual units function as a whole. It is therefore necessary to work strategically towards maintaining a basic level of fitness year-round which can then be developed and maintained throughout the competitive season.

COMPONENTS OF CONDITIONING

A handler needs to understand the integral components of a conditioning regime as these might, potentially, relate to injury. There is scant information regarding the conditioning of the canine athlete so we have to extrapolate from the human and the equine field. The nature of the training should ultimately be discipline or sports dependent, since the demands of a 7-hour endurance sled race are very different from those of a short duration Greyhound sprint race.

Conditioning describes the physical requirements and physiological adaptations that arise from activity interventions, which, ultimately, lead to improved performance in any given sport. A number of general principles apply:

Specificity: How individual muscles adapt to specific training undertaken.

Individuality: How each individual dog responds.

Reversibility: Loss of training benefit when stopped.

If an unvaried training regime is applied all year round, the individual would soon become stressed and tired, and prone to injury. It is therefore important to vary the intensity of training throughout the year, e.g. conditioning, pre-competition, competition and rest:

Conditioning stage: The emphasis is on developing both aerobic and anaerobic fitness, strength and power.

Pre-competition stage: The emphasis shifts slightly to work on skill or performance

Competition: Conditioning should take a back seat while the focus is on performance.

Often inadequate attention to the conditioning stage is encountered in the field of canine sports medicine. Owners and veterinary surgeons alike have a poor understanding of what constitutes a truly 'fit' dog and how this can be achieved.

The tendency is to move into the pre-competition or competition stage, leaving the dog inadequately prepared for the demands of competition and, therefore, more prone to injury. It is essential to vary the training load, allocating easy days and easy weeks, to give the athlete adequate time to recover, e.g. train hard for 4 days out of 7 and 3 weeks out of 4.

Stimulating structural and functional changes to improve performance is the major objective of conditioning. To achieve this a conditioning programme must be drawn up, and adhered to, with a focus on:

- The frequency and length of the training sessions.
- The type of training.
- The speed, intensity, duration and repetition of the performance.
- Rest intervals.

SPECIFICITY

The type or adaptation that occurs both within the muscle, and the cardiovascular system, reflects the type of conditioning that is undertaken. In this way, a specific anaerobic exercise used in strength/power training will bring about adaptations in the strength and power function of the system, but will not help endurance. Conversely, aerobic conditioning methods will improve oxygen carrying and delivery capacity to the muscle, but will not increase strength.

Conditioning changes are also very muscle specific. For example, different muscles are used in swimming and walking so if the conditioning programme only consists of swimming, the dog will not be able to run any faster on land.

For this reason, whole body conditioning should be undertaken initially. But once a basic level of fitness is achieved, the most important component, in terms of fitness of each discipline, should be identified and the athlete trained accordingly. There is no advantage for endurance athletes to do large amounts of power training, nor for athletes involved in disciplines requiring strength to do a vast amount of endurance work.

As can be seen from the diagram below, agility draws upon components of both strength and endurance. The dog must be able to run around the ring repeatedly, which is an aerobic activity. However, he must also be able to increase energy delivery at the point of take off for a jump or moving up the A-frame, which calls on anaerobic energy delivery. Therefore both types of work must be incorporated into his conditioning and training programme.

Strength versus endurance training

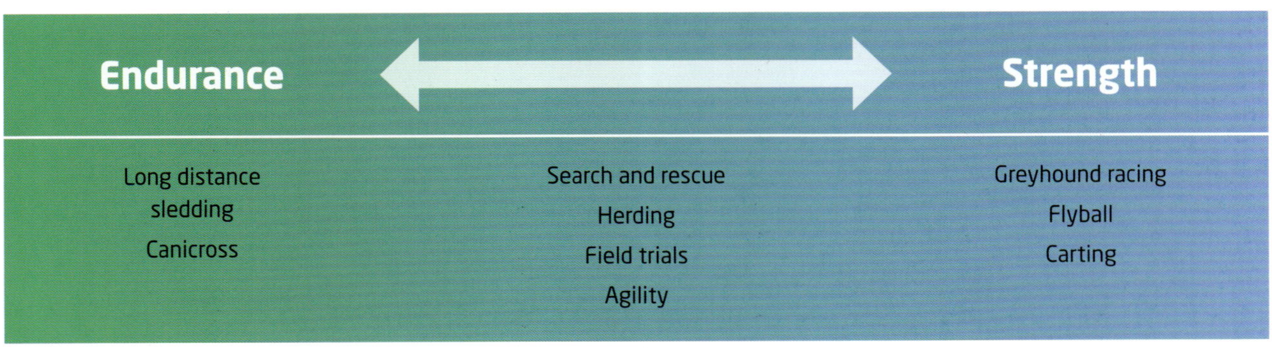

OVERLOAD

Overload training allows an athlete to perform work at greater intensity, or to perform a greater volume of work at a given intensity. The principles include:

- Applying stress to the body over and above that which is normally encountered.
- Allowing adequate recovery to produce a training effect, i.e. giving the muscles and the heart and lungs time to adapt.
- Increasing training load by changing the volume (quantity and duration) or the intensity (quality) of training.
- Only increasing volume or intensity at a given time.
- Progressing new training activities slowly.
- Monitoring outcomes closely.

INDIVIDUALITY

There are significant individual differences between dogs in terms of both phenotype and psyche. Some dogs will require a substantial amount of conditioning and skill training, whilst others will succumb to over-training very easily.

REVERSIBILITY

Detraining, or loss of performance adaptations, occur very quickly when a dog stops training. It has been found that 1-2 weeks of detraining is enough to reduce both metabolic and exercise capacity. In just 3-4 weeks the number of capillaries in trained muscle drops by 25 per cent. VO2max (maximum aerobic metabolic rate) declines by 25 per cent, as does cardiac output in the same timescale. In humans this equates to a loss of aerobic capacity at a rate of 1 per cent per day. This reiterates the importance of maintaining a background level of fitness in the off-season.

CONDITIONING METHODS

Conditioning methods include:

Aerobic

Anaerobic

Strength and power work

Proprioceptive training

Discipline specific training

Agility or flexibility training

A balanced programme will address all of these components, within the conditioning programme, with the emphasis placed on varying each individual component depending on both the stage of conditioning and individual requirements.

AEROBIC OR ENDURANCE TRAINING

Aerobic conditioning generally involves sustained exercise at moderate but not maximum heart rate. The aim is to improve the delivery of oxygen to muscle, and the ability of muscle to use oxygen as delivered. The level of exercise must be high enough to stress the cardiovascular system – typically 60-80 per cent of maximum heart rate (300-318 beats per minute for an adult dog). The maximum heart rate (HRMax) achieved during exercise does show variation between species of dog – from 300 beats per minute in crossbreds to 330 beats per minute in the Greyhound. By extrapolating across from human values, the following figures can be assumed:

Early training range:
Training at 70 per cent HRmax – 50 per cent VO2Max

Moderate or medium intensity training:
Training at 80 per cent HRMax – 70 per cent VO2max

High intensity training:
Training at 90-100 per cent HRMax – 80-100 per cent VO2max

EXERCISES FOR STRENGTH TRAINING

Metabolic changes
Cardiovascular changes
Muscle changes

METABOLIC CHANGES

With aerobic conditioning programmes, an increase in mitochondrial numbers occurs within the muscle. This, in turn, increases the amount of enzymes involved in aerobic metabolism, allowing the body to produce more ATP (adenosine triphosphate, the high-energy molecule) aerobically before high levels of lactate accumulate. Mitochondrial numbers can increase by up to 50 per cent within 3 weeks of starting training. Aerobic or endurance training also increases the dog's ability to use fat as an energy source. This adaptation reflects:

- The increase in blood flow through conditioned muscle.
- The increase in fat digesting enzymes.
- The increase in mitochondrial numbers.
- A drop in concentration of stress hormone in trained muscle.

This ability to use fat as an energy source, rather than glycogen/glucose, is extremely important because it conserves muscle glycogen stores and delays fatigue. At the same time, aerobic conditioning helps with efficient carbohydrate metabolism. The net result is a reduced dependence on carbohydrate metabolism and an increased dependence on fat.

Within the muscle, specific changes are seen in response to aerobic conditioning. These include an increase in size of the aerobic or slow twitch type 1 muscle fibre (see Muscle structure, page 45). There is also an increase in myoglobin levels.

Aerobic or endurance work should bring about changes to the cardiovascular system as well. These include an increase in heart size, and in the heart's efficiency as a pump. Many athletes – human, equine and canine – have an audible heart murmur. This does not mean that their heart is not working but rather that is has grown in size.

The heart wall is made of muscle, and like any other muscle, cardiac muscle increases in size when trained. This means that the heart wall thickens and the size of the heart chamber expands, so it increases in overall dimensions. The valves, however, are not made of muscle and will increase in size as the heart grows. Often they become stretched open and allow blood to flow backwards through them. This creates turbulence, which is audible as a 'murmur' when the heart is auscultated.

Some studies show that athletes with murmurs are more likely to win races than those without. But it is important to bear in mind that this type of murmur is created by very different circumstances than those that result from pathological changes

Aerobic conditioning allows more blood, and more oxygen, to be pushed around the body.

within the heart and are associated with heart failure. Endurance training, in particular, is effective at increasing chamber size whilst strength or anaerobic training is more effective at increasing the thickness of the heart wall.

These changes within the heart result in the organ becoming a stronger and more effective pump, i.e. it can push more blood around the body at slower heart rates because each pump of the heart moves more blood than an untrained heart. This, in turn, reduces the amount of work that the heart has to do and the amount of oxygen that is actually used by heart muscle itself.

One of the other effects of aerobic training is to produce more blood through increasing plasma volume; up to 20 per cent increase in plasma volume is seen in response to endurance training. This reflects an increase in a protein, known as albumin, and is one of the reasons why more protein is required in the diet in early conditioning. An increase in plasma volume makes the heart work more efficiently, and it also helps the dog control his body temperature by absorbing the heat produced by exercise.

Perhaps the most significant response to aerobic or endurance programmes is the change in cardiac output – the amount of blood, and therefore oxygen, pushed around the body. This means that more blood, and therefore oxygen, is delivered to the muscle for aerobic work. At the same time, the number of capillaries (small blood vessels) within the muscle increases dramatically so each muscle cell is closer to the source of oxygen and can extract it from the circulation more easily.

Aerobic exercise also brings about changes within the lungs. The muscles involved in moving the chest increase in size allowing the dog to breathe more deeply, thus filling the lungs with more oxygen. The breathing or respiratory rate also slows so, at high levels of exercise, the dog, proportionately, does not breathe as fast as the untrained dog. This allows the lungs more time to fill with air, and also reduces the amount of energy used up in breathing.

The net result of these changes is the more rapid delivery of oxygen to the muscle, an improved ability to remove oxygen from the blood and more efficient temperature control. Lean body mass should also increase and, potentially, psychological benefits will also be seen with the dog becoming happier in himself. Other changes include purposeful structural adaptations, such as increased bone density, improved elastic efficiency of ligaments and tendons, and an increase in size of the ligaments and tendons.

Aerobic training can occur in two forms, namely continuous training and interval training.

CONTINUOUS TRAINING

With continuous training, exercise is sustained at the same intensity for a variable duration of time – aiming for 60-80 per cent heart rate maximum (HRmax). An example would be continuous trotting for 40 minutes. This develops aerobic capacity and involves repetitive whole body movements, such as walking or running.

The aim is to maintain heart rate at a constant level so, ideally, heart rate monitors should be used. However these are difficult to use, in practice, as they require an area of coat to be clipped over the heart in order to achieve accurate readings.

INTERVAL TRAINING

Steady, continuous exercise is interspersed with short periods of higher intensity work followed by a recovery period. The aim is to work at 85 per cent of HRmax reducing to 35-40 per cent of HRmax in the recovery period. This technique is particularly good for sports such as flyball and agility where short intense bursts of anaerobic activity are required over and above a basic aerobic level of fitness. It allows the body to exercise intensively without lactate building up and is, thus, a very effective form of aerobic training or conditioning.

An example would be:

5 minute warm up, 1 minute running and 2 minutes slow trotting, repeated 5 times as a set.

Depending on the fitness of the dog, the set could be repeated up to 3 times in an exercise session.

Other variables would be reducing the recovery interval from 2 minutes to 1 minute, increasing the number of repetitions or increasing the speed of the sprint.

Interval training can also enhance anaerobic capacity or strength due to the sprint component.

PRACTICAL AEROBIC TRAINING

Aerobic or endurance sessions should be performed 3-4 times a week. A minimum of 2 sessions a week is essential. Dogs should exercise at 60-80 per cent of their maximum heart rate for 30-40 minutes at a time. Initially, at the start of training, this may represent fast walking or moderate trotting, depending on the dog's basic level of fitness. As time progresses, the dog should increase to a fast trot or canter.

Bear in mind that once the dog has adapted to the exercise, there is no further benefit from performing the exercise at the same level. So if the dog starts out by walking for 30 minutes in week one, by week 3 (9 sessions later), he should be trotting at a moderate pace, and after another 9 sessions he should be able to trot fast and for 45-50 minutes.

Generally, the higher the intensity of training – whilst remaining in the aerobic zone – the more effective it is. However, you need to be aware that excessive training intensity, and abrupt increases in training volume, can lead to injury. Therefore, with an unfit dog you will need to start slowly and progress gradually.

ANAEROBIC OR STRENGTH TRAINING

Anaerobic changes in response to training include the development of increased levels of anaerobic substrate – ATP, creatinine and glycogen in resting muscle. This, in turn, can bring about significant increase in muscle strength. The other important adaptation is the increase in concentration of enzymes associated with anaerobic metabolism of glucose. There is also an increase in the ability to generate high levels of lactate at extreme exercise. Finally, an increase in diameter of the fast twitch, type 2 muscle fibre (see Chapter 4: Muscle structure, page 45) is seen.

These changes are best achieved by intermittent, or interval training, when short periods of intense training are separated by periods of rest or recovery. Muscles must be worked to their maximum force generating capacity. The principle of such training is to achieve a level of lactic acidosis with one effort, and then allow the body to recover from it.

The goal of strength, or anaerobic, training is to gradually and progressively overload the muscle in order to stimulate protein synthesis, which results in an increase in diameter of the muscle fibre. This, in turn, increases muscle strength. Muscle strength is the amount of force that may be exerted by an individual in a single, maximum muscle contraction. Power is the maximum amount of work an individual can perform in a given unit of time.

The most common form of strength training is resistance activity, where the dog's muscular activity is performed against an opposing force, i.e. there is a force trying to stop the dog from moving. Examples include accelerating upwards against gravity, moving against an inert object, pushing against friction and braking against momentum.

Strengthening exercises are isometric if the joint does not move during the exercise and the muscle length stays the same. Isometric strengthening exercises are generally used when the muscle is very weak and are more likely to be part of a rehabilitation programme rather than a conditioning programme. One example would be a standing weight shift where the extensor muscles contract against gravity but do not move the limb.

During isotonic exercises, the body part moves against the force and the part is strengthened across the entire range of movement. In humans this is most commonly performed through lifting weights. This is more difficult to achieve in dogs. Distal limb weights can be used, but it is difficult to calculate an appropriate weight, and the dog cannot tell you when he is feeling pain.

It is easier to use the dog's own body as the weight, e.g. performing a wave or a high five. Getting the muscle to contract or lengthen against a constant force can also be used, e.g. placing a theraband (an elastic resistance strap) on the limb. Strength training is more effective when the muscle is lengthening against a force, e.g. pulling against a theraband or walking down a steep gradient.

Strength training exercises can be divided into two basic groups. The first group involves the use of largely static exercises to strengthen a specific body part, e.g. waving or a high five to strengthen the forelimb, carting or pulling an object to strengthen the hindlimbs. Care must be taken with this type of specific exercise regime, ensuring that a balanced approach is taken to strengthen all muscle groups through choosing different sequences of exercises. However, if specific muscle imbalances exist, targeted strength training can be used to even these out.

The second group of exercises is performed largely outdoors and serves to strengthen the whole body in a balanced fashion. Such exercises include running through deep water, running up sand dunes and jumping.

Exercises for strength training

Forelimbs	Hindlimbs	Core	General
Waving/High5	Dancing	Balance board	Walking in deep sand
Wheelbarrow	Jumping vertically	Diagonal standing	Walking in deep water
Digging	Pulling against a theraband	Crawl	Trotting over poles
Backwards walking up hill	Running up hill/sand dunes	Balance ball	
	Carting/Sledding		

Rapid and repeated transitions between walk and canter will also help to develop muscle power. Interval training, where the sprint work is performed at maximum intensity – often involving an uphill gradient – can be a good way of increasing muscle strength.

Since a by-product of anaerobic exercise is lactic acid, and since muscle fibres are worked to their maximum, anaerobic training results in low-grade muscle damage and can lead to significant muscle soreness. It has the potential to cause significant harm compared to aerobic methods and should therefore be undertaken with care. It is particularly important that the body is given sufficient time to heal and repair between anaerobic training sessions otherwise there is an increased risk of injury.

The efficiency of an anaerobic training regime can be increased through making sure:

- There is an adequate warm up period before starting the exercise regime to increase body temperature and tissue metabolic rate.
- Care is taken to make sure the exercise is performed well and in a controlled manner.
- The animal is not in pain.
- The exercises start slowly and increase in effort, i.e. perform the exercise with minimal resistance, initially, so the body learns which muscle to activate, in the right order, with minimal effort.
- The exercises are combined with a stretching regime to maintain range of motion.
- The muscles are strengthened through their full range of motion.

PRACTICAL ANAEROBIC TRAINING

This should consist of:

- 1-2 weekly sessions a week of whole body anaerobic conditioning, e.g. uphill sprinting, strenuous interval training. Sessions should be spaced out by 72 hours.
- 1-2 weekly sessions of focused strength training, working individual muscle groups.

Choose either one from the first group and two sessions from the second group or vice versa.

Remember more is not necessarily better. If a dog builds too much muscle, e.g. develops massive shoulders, this will limit shoulder flexion and extension and, in turn, reduce stride length. The dog will then need to take more steps to cover the same ground, which is less efficient in energy terms. This type of over-development can occur in response to non-functional training, e.g. swimming to excess or running in very high levels of water.

PROPRIOCEPTIVE TRAINING

The term proprioception comes from the Latin *'proprius'* which means 'one's own', and the word perception. It therefore describes how the body sees and controls itself in space. Sensory feedback from the receptors in the legs provides information regarding joint position, movement, vibration and pressure. This is combined with information from the eyes and the vestibular system to create a response that keeps us upright and moving in the correct direction.

Like all neural pathways, the proprioceptive pathway can be trained through the introduction of exercises that work the connections between the receptors in the legs and back, and the central

Check out the many different surfaces a dog has to negotiate when he is running a course.

nervous system. Proprioception keeps joints stable and helps co-ordinate movement patterns.

Following injury to the musculoskeletal system, proprioception is often badly affected, so exercises to restore proprioception form the mainstay of early rehabilitation exercise regimes. Changes in proprioception affect balance and muscle strength, and slow the body's response to changes in the external environment, which leads to loss of balance.

Agility is extremely challenging, in terms of proprioceptive control, due to the need to change both speed and direction in a fraction of a second. Terrain underfoot is also constantly changing between ground and equipment contact, which also provides a proprioceptive challenge. This is enhanced when the going is poor, e.g. wet and slippery ground or moving over a poor contact surface. Therefore it is essential that proprioceptive training forms part of every conditioning programme. It assists with skilled movement, and reduces the amount of force required by the muscle to stabilise the limbs, thus reducing fatigue.

Exercises to assist with proprioception include:

- Slow walking.
- Walking over novel terrain.
- Ladder walking.
- Backwards walking.
- Balance board/cushion.
- Camping/air mattress.
- Fitness balls.

PRACTICAL PROPRIOCEPTIVE TRAINING

Proprioceptive training requires intense concentration and therefore should be carried out for short periods of time – generally no more than 5 minutes in one session. As with the training of any neural pathway, it must be repeated at regular intervals to provide learning and retention. Therefore it is recommended that short periods of proprioceptive training are undertaken on a daily basis, e.g. 5 minutes twice a day.

Since it is mentally, rather than physically fatiguing, it should not result in muscle damage or injury and therefore recovery time or prolonged rest between sessions is not required.

AGILITY OR FLEXIBILITY TRAINING

Making sure that joints can move through their full range of motion is essential for maximising stride length and therefore performance. Athletic activity, even if it does not progress to injury, increases tissue stiffness and makes structures less flexible.

This is a normal response to training, but one that does need to be countered with regular stretching to maintain performance and prevent injury.

Tissues which have been injured are much more likely to be stiff and less flexible. Muscle spasm, pain, inflammation and stiffness can all limit joint range of motion. This, in turn, makes the muscle-tendon unit less stretchy, which can have a knock-on effect on surrounding joints and muscles. For example, the back can stiffen and the muscles shorten following inflammation in the knee or stifle joint. Some dogs are inherently stiffer than others and will require more intense stretching. Flexibility can be limited by a number of factors:

- Osteoarthritic changes within the joint.
- Fat or excessive muscle which limit movement of individual joints.
- Scar tissue.
- Connective tissue – ligaments/joint capsule.

When considering flexibility, it is important to differentiate between static and dynamic movement:

Static flexibility is the amount of movement that a joint can undertake when moved from A to B passively. If the value is reduced, it may lead to an increased risk of injury.

Dynamic flexibility is the movement generated under the force of a contracting muscle. This is extremely important for determining athletic activity as (stated previously) any restriction in dynamic flexibility can reduce stride length and therefore speed.

Agility places a dog's joints into extreme range of motion; good flexibility is therefore crucially important in order to prevent injury and improve performance. Traditionally, stretching has been the mainstay of maintaining flexibility. However, if the muscle tightness is secondary to nerve activity or trigger points in the muscle, these may have to be addressed first (though acupuncture/chiropractic/physiotherapy) before stretching can be effective.

The benefits of stretching include:

- Increased muscle and joint flexibility.
- Increased muscle relaxation.
- Decreased muscle soreness.
- Improved circulation.
- Prevention of adhesions.

Flexibility, which can be developed with a stretching programme is key to preventing injury and enhancing performance.

Injuries are more likely to occur when a dog is suffering from fatigue.

You need to take on board the principles of stretching (see Chapter 10: Physiotherapy Techniques), but it is equally important to design a stretching programme specifically for the individual concerned. The dog should be well warmed-up prior to starting the stretching programme, e.g. through walking or jogging. In addition, heat packs can be applied to the target area before starting work. Different muscles need to be stretched for different lengths of time but, in general, start by holding the stretch for 15-20 seconds and work up to 30-60 seconds. Remember stretching should always be pain-free.

PRACTICAL FLEXIBILITY TRAINING

For most dogs, 3-4 sessions focusing on flexibility should be sufficient. Once a dog demonstrates good flexibility, 2 sessions a week will suffice. Some dogs are naturally much tighter, and may require daily stretching. Before stretching, make sure the dog is warmed-up and then undertake a 5-10 minute stretching routine.

Your must never:

- Stretch before exercise: This increases the risk of injury, possibly by making the tissues too relaxed and therefore unable to respond to the challenge of exercise.
- Cause pain or discomfort.

FATIGUE

Significant debate exists as to where fatigue exactly occurs, i.e. is it in the muscle, is it in the nervous system, or is it a purely psychological phenomenon?

Fatigue occurs when exercise continues to the point when muscle and liver glycogen stores are compromised. This can occur even though there is enough oxygen in the system to continue to exercise aerobically. Fatigue represents the decline in muscle tension, or force capacity, with repeated stimulation or during a given time period.

In humans, this definition also encompasses a perception of increased difficulty in achieving an exercise outcome. Since horses in intense training can also lose their competitive edge (over-training) without any apparent organic disorder, it is likely that central or physiological fatigue exists in animals as well.

For muscle to function, a series of events occur leading from the higher centres in the brain, via the spinal cord and motorneurons, and ending with the individual cross-bridges generating force. A failure at any point will lead to loss of force, which involves:

- Reduced glycogen content of the active muscle in the face of adequate oxygen supply.
- Lack of oxygen and increased blood and muscle lactate.
- Lack of response within the muscle to the nerve stimulus.
- Fatigue at the neuromuscular junction when an action potential fails to cross from the motor neuron to the muscle fibre due to changes in electrolyte gradients.
- Interference with the contractile process due to altered Ca 2+ uptake by the sarcoplasmic reticulum.
- Elevation in muscle temperature.

RECOVERY

In recent years there has been an increasing amount of information regarding the correct management of the athlete during the recovery period in order to maximise the response to training and to prevent injury. Often the athlete will have to perform several runs close together, thus rapid recovery from exhaustive activity is extremely important.

During the recovery phase the following should be achieved:

- Restoration of function.
- Neuromuscular recovery.
- Tissue repair.
- Resolution of muscle soreness.
- Psychological recovery.

Recovery can be assisted by adequate cooling down and providing the right nutrients – including water – at the right time. Massage should also be considered at this stage to assist with muscle recovery.

OVER-TRAINING

Over-training must be avoided as it can lead to prolonged muscle soreness and poor performance. It can also predispose the dog to immunosupression and increase the risk of respiratory disease. It can be associated with changes in thyroid hormone levels, and can increase the level of circulating cortisol (stress hormone).

Loss of body mass can also be a sign of over-training, as can loss of appetite. But often the most common, initial sign is a decline in performance. Body weight, appetite, mental attitude and general behaviour can be used as markers to prevent over-training. Signs of over-training can also include increased muscle soreness and prolonged recovery times.

Over-training can be prevented through providing adequate rest and recovery periods, and by providing enough variation, including periods of play, in the conditioning programme.

WARMING UP AND COOLING DOWN

Warming up prepares the body for exercise. The type of exercise about to be embarked upon should determine the type of warm up. The most effective warm up should consist of both general and specific exercises:

General exercises should include jogging, gentle stretching and resistance exercises.

Specific exercises include movements specific for the sport, e.g. jumping and weaving for the agility dog, rapid gait transitions for the trialling dog, gentle sprinting for the racer.

The possible benefits include:

- Increased blood flow to muscle.
- Increased oxyhaemoglobin breakdown and improved oxygen delivery to muscle.
- Increased capacitation and reduced vascular resistance.
- Increased release of oxygen from myoglobin.
- Enhanced cellular metabolism.
- Reduced muscle viscosity leading to smoother contraction and increased mechanical efficiency.
- Increased speed of impulse propogation.
- Increased receptor sensitivity.
- Improved range of motion.

- Decreased stiffness.
- Increased relaxation and focus.
- Enhanced cardiovascular response to sudden exercise.

No data exists on the most appropriate duration or intensity of the warm up period. Thus, a handler needs to monitor each and every competition dog and determine what appears appropriate for each individual. The warm up effect lasts 30 minutes, therefore too early a warm up should be avoided. This can be an issue in disciplines such as agility where large numbers of competitors have to queue for their turn. If the dog is sitting, any benefit of warm up is lost.

Recent human studies have shown that an effective warm up can reduce the risk of injury by 50 per cent. The exact mechanism of this is unknown, i.e., is it a purely physiological effect, or is it due to altered levels of neuromotor control, focus and muscle strength?

The evidence underlying the benefits of warming up through stretching is scanty. In fact, it appears that including a stretching programme as part of a warm up regime can be counter-productive and predispose to injury. There does appear to be benefit in readying both the musculoskeletal and cardiovascular systems to exercise through gentle activity over the terrain, or equipment that they will be used in competition *(Fradkin et al, 2010, Huang et al, 2011)*. Appropriate warm up regimes are also thought to assist with injury prevention *(Bien, 2011)*.

Most serious sportsmen undergo a warm down or cool down recovery period. The duration is variable and largely dictated by the duration of the competition, but it generally varies from 5-15 minutes. Generally a slow jog or walk, followed by appropriate stretching, should be carried out. Again, there is conflicting evidence regarding its effectiveness.

Some texts advocate the use of cold therapy in recovery. In practice, if a dog has pre-existing injuries from which he has recovered, such as tendon or ligament strain, or if one or more joints are compromised with reduced movement, the application of ice therapy following exercise can prevent further damage and inflammation.

Another important component of the cool down period is allowing the dog to mentally relax, which may be as important as the effect on the musculoskeletal system. During competition, the dog is expected to be alert and focused at all times. By default, he will be in sympathetic overdrive, or in fight and flight mode, with high levels of circulating stress hormones. This allows adrenalin to be released, the heart rate to increase, the airways to dilate and improves the use of muscle glycogen. At the same time it diverts blood away from the intestines to the muscle.

After completing a round, agility dogs are often rewarded by tugging, which continues to wind them up – and further promotes these physical responses. This is likely to be associated with further endorphin release, which acts as a stimulant. So, if the dog is then immediately put back in his crate, he never has a chance to calm down. This, in turn, prevents the tissues from relaxing and impedes blood flow patterns returning to normal. Over time this can result in stressed dogs that never learn to relax, making for tight tissues that are more prone to injury.

Following exercise there should be a switch to rest and repair where the parasympathetic nervous system takes over. This allows the muscle to relax and restore its supply of glycogen ready for the next period of exercise. If this does not occur, the athlete may start to show adverse signs, such as muscle soreness and fatigue, increased resting heart rate, lack of sleep, and poor absorption of nutrients from the diet. If taken to the extreme, the heart rate will eventually slow down, the body will become unable to use glycogen, and the capacity for exercise drops right off.

Therefore each cool down period should also focus on calming techniques to teach the dog to switch off and relax. High intensity games should be avoided, and replaced with slow, gentle stroking coupled with slow walking in a calm environment. Once the dog has settled both in terms of heart rate and mental drive – then and only then – should he be kennelled. Adequate provision of water and easily digestible nutrients are also critical in the cool down period to assist with preventing muscle damage and soreness.

A comprehensive conditioning programme takes a minimum of 6 weeks to complete in a relatively fit dog. A young dog, an unfit dog or an elderly dog will often take up to 12 weeks to complete a basic conditioning programme. Once this has been achieved, the focus can shift on to skill or discipline specific training (see Chapter 7).

Before embarking on a conditioning programme, it is useful to carry out a quick health check which includes:

- Gait analysis.
- Resting heart and respiratory rate.
- Musculoskeletal assessment.
- Laboratory analysis to test levels of red and white blood cells and functioning of the thyroid hormone.

This ensures that the dog is in the best possible condition prior to starting training.

On pages 71-73 there are rough guides to daily training regimes in a 6 and 12 week conditioning programme.

These are just guidelines; individual variation will mean that some dogs will require several more weeks to achieve their target whilst others will be able to progress more quickly. Towards the end of the conditioning period, skill training can be introduced, potentially on the days which focus on strength training. It is important that the one rest day is maintained.

References

Bien D.P., R*ationale and implementation of anterior cruciate ligament injury prevention warm up programmes in female athletes*, J Strength and Cond Research 2011, 25, 271-285

Davis et al, *Effect of training and strenuous exercise on haematological values and peripheral blood leukocyte subsets in racing sled dogs*, JAVMA 232; 6: 2008

Evason et al, *Alteration in thyroid hormone concentrations in healthy sled dogs before and after athletic conditioning*, AJVR 65; 3: 2004

Fradikin A.J. et al, *Effects of warming up on the physical performance: a systematic review with meta-analysis*, J Strength Cond Research, 2010: 24, 140-148

Hill R.C. et al, *Mild food restriction increases the speed of racing greyhounds*, Jvet int med,1999; 13: 281

Hill R.C. et al, *Effect of increased dietary protein and decreased dietary carbohydrate on performance and body composition in racing greyhounds*, Am J Vet Med Assoc 2001b. 62: 440-447

Hinchcliff K.W. et al, *Effect of racing on serum sodium and potassium concentrations an acid -base status of Alaskan sled dogs*, JAm Vet Med Assoc, 1997a; 210, 1615-1618

Hinchcliff K.W. et al, *Exercise associated hyponatremia in Alaskan sled dogs:urinary and hormonal responses*, J App Physiology, 1997c 83: 824-829

Huang J.S. et al, *Sling exercises and traditional warm up have similar effects on the velocity and accuracy of throwing*, 2011, J Strength Cond Research: 25, 1673-1679

Reynolds A.J. et al, *Effect of diet and training on muscle glycogen storage and utilisation in sled dogs*, J App Physiology, 1995; 79: 1601-161607

Reynolds A.J. et al, *Effect of post exercise carbohydrate supplementation on muscle glycogen repletion in trained sled dogs*, Am J Vet Res 1997; 58: 1252-1256

Toll P. et al, *The effect of dietary fat and carbohydrate on the sprint performance in racing Greyhounds*, Proceedings of the 8th International Racing Greyhound Symposium, North Am Vet Conference, Gainsville, FL: NAVC 1992 1-3

6 week conditioning programme

Week	Monday	Tuesday	Wednesday	Thursday	Friday	Saturday	Sunday
1	Aerobic - 30min trotting	Strength training - 10min	Aerobic - 30min trotting	Strength training - 10min	Rest - 2-3 slow walks, medium length	Aerobic - 30min	Long walk/ lots of play
	Proprioception - 2x5min	Proprioception - 1x5min	Proprioception - 2x5min	Proprioception - 1x5min		Proprioception - 1x5min	Proprioception - 2x5min
		Stretching - 1x5min		Stretching - 1x5min			Stretching - 1x5min
2	Aerobic - 35min trotting	Strength training - 10min	Aerobic - 35min trotting	Strength training - 10min	Rest - 2-3 slow walks, medium length	Aerobic - 35min	Long walk/ lots of play
	Proprioception - 2x5min	Proprioception - 1x5min	Proprioception - 2x5min	Proprioception - 1x5min		Proprioception - 1x5min	Proprioception - 2x5min
		Stretching - 1x5min		Stretching - 1x5min			Stretching - 1x5min
3	Aerobic - 40min trotting	Strength training - 10min	Aerobic - 40min trotting	Strength training - 10min	Rest - 2-3 slow walks, medium length	Aerobic - 45min trotting	Long walk/ lots of play
	Proprioception - 2x5min	Proprioception - 1x5min	Proprioception - 2x5min	Proprioception - 1x5min		Proprioception - 2x5min	Proprioception - 2x5min
		Stretching - 1x5min		Stretching - 1x5min			Stretching - 1x5min
4	Aerobic - 50min trotting	Strength training - 15min	Aerobic - 50min trotting	Strength training - 15min	Rest - 2-3 slow walks, medium length	Aerobic - 55min trotting	Long walk/ lots of play
	Proprioception - 2x5min	Proprioception - 1x5min	Proprioception - 2x5min	Proprioception - 1x5min		Proprioception - 2x5min	Proprioception - 2x5min
		Stretching - 1x5min		Stretching - 1x5min			Stretching - 1x5min
5	Aerobic - 60min trotting	Strength training - 15min	Aerobic - 60min trotting	Strength training - 15min	Rest - 2-3 slow walks, medium length	Aerobic - 65min trotting	Long walk/ lots of play
	Proprioception - 2x5min	Proprioception - 1x5min	Proprioception - 2x5min	Proprioception - 1x5min		Proprioception - 2x5min	Proprioception - 2x5min
		Stretching - 1x5min		Stretching - 1x5min			Stretching - 1x5min
6	Aerobic - 80min trotting	Strength training - 20min	Aerobic - 30min trotting	Strength training - 15min	Rest - 2-3 slow walks, medium length	Aerobic - 35min trotting	Long walk/ lots of play
	Proprioception - 2x5min	Proprioception - 1x5min	Proprioception - 2x5min	Proprioception - 1x5min		Proprioception - 2x5min	Proprioception - 2x5min
		Stretching - 1x5min		Stretching - 1x5min			Stretching - 1x5min

12 week conditioning programme

Week	Monday	Tuesday	Wednesday	Thursday	Friday	Saturday	Sunday
1	Aerobic - 20-30min walking	Strength training - 2min	Aerobic - 20-30min walking	Strength training - 2min	Rest - 2-3 slow walks, short length	Aerobic - 20-30min walking	Rest - 2-3 slow walks, short length
	Proprioception - 2x5min	Proprioception - 1x5min	Proprioception - 2x5min	Proprioception - 2x5min		Proprioception - 2x5min	Proprioception - 2x5min
		Stretching - 1x5min		Stretching - 1x5min			Stretching - 1x5min
2	Aerobic - 20-30min walking	Strength training - 2min	Aerobic - 20-30min walking	Strength training - 2min	Rest - 2-3 slow walks, short length	20-30min walking	Rest - 2-3 slow walks, short length
	Proprioception - 2x5min	Proprioception - 2x5min	Proprioception - 2x5min	Proprioception - 2x5min		Proprioception - 2x5min	Proprioception - 2x5min
		Stretching - 1x5min		Stretching - 1x5min			Stretching - 1x5min
3	Aerobic - 30-35min walking	Strength training - 4min	Aerobic - 30-35min walking	Strength training - 4min	Rest - 2-3 slow walks, medium length	Aerobic - 30-35min walking	Medium walk/ play
	Proprioception - 2x5min	Proprioception - 2x5min	Proprioception - 2x5min	Proprioception - 2x5min		Proprioception - 2x5min	Proprioception - 2x5min
		Stretching - 1x5min		Stretching - 1x5min			Stretching - 1x5min
4	Aerobic - 40min walking interspersed with 5-10min trotting	Strength training - 5min	Aerobic - 40min walking interspersed with 5-10min trotting	Strength training - 5min	Rest - 2-3 slow walks, medium length	Aerobic - 40min walking interspersed with 5-10min trotting	Medium walk/ lots of play
	Proprioception - 2x5min	Proprioception - 2x5min	Proprioception - 2x5min	Proprioception - 2x5min		Proprioception - 2x5min	Proprioception - 2x5min
		Stretching - 1x5min		Stretching - 1x5min			Stretching - 1x5min
5	Aerobic - 40min walking interspersed with 10min trotting	Strength training - 5min	Aerobic - 40min walking interspersed with 10min trotting	Strength training - 5min	Rest - 2-3 slow walks, medium length	Aerobic - 40min walking interspersed with 10min trotting	Long walk/ lots of play
	Proprioception - 2x5min	Proprioception - 2x5min	Proprioception - 2x5min	Proprioception - 2x5min		Proprioception - 2x5min	Proprioception - 2x5min
		Stretching - 1x5min		Stretching - 1x5min			Stretching - 1x5min
6	Aerobic - 50min walking interspersed with 10min trotting	Strength training - 7min	Aerobic - 50min walking interspersed with 10min trotting	Strength training - 7min	Rest - 2-3 slow walks, medium length	Aerobic - 50min walking interspersed with 10min trotting	Long walk/ lots of play
	Proprioception - 2x5min	Proprioception - 2x5min	Proprioception - 2x5min	Proprioception - 2x5min		Proprioception - 2x5min	Proprioception - 2x5min
		Stretching - 1x5min		Stretching - 1x5min			Stretching - 1x5min

7	Aerobic - 45min walking interspersed with 15min trotting	Strength training - 8min	Aerobic - 45min walking interspersed with 15min trotting	Strength training - 8min	Rest - 2-3 slow walks, medium length	Aerobic - 45min walking interspersed with 15min trotting	Long walk/ lots of play
	Proprioception - 2x5min	Proprioception - 2x5min	Proprioception - 2x5min	Proprioception - 2x5min		Proprioception - 2x5min	Proprioception - 2x5min
		Stretching - 1x5min		Stretching - 1x5min			Stretching - 1x5min
8	Aerobic - 40min walking interspersed with 20min trotting	Strength training - 10min	Aerobic - 40min walking interspersed with 20min trotting	Strength training - 10min	Rest - 2-3 slow walks, medium length	Aerobic - 40min walking interspersed with 15min trotting	Long walk/ lots of play
	Proprioception - 2x5min	Proprioception - 2x5min	Proprioception - 2x5min	Proprioception - 2x5min		Proprioception - 2x5min	Proprioception - 2x5min
		Stretching - 1x5min		Stretching - 1x5min			Stretching - 1x5min
9	Aerobic - 30min walking interspersed with 30min trotting	Strength training - 10min	Aerobic - 30min walking interspersed with 30min trotting	Strength training - 10min	Rest - 2-3 slow walks, short length	Aerobic - 30min walking interspersed with 30min trotting	Long walk/ lots of play
	Proprioception - 2x5min	Proprioception - 2x5min	Proprioception - 2x5min	Proprioception - 2x5min		Proprioception - 2x5min	Proprioception - 2x5min
		Stretching - 1x5min		Stretching - 1x5min			Stretching - 1x5min
10	Aerobic - 20min walking interspersed with 40min trotting	Strength training - 10min	Aerobic - 20min walking interspersed with 40min trotting	Strength training - 10min	Rest - 2-3 slow walks, short length	Aerobic - 20min walking interspersed with 40min trotting	Long walk/ lots of play
	Proprioception - 2x5min	Proprioception - 2x5min	Proprioception - 2x5min	Proprioception - 2x5min		Proprioception - 2x5min	Proprioception - 2x5min
		Stretching - 1x5min		Stretching - 1x5min			Stretching - 1x5min
11	Aerobic - 15min walking interspersed with 45min trotting	Strength training - 12min	Aerobic - 15min walking interspersed with 45min trotting	Strength training - 12min	Rest - 2-3 slow walks, short length	Aerobic - 15min walking interspersed with 45min trotting	Long walk/ lots of play
	Proprioception - 2x5min	Proprioception - 2x5min	Proprioception - 2x5min	Proprioception - 2x5min		Proprioception - 2x5min	Proprioception - 2x5min
		Stretching - 1x5min		Stretching - 1x5min			Stretching - 1x5min
12	Aerobic - 10min walking interspersed with 50min trotting	Strength training - 12min	Aerobic - 10min walking interspersed with 50min trotting	Strength training - 12min	Rest - 2-3 slow walks, short length	Aerobic - 10min walking interspersed with 50min trotting	Long walk/ lots of play
	Proprioception - 2x5min	Proprioception - 2x5min	Proprioception - 2x5min	Proprioception - 2x5min		Proprioception - 2x5min	Proprioception - 2x5min
		Stretching - 1x5min		Stretching - 1x5min			Stretching - 1x5min

Chapter Seven:

SKILL TRAINING: TAPER AND FATIGUE

Pursuit of sport is a centuries-old concept; it is essentially a foundational activity which we have adapted and reformed to be ingrained in our daily culture. Defining sport is broadly individualistic, and that's the beauty behind the concept today – there is no limitation on what it means to you. However, the basic intent behind centuries of application remains the same: a sport is an athletic activity wherein competitors play.

The keywords here are *athletic* and *play* – whether you consider dog agility a sport or not, the competitive structure remains the same. It is important to respect that, despite variation in pursuit of the sport (from a few weekends a year, to the full-round professional), the demands of the game do not change: you are asking your dog to perform an athletic requirement.

In some sports such as canicross, the handler must be as fit as the dog and their conditioning will have been done in parallel. In this way the handler has an understanding of what is required to be 'performance' or 'competition' fit, and will have trained both themselves and their dog. In agility, however, particularly at a lower level, there is less of an onus for the handler to be fit. Many assume that the dog is a natural athlete and expect him to perform in the agility ring without sufficient preparation. They have neither the understanding

There are a number of conditioning exercises that can enhance performance.

nor the practical experience of what getting fit means, and why lack of fitness makes some of the agility obstacles insurmountable.

Advanced development of a team comes down to understanding these requirements and the ability to place them into context. As with any sport, time spent surrounding the competitive ring often defines the time spent in it. We have so far established a network of coaches, peers, and veterinary professionals; hours have been invested in grasping the fluidity of movement, communication, and control. At this point, the level of groundwork undertaken allows a natural progression into *thoughtful* teamwork. Refining this is now a consequence of strategy, application and experience; this is applicable to a new dog who has grasped basic concepts, as well as those preparing for a specialised event.

STRATEGIES FOR PERFORMANCE AND SKILL ENHANCEMENT

Once a dog has been properly conditioned, strategies for performance and skill enhancement can be embarked upon. One of the key principles in optimising sports performance is inclusion of rest and recovery periods. These translate to literal gains made off the agility field; utilising principles of fatigue and tapering result in physiological adaptations that enhance athletic capabilities.

THE EFFECT ON MUSCLES

In Chapter 4: Optimising Energy and Exercise we discovered that an individual skeletal muscle body is made up of multitudes of microscopic muscle fibres. These fibres as classified as either slow or fast twitch depending on their speed of contraction.

This is relevant to fatigue, as one type of muscle fibre will tire more quickly due to the differences in energy production previously described. Typically, fast twitch muscles fatigue more quickly, as the energy used to power muscle contraction is produced in a smaller quantity. Additionally, lactic acid is released as a by-product. Accumulation of lactic acid result can impair muscle contraction and results in a burning feeling.

However, studies have demonstrated that dogs may be unique with regard to capabilities of fast and slow twitch muscle fibres. It is possible that the fast twitch muscles of a canine have a better aerobic capacity compared with other species. Complicating matters, canines have hybrid fibres that contain fast and slow twitch characteristics.

Through the study of cadavers, anatomists have assigned specific actions to certain muscle bodies. These actions are based on where the muscles attach to the bones and become evident when the muscle contracts, e.g. the sartorius can be involved in both stifle flexion and extension. However, theory and practice are two very different things and many muscles have multiple actions depending on joint position, and how much work they are required to do (e.g. standing, walking, running). So although muscle actions can be isolated for study purposes, this is not the case in the moving animal. This is why movement is so complex, and is why it is so important to train functionally, e.g. we train running by running, jumping by jumping and not by swimming.

Muscle adaptations to activity

	Fast twitch	Slow twitch
Activity	Short burst, high intensity (flyball box turn, shoulder movement through weave poles)	Endurance (canicross, sled-dog events, flatwork)
Muscle contraction	Generates a higher amount of force in a short period of time	Takes longer to generate the same amount of force
Energy production	Can utilise anaerobic metabolism which provides energy quickly but in a limited capacity; happens when oxygen demand exceeds supply	Uses aerobic metabolism; provides energy in higher yield and more sustainably over time but is slower in delivery
Role in fatigue	Less resistant to fatigue	More resistant to fatigue

CONDITIONING ADAPTATIONS

It is important to consider the multiple functions of muscles when conditioning; not only is it valuable to strengthen the appropriate muscles, these muscles need to contract at the precise time for the correct action.

Poor application of conditioning principles can cause the wrong muscles to contract at an inappropriate time for the desired movement, or cause an over-reliance on the incorrect muscle group. An athlete is then predisposed to more rapid fatigue, or even injury, as two opposing muscle contractions fight each other to perform an action.

Dogs are particularly good at performing subtle adaptations that alter their pattern of movement, without appearing overtly lame. Prior to starting a conditioning programme, it is advisable to check advanced exercises with a qualified rehabilitation professional as what you are planning may be unnecessarily extreme, or may not have the desired effect. The untrained eye is unlikely to spot a problem, such as dog avoiding engagement of a muscle group, for example.

UNFORSEEN CONSEQUENCES

The multiple function of muscles means that there may be unforseen consequences. For example, the action of the bicep brachii in the canine is to flex (bend) the elbow and to extend (reach out) the shoulder. This muscle is subject to normal force during deceleration, or upon the landing phase of an agility jump. Fatigue and other factors contribute to overloading and potential injury, such as the style of a trained behaviour, inadequate conditioning, suboptimal physical and mental control, or handler error.

TYPES OF FATIGUE

Regarding our own lives, fatigue can become cumulative and is often inconvenient, resulting in a lack of focus, lethargy, and general exhaustion. We take this as a sign to slow down, changing variables such as nutrition and sleep in order to balance our bodies. Fatigue therefore has a purpose, helping to regulate stable function throughout all body systems. Athletes can use this information to help enhance their performance through applied training and recovery. Conversely, a lack of understanding and respect for fatigue boundaries can impair performance.

On a basic level, fatigue can be defined in several body systems, including neurological, respiratory, and musculoskeletal. Thus, contributors to fatigue can be broken down into two components: psychological and physiological, hence the earlier reference to physical and mental control.

Psychological fatigue can be a reflection of the environment. Factors such as stress, lack of sleep, and ambivalence resulting from training overload can all result in poor performance. Recovery times increase due to depleted physiological factors that are unavailable to balance any deficiency; this is compounded when recovery is incomplete.

Physiological fatigue is a reflection of the demand placed upon the organ systems themselves, either through training principles or underlying medical conditions. It is helpful to further evaluate how these systems function from an athletic perspective in order to understand where fatigue can occur.

THE EFFECT ON THE RESPIRATORY SYSTEM

Exercise stimulates a number of changes within the respiratory system. Fundamentally, tissues (such as the muscle you are contracting to move) require oxygen to function. Exercise demands more oxygen from the tissues, depending on the condition of the animal and the intensity of an activity. If more oxygen is needed, the breathing rate must increase. How is this done?

Firstly, let us practice control of breathing: take a deep breath, and let it out slowly. Two processes were involved in this: active (inhalation) and passive (exhalation). During a breath-in, a muscle called the diaphragm is recruited; this muscle separates the chest and abdomen into two separate cavities. By contracting and changing chest volume, the diaphragm allows changes in atmospheric pressure between the chest cavity and the environment to occur which then regulates breathing.

Using muscle to expand the chest cavity causes pressure inside the chest to be lower than that of the outside; thus air will find it easier to move into an area of lower pressure and fill the space. This is why inhalation is an active process; it requires work to create this negative pressure gradient.

Again, take a deep breath – and then stop halfway; this illustrates that the chest can expand in varying rates and does not always fill to the same capacity.

Exhalation is typically a passive process; the characteristics of the respiratory anatomy allow carbon dioxide to escape the lungs without extra work. The body wants to equalise the pressure gradient as we have now filled the lungs so much, the pressure within them is greater than the environment. However, during exercise it is possible to add an active component to exhalation by contracting the abdominal muscles, which will help force air out at a faster rate.

It is reasonable to assume that fatigue of the abdominal muscles or diaphragm will affect the efficacy of breathing. However, with regard to the diaphragm, respiratory muscle fatigue is unlikely to occur in a healthy dog who is well suited to doing work over time due to the aerobic nature of the muscle function (Millis, D.L., Levine, D., *Canine Rehabilitation and Physical Therapy Exercise*, 2014).

However, work requires available energy, and these are factors we influence in the canine athlete with respect to nutrition and level of conditioning.

THE EFFECT ON THE CARDIOVASCULAR SYSTEM

As a result of conditioned exercise, adaptive changes occur to the cardiovascular system in order to improve function and recovery. What happens *during* exercise?

Remember, there is now an increased demand for oxygen; we have established how the respiratory system responds to this – but how does the cardiovascular system respond?

- The heart rate increases.
- The heart contracts with more strength.
- The amount of blood ejected from the heart in a single stroke (beat) increases; this is the blood that delivers oxygen to the tissues.
- The amount of time it takes for the blood to flow back to the heart (after it has delivered its oxygen and is returning to receive more) is decreased.

An increased amount of blood is shunted to skeletal muscle. In humans, 15-20 per cent of total blood flow goes to skeletal muscle at rest, during exercise this becomes 80-85 per cent (Laughlin, M.H., *Distribution of skeletal muscle blood flow during locomotory exercise*, Adv Exp Med Bio, 1988).

These changes all allow an increased percentage of oxygen uptake, in conjunction with the respiratory system.

THE EFFECT ON THE MUSCULOSKELETAL SYSTEM

A muscle cannot contract for an infinite length of time, which means it cannot perform an action for an infinite length of time. Therefore, muscular fatigue can be defined as repeated use leading to a decline in performance. Although some evidence exists for involvement of the central nervous system, it is generally agreed that fatigue arises from within the muscle itself, and is a reversible phenomenon.

We have established that during athletic activity, the percentage of blood flow to skeletal muscle increases. One reason for this is because this area of the body now requires more energy, and therefore more oxygen to help produce it.

Interestingly when a muscle contracts to its maximum ability, the blood flow is partially or fully occluded by the strength of the contraction, essentially squeezing the blood vessels shut. Over time, this can limit the amount of oxygen delivered to the tissues if the muscle undergoes repeated and full contractions during intense exercise. This, in turn, decreases the amount of energy available for work. Ultimately, it is energy that is the limiting factor in muscle fatigue.

Ambient temperature can also influence how quickly a muscle tires; this is relevant especially for those in regions where heat exhaustion is a significant factor. Muscle temperature and core temperature increases; in addition there is increased competition for blood flow, typically shunted towards skeletal muscle (Allen, D.G., Lamb G.D., Westerblad, H., *Skeletal muscle fatigue: cellular mechanisms*, Physiological Review, 2009).

Attention to intensity and duration of training, hydration, adequate recovery and a cool down period are especially critical on hot days. Conversely, in cold climates where practices are held throughout the winter, close attention should be paid to a warm up in order to increase the temperature of the musculature for work, stimulate blood flow, and help open vessels in the lungs for respiration. It is also important that the dog does not get too cold between runs.

How does this relate to training or competing? Arguably, this is the most relevant type of fatigue with regard to influencing the canine athlete. Using appropriate sports strategy – which involves a balanced training programme and adequate rest periods – we can help to maximise power output and speed in the canine. A balanced training system would include strength, skills, and sprint training, incorporating input from physiotherapy professionals, coaching feedback, and endurance training. It may be useful to keep a diary detailing type and intensity of training (see sample diary, page 84).

On a simplistic level, controlling fatigue helps with injury prevention. If tired, balance and focus is affected, which begins to affect performance. Memory retention is also inhibited, as the body begins to focus on maintaining basic function. If an exercise is repeated until a dog is tired, the functional challenge is removed from the exercise. A blind cross, if repeated until successful, may not be a measurable level of success when compared to a competitive standard. At fatigue point, the skill has been performed more slowly and with unrealistic timing.

A better strategy would be to break down the exercise, review video footage, and later test yourself by putting the same exercise into practice – but with a variation – enabling mental challenge on each attempt. The same principle applies with regard to re-setting a jump if it is repeatedly knocked by a young dog. If fatigue and inexperience is a factor, repeating the exercise will result in stress for the dog and frustration on the part of the handler.

The same concept applies during competition, and is worth remembering pre-run, post-run, and pre-competition:

- Do not over-utilise the practice jump.
- Plan a reasonable amount of runs for the weekend.
- Allow recovery periods between rounds.

Bear in mind that short-term gains, earned by practiscing a weak skill (cramming), will only increase the time needed for recovery. This affects the structure of your season both from a physical and mental perspective; it is only a short-term solution which does not lend itself to confidence in teamwork.

TAPERING

Little improvement occurs in aerobic performance during the competitive season. Rather, our success or performance during the competitive period is a reflection of all the hard work carried out in the previous months. During competition, human athletes work very hard to prevent physiological and performance deterioration as the season progresses. They often taper both training intensity and volume to reduce the stress of daily training and to optimise performance.

Tapering is defined as the reduction of exercise before a competition. The duration of taper is not exact and will often vary from dog to dog and from season to season. The programmes (see page 79) are a guideline; the optimum taper varies with adaptiveness, recovery, and experience running in events. You will need experiment to find out what timeline best suits your dog; athletes vary in their ability to recover, as well as in their ability to maintain physical improvements.

There are a number of studies detailing the benefits of tapering; these are based on human sports literature and more research is needed in support of the working dog. However, it is

Taper programme

Three weeks to go	Two weeks to go	One week to go
Cardiovascular session - e.o.d	Cardiovascular session - e.o.d	Cardiovascular session - 2 sessions with nothing in the 48 hours before competition
Skill/agility training - 2 sessions	Skill training - 1 session	Skill session - short (50% normal training time) with nothing in the 48 hours before competition)
Strength training - 2 sessions	Strength training - 1 session	Strength training - Short session or no session (nothing in the 48 hours before competition)

generally agreed that tapering:

- Improves performance (upwards of 6 per cent, with a 3 per cent average; this gain is an advantage in a timed event.
- Counteracts the effects of cumulative fatigue; this is the main goal of a taper whilst keeping training-induced athletic adaptations.
- Increases glycogen storage (increasing energy stores for the event at hand and thus affecting muscle contraction).
- Increases the density of red blood cells (these carry oxygen and thus also will help increase available energy).

A 1-3 week taper exponentially reduces training volume by 40-60 per cent, whilst maintaining training intensity, appears to provide the most efficient strategy to maximise performance gains. That means, you train just as hard but reduce the number of weekly sessions.

From a physiological perspective, 4-7 days of taper should allow liver and muscle glycogen (energy) stores to be fully replenished. This amount of time should also be enough to get rid of any muscle soreness and allow minor injuries, such as the tearing of muscle fibres, to heal.

SKILL ACQUISITION

Business corporations now commit resources to team building, and in sports no successfully rated team gains experience and cohesion only on the playing field. Likewise, the development of an agility team does not come through sheer repetition of a desired skill. However, this happens all too often in dog agility, sometimes in pursuit of a handler skill or resulting from miscommunication in obstacle development. Ideally, this should be eliminated in foundation training, which advances understanding and contextualisation for both handler and dog.

Psychological pop culture claims it takes 10,000 hours of practice to excel in a modality. While the theory is questionable, it is a reasonable way to view structuring an agility career with some adjustment. Simply put, 10,000 hours of equipment-type practice is not feasible in the lifetime of a dog; this time needs to go elsewhere. How then, is a specific skill best acquired?

Firstly, we need to re-define the idea of training to that of a modality used in other sports. Within this context, the term 'in training' refers to studying footage, evaluating strategies for edge and efficiency, sports-specific conditioning, and dedicated practices – not just time spent in hand with the dog and a reward.

Applying principles of tapering and fatigue, while acquiring strength, power and core control in balance with skill training, helps optimise performance. A well-rounded athlete utilises available resources, i.e. a network of peers, coaches, veterinary professionals, as well as time *off* the field of competition to improve the quality of time spent *on* it. Thus cumulative impact of a sport is minimised and, hopefully, longevity of a competitive career results.

No one team fits in an ideological box; while the ideas below are broad outlines, team partnerships are unique and vary with methodologies, resources, and experiences. Understanding the physical and mental requirements of an agility round helps you maximise strength, power, and speed in a behaviour. Use this information to help dictate how to train, but use self-evaluation to dictate what to train.

It seems the sport of agility is well named; from a physiological perspective, agility is the ability to change direction of the body with efficacy and efficiency, often in opposing directions (Hausswirth, C. and Mujika, M., *Recovery for performance in sport,* France: Institut national du sport et de l'éducation physique, 2013).

A number of factors are involved in agility. Balance and coordination are developed and continue to be challenged by advancement of skill. Other influencing components include power, and the now-popular term, 'core control'. Altering any one of these: balance, coordination, power, or core control will have an effect on agility.

Power is the ability to contract a muscle to its maximum point in order to generate an explosive burst. It is made of two components:

Strength: the maximum force applied against a load. In agility, this means how hard does a dog push against the ground, in one muscle contraction, in order to receive energy back for movement.

Speed or rate: how quickly a muscle can contract (see Chapter 4).

Why is power important? Essentially, power represents the amount of energy available to do work in a unit of time and is expressed in watts. It is calculated by multiplying force by distance, then dividing by time. Obviously, these are all very important considerations in agility where the winning run is dictated by control and timing! Power is particularly influential for acceleration and jumping.

Core control (or stability) refers to the ability of the body to engage appropriate trunk and abdominal muscles during movement. Essentially, is the body well controlled in these areas while moving through space? This is relevant to skill performance in terms of efficacy and injury prevention.

This is why balanced and sports specific conditioning is of crucial importance. If you are developing strength, speed, and core stability, you need to be training the correct muscle groups. If not, you may be targeting development of the wrong movement for your sport. Before engaging in a conditioning programme, it is worth considering the material and discussing its relevance to the skill at hand. Does it make sense? You don't have to be a medical professional to ask a question; never hesitate, you are your dog's own advocate.

For convenience, anatomists break down muscle into memorisable components, naming specific groups and defining their functions. It is important to remember these are useful, but arbitrary separations. Realistically, the body moves as a unit

Exercises for strength and power

Strength Core	Strength	Power
Walking up steep hills	Walking over cavaletti rails	Down to sprint
Walking up sand dunes	Standing on balance cushions	Down to jumping onto a box
Crawling under a bar or through tunnels	Standing on a balance ball	Interval training
Running over uneven terrain	Running over uneven terrain	Running over uneven terrain
Walking in water	Diagonal leg lifts	Sprinting up hill
Dancing - strengthen hind limbs	Sitting on a balance cushion	Trotting in shallow water
High 5 - strengthen forelimbs	Rolling a ball	Trotting over poles, particularly if placed on an incline and decline

Be careful about incorporating wing wraps into a training programme too early.

with muscle and sinew interwoven; the throwing arm of a pitcher will never be completely isolated from the movement through his feet.

PUTTING IT INTO PRACTICE

As we start to focus on skills, we are putting into context the foundation already laid. For example, your dog understands acceleration, deceleration, and bending. It has been appropriately conditioned and can now utilise these ideas for purpose. Your dog has also learnt to control these movements with your involvement and under the stress of excitement. As a trainer, you are now aware of how your dog moves during acceleration, deceleration, and bending; teamwork is also a developing and handler influence has been introduced as a concept.

Now, if you understand how your dog moves and how this relates to the skill you are developing, rapid understanding and contextualisation can occur. Adjustments can be made in your training based on the initial response to the introduction of a behaviour.

If this sounds complicated, let us look at a few examples:

Wraps

The foundation skills that are involved in wrapping a jump are bending, and deceleration. They are completely different to the skill of jumping and, as such, are almost impossible to train together.

It is tempting to apply this to equipment at a young age, as the idea of a wing wrap is low impact. However, be cautious with over-training in this scenario. It is too easy to train a gait pattern that is less efficient, as a puppy is not able to combine this skill with jumping. The error factor will also be cumulative. Initially the pup will not be balanced in the jump, and when the jump is combined with the wrap, the lack of balance will be compounded – as will the potential damage to the tissue. It will also increase the psychological demands of performing the task, leading to more rapid fatigue and potentially causing the pup to be over-faced.

Remember, one factor of jumping involves power. A puppy at this point has not developed the strength and speed to maximise his power output; therefore at this stage it will not be a component of your wing-wrap and will have to be added later.

Additionally, the repetition of multiple wing-wraps can have a negative effect on bending. Occasionally, dogs develop a pattern of movement wherein they turn at a sharp angle, and flip the lower spine around the pole or cone; this style is not corrected during the addition of a jump bar. Deceleration then has to be reinforced at height, as the temptation will be to jump towards a target (the wing wrap), rather than bend around the obstacle. Early take off may also be a later consequence.

Why is appropriate bending desirable in this scenario? It will allow continuation of core stability through deceleration, take off, and landing. Upon landing, it will help set the dog up for the right muscles to engage in powering for acceleration towards the next obstacle. Lastly, it assists in distribution of shock absorption to the relevant areas.

As previously stated, dogs are very capable of small gait adaptations that are less efficient. Likewise, these gait adaptations can be 'trained' very quickly by the handler. A wing wrap is not a difficult concept to understand and can easily be added to a mature dog's repertoire. Like any training method, balance is important.

Running Dog-walk

A running contact does not have to involve continual repetition of a single behaviour with minute adjustments. However, what it does involve is study. As a handler, the striding on the contact should be studied prior to starting work in order to replicate this same striding pattern in your dog.

It may seem as if the gait pattern required of a running dog-walk is consistent and unchangeable but multiple variables are actually involved on course, which can be equated to the components of jumping. Deceleration and acceleration are in constant balance, depending on the entrance and exit approaches to the contact. These are influenced by the method of training chosen, the handler's style of turning the dog afterwards, plus a myriad of other factors which are too numerous to list here. Bearing this in mind, you need to observe the following variables when you are watching footage:

- Striding (speed, number, length, over both apex).
- Adjustment of stride dependent on:
  Entry (speed, angle)
  Perception of exit
  Handling of exit
  Desired contact behaviour
  (method of training).
- Foot placement on contact entry.
- Foot placement on contact exit.

Experienced dogs are able to adjust their contact exit mid-plank if their initial approach was not ideal; a younger dog will typically miss the contact. Do not panic and allow time for latent learning.

Understanding physiological barriers and manipulation of foundation, conditioning, and skill protocols allows an improved level of agility – in all definitions.

Purposed training helps rapid contextualisation; it also decreases the amount of ring experience needed, as well cumulative impact for your canine partner. Communication can be refined easily and is not a new variable with regard to understanding movement. On the part of the handler, this allows adjustment of a training plan to achieve a desired behaviour. On the part of the dog, this allows greater focus on skill enhancement and reinforces foundation principles.

Observation is key when teaching the correct stride pattern for a running dog-walk.

Training Tips

- **Keep a diary to evaluate your training balance (length of time, skill used)**
- **Video training sessions (note success, evaluate why a result was incongruous with expectation)**
- **Observe other teams**
- **Put skills into context when applicable, avoid over-training a gait pattern**
- **Allow time for mistakes and latent learning**
- **Ensure variability when acquiring or refining skills; avoid repetition**
  - If repeating for handler skill, change the set-up slightly; whether it the same skill in another area of a course, the challenge done in the opposite direction, or the angles varied
  - If the dog or the handler needs more repetition for understanding or confidence, break down the behaviour into smaller components

Sample training diary

Date	Duration	Type/Skills	Further notes	Intensity
June 14	10 minutes	Bending work, both independent and shaping. Short jumping sequences, slightly changed approaches. Standard height.	Did well, is slightly better on left – make sure to balance.	Moderate
June 16	30 minutes	Hill run; had to stop often for traffic.		Low
June 22	10 minutes	Running dog-walk, brought up to full height. Did five repetitions; and fatigued in last causing a miss. Worth putting into sequence rather than independent practice – first four hits variable but in, seems to understand criteria.	Review of video footage shows occasionally struggles with control on second apex; this affects where feet hit – should improve with experience.	High

SUMMARY

There is much to consider in the field of skill training, and the impact this has on the agility dogs. But keep the following guidelines in mind:

- Agility requires athletic skills – requirements of a round do not change with individual goals.
- Repetition does not equal retention.
- Time spent outside the agility ring defines the time spent in it.
- Training is an inherent constant gained through thoughtful application of study and experience.
- Variability prevents injury.
- Keep it fun!

Ultimately, play the game – think about it, and play the game. Any goal in an agility round (and you have created one by merely entering) involves individual potential, and therein lies the fun. If you are looking for a challenge: this is it.

References

Allen D.G., Lamb G.D., Westerblad, H., *Skeletal muscle fatigue: cellular mechanisms*, Physiological Review 88: 287-332, 2009

Hausswirth C. and Mujika, M., *Recovery for Performance in Sport*, France: Institut national du sport et de l'éducation physique, 2013

Laughlin M.H., *Distribution of skeletal muscle blood flow during locomotory exercise*, Adv Exp Med Bio 227: 87-101, 1988

Millis, D.L., Levine, D., *Canine Rehabilitation and Physical Therapy Exercise*, Philadelphia, PA: Elsevier, pp.163-168, 2014

Chapter Eight:

WHY DO DOGS GET INJURED?

In order to prevent injury, it is essential to have an understanding of what causes them in the first place. Within the field of agility, a number of risk factors can be identified including:

- Nutritional issues.
- Temperament issues.
- Conditioning issues.
- Skill training issues.
- Equipment contact injury.
- Ground surface.
- Climatic conditions.
- Warming up and cooling down.

When one or more of these factors come together they can coalesce to form a 'perfect storm' of injury (Fig 1). Therefore it is important to address all factors within our control to mitigate such injuries and, thus, minimise the impact of factors such as climate and running conditions which are outside our control.

Ideally a systematic review should be carried out on the dog/handler unit covering:

- Nutrition.
- Conditioning and training regime.
- Gait analysis.
- Musculoskeletal examination.
- Review of running surfaces.
- Psychological adaptations of owner and dog to competition and training.

This review helps to identify the problem(s) and allows specific measures to be implemented to reduce the future risk of injury. Once implemented,

Risk factors

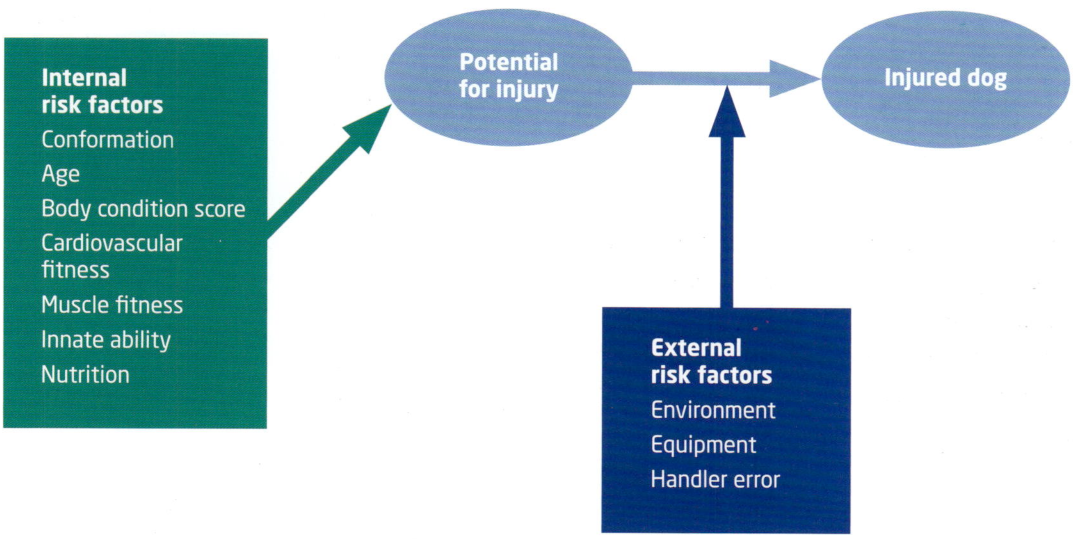

the effectiveness of preventative measures must also be evaluated, e.g. if changes are made to the training routine, it is important to evaluate whether these changes are effective, ineffective or even potentially harmful to the athlete. Often the best way to assess the effectiveness, or otherwise, of a particular technique is regular assessment of the athlete by a qualified professional prior to the start of training, 6 weeks after the onset of training and a further 6-8 weeks after that to ensure that the athlete is meeting the demands of competition.

INTERNAL RISK FACTORS

Some internal risk factors, such as conformation, are difficult to influence. In the same way that the body morphology and physiology of some humans is better adapted to particular sports, the same is true of our dogs.

CONFORMATION

Anatomical factors such as limb length, muscle fibre type, and the elastic potential of our muscle tendon unit, will govern athletic potential and is fairly inflexible. If we consider the two extremes: the racing Greyhound and the sled dog, it is immediately obvious that even though they belong to the same species that they are inherently different.

The Greyhound is the 100 metre sprinter, strong, powerful and built for speed. Such an athlete can release a vast amount of energy in a short period of time, but is completely incapable of sustaining it beyond 30-40 seconds. At the opposite end of the spectrum we have the sled dog, the marathon runner that can move extremely efficiently, conserving energy for hundreds of miles. Neither breed would perform well in the other's sport.

All other dogs lie somewhere in-between on the spectrum, though with most having more in common with the sled dog than the Greyhound. Even within the Border Collie/Working Sheepdog community, there are significant differences in phenotype; some Collies have plenty of muscle and bone whilst others are much leaner and lighter with minimal muscle development.

When we then consider other breeds involved in agility, some are inherently more athletic than others. Whilst breed should not be a barrier to competition, in some cases, it has to be accepted that conformation will be limiting to performance. For example, dogs which have an over-abundance of forelimb musculature and a more forward shift in centre of gravity, such as the Boxer and the Mastiff, do not have the range of motion in the shoulder joint that is seen in a Border Collie. This, in turn, restricts their stride length and makes them less agile.

Breeds that have a very upright forelimb angulation, such as the Poodle, tend to be less able to shock absorb their joints and become more susceptible to compressive injuries. Looking at the hindlimbs, whilst greater rear angulation allows for greater stride length and improved athletic potential, this type of conformation is more difficult to stabilise and requires better

The Poodle is more vulnerable to concussive injuries.

The Boxer lacks range of movement in the shoulder joint.

proprioceptive acuity on behalf of the dog.

The 'ideal' agility gait must be efficient in terms of stride length so that that the dog can cover the ground in as few strides as possible, thus conserving energy and improving speed. It must be balanced to allow the dog to turn quickly and land in a controlled manner. Finally, it must be capable of explosive power at the point of take off to allow the dog to clear a jump. All of these factors must be trained for and can be inhibited by muscle or joint pain, muscle weakness and restricted range of motion.

Weight to height ratio is another important contributing factor to athletic ability. The body weight ratio is the body weight divided by the height at the withers. The higher the ratio, the greater the risk of injury.

AGE

Care must be taken when training the very young and the older dog. Young dogs have poor endurance and take time to become well balanced and coordinated. Young dogs can be ruined, both physically and psychologically, by putting too much pressure on them too young. From an anatomical perspective, their joints are very soft and easily damaged. In addition, their muscles have not yet reached their maximum strength and power and are less able to protect the joints. Too much high impact, repetitive work, such as extended sessions of jumping or weaving, can be extremely damaging in the young dog.

At this age, long and repetitive training sessions can also be taxing mentally. It is easy to sour a juvenile by over-facing him and expecting too much of him early on. Sessions should be short, low impact and fun.

At the other end of the spectrum, older dogs are inherently stiffer as tissues become less elastic with age. This affects their flexibility and balance and makes then more prone to injury. This is accentuated under poor climatic conditions or if the ground surface is below standard. Cardiovascular function also deteriorates with age and thus aerobic capacity is reduced. This does not mean that an older dog should not compete, rather that the handler needs to be more careful and sympathetic to the dog's physical and mental fitness. It may be necessary to compete less often or in easier classes.

BODY CONDITION SCORE (BCS)

Ideally athletes should sit at body condition score 2.5/5. If this drops to 2, then potentially the dog has insufficient energy reserves to continue performing all day, and day after day. This is more likely to happen when there is limited time between bouts of athletic activity, allowing insufficient time to replenish energy stores.

If the handler is not careful, this can be self-perpetuating with the body starting to break down its own muscle to meet calorific demands, leading to a further drop in BCS. If the BCS is too low, it can also result in insufficient energy reserves to meet the immediate demands of exercise, leading to a drop in performance, loss of strength and a loss of mental clarity, which can lead to increased risk of equipment-associated injury.

Conversely, a high body condition score increases the weight to height ration, increasing the load on the joint and, thus, the risk of injury. The excess weight has to be moved around the ring; this is inefficient in terms of energy requirements, and predisposes to injury. Adipose or fat is inflammatory in its own right and, again, this can contribute to pain and inflammation in the athlete. Excess body fat also inhibits the muscles response to insulin and, therefore, the ability of the muscle to take up glucose. Equally, a high body condition score and low lean body mass to fat ratio indicates that a dog has not been properly conditioned and will not be capable of performing well in training or competition.

CARDIOVASCULAR FITNESS

A lack of adequate conditioning leads to insufficient cardiovascular adaptations to ensure that most of the round is undertaken under aerobic conditions. Without proper conditioning, there is an inadequate blood flow so oxygen delivery to the muscles is prejudiced. This is coupled with the heart having to pump faster and less efficiently during exercise, which, in turn, increases the risk of muscle soreness and damage and leads to prolonged recovery times. If this is repeated on a frequent basis, it can predispose to muscle shortening, loss of range of motion, further inhibition of muscle perfusion and, ultimately, failure of tissue adaptation and repair which leads to injury.

Since cardiovascular function deteriorates with age, this problem is accentuated in the older athlete and it is imperative that these dogs undergo adequate conditioning prior to competing.

MUSCLE CONDITIONING

A lack of proper conditioning also affects muscle power and strength. It affects the fine-tuning of muscle contraction and makes the athlete less efficient at dealing with lactic acid. This, again, leads to post exercise stiffness and a disruption in the balance of damage and repair within body tissues.

INNATE ABILITY

Although dogs, in general, have greater aerobic capacity and athletic potential than humans, this does not mean that all dogs are great athletes. Athletes, by default, are generally obsessive and high drive individuals. These traits are often as important as physical performance in determining how well an athlete does in competition, and it is why so much money is spent on sports psychology in the human field.

Without the desire to win, and the ability to continue focusing when the same manoeuvre is performed time and time again in training, it is difficult to succeed. Not all dogs can cope with this pressure, and can become dull, lack lustre and withdrawn, or remain permanently on a stress induced high, which does not allow the tissues to repair.

There is little joy in training an athlete that has no interest in performing. It is difficult to become a team and, inevitably, the handler will become frustrated or stressed whilst the dog becomes withdrawn or less and less inclined to perform. When choosing a dog for agility, think about breed characteristics that make one dog more suitable than another – but also choose a type of dog that matches your personality.

A dog must have the mental strength and focus in order to compete at the top level.

If the handler is highly-strung and nervous, it helps to have a canine partner who is calm and focused. Other dogs, particularly some of the Collies, need a strong, confident handler that gains their respect and trust. Think carefully before selecting your team-mate to make sure you will be compatible in terms of personality.

NUTRITION

Achieving the correct nutritional balance is intrinsic to good performance. The ratio of protein:fat:carbohydrate in the diet will dictate energy supply and replenishment, tissue repair and adaptation, and aerobic potential. A mismatch of nutrients can lead to poor performance and increased risk of injury. Studies have shown that a low protein diet (less than 18 per cent) can increase the risk of injury and prevent training adaptations, such as an increase in VO2max and increases in red blood cell production *(Kronfeld et al, 1989)*. Low protein diets also can lead to muscle breakdown. Inadequate fat in the diet can have a negative effect on aerobic potential and can also lead to rapid fatigue.

Timing of feeding is also critically important. During exercise, blood is diverted away from the stomach and intestines to the muscles. Therefore if dogs are fed too close to exercise, they will not only have to carry around the extra weight of the food but also will not be able to utilise it properly. This can lead to surgical emergencies such as gastric dilation and torsion, but also to less life threatening but equally debilitating conditions such as chronic diarrhoea.

Feeding soluble carbohydrates following exercise can help restore muscle glycogen supplies and maintain energy output and enhance muscle recovery. It is equally important to ensure a correct level of hydration at all times – as little as 2 per cent dehydration can affect athletic performance.

EXTRINSIC FACTORS

Many extrinsic factors can predispose to injury. These include climatic conditions, ground surface, handler issues, equipment issues and course design. Training can as arduous as competing; in fact, it may be even more demanding as the same course or combination of manoeuvres are trained over and over again.

There is also a tendency for certain designs to become fashionable. For example, continually going round the back of jumps which leads to pressure being placed on the same structures repeatedly. Other course design features that can predispose to injury include inappropriate spacing between jumps and failure to erect tunnels and tyres correctly.

With respect to the equipment, injury can occur by having different contact surfaces on equipment, set up for different rounds. These may have different coefficient of friction, changing proprioceptive feedback and affecting conditions of performance. In this way, the dog's whole system has to continuously adapt to different conditions of performance which can be extremely challenging to a young, unskilled, poorly trained or injured dog. It maybe sufficient to change a dog from one who is living with some discomfort or pain into one that is clearly physically injured and lame.

Different ground surfaces provide the athlete with different challenges. Deep sand is extremely demanding in terms of energy required for movement. It places significantly higher demands on the muscle-tendon unit and predisposes to soft tissue injuries, ligament tears and back issues. The deeper the sand, the greater the challenge. Often dogs that have competed outdoors all summer will injure themselves in the autumn when they change to indoor training and insufficient time has been given for their bodies to adapt.

Grass rings have their own set of challenges. In general, the harder the ground, the greater the amount of concussive damage. As a result, toe dislocations and joint inflammation are more likely to be seen following too much work on hard ground. Wet grass and mud is generally very slippery and make it difficult for the dogs to keep their dynamic stability and not slip or slide. Equally, deep ruts or holes in the ground can cause instability in the limb and take structures to the outer range of motion with an increased incidence of severe injuries, such as fractures.

Equipment injury is another extrinsic factor that plays an important role in whether a dog is injured or not. In the survey carried out by Levy et al for *Clean Run* magazine in 2007, dogs were found to be most frequently injured by contact either with an obstacle or the ground. Slips were the predominant cause of non-contact injuries, but overuse injuries were reported frequently as well. A total of 27 per cent of all injuries occurred on the A-frame whilst 23 per cent of injuries occurred on the dog-walk, with hurdles being the next most common cause of injury. Shoulders, backs and digits were the most commonly injured body parts.

Certain factors can help mitigate equipment injury, such as ensuring tunnels are correctly erected, jumps are correctly spaced, contact surfaces are uniform, and that materials used in construction are the same for each round. The height and pitch of the A-frame can increase or decrease the challenge both on the incline and decline. During training certain factors, such as repeating contacts over and over again, particularly standing contacts where the dog decelerates rapidly is particularly injurious to joints.

Injuries can also be caused by the handler rewarding the dog with tugging. Excessive tugging, or the extreme of circling the dog through the air at the end of a toy, commonly leads to soft tissue injuries of the neck and trunk.

Handler error can also predispose a dog to injury. If the handler misreads the course, or fails through inappropriate body alignment to set the dog up correctly for an obstacle, it can lead to rapid deceleration and change of direction, poor angle of entry and inadequate stride length for take off.

Handlers often fail to read their dogs correctly and continue to run them when they are tired or in pain. This is not helped when multiple qualifiers are staged over a short space of time. Most injuries occur when we are tired and cannot control joint or limb position. This allows the joints to move to their outer range of motion, which places extreme

A sand surface can be very demanding - the deeper it is, the more energy is required.

A grass surface poses problems if it too hard, or if it is wet and slippery.

stresses on ligaments, tendons and muscles, often leading to disruption to their substance or even complete tears. A good bond and understanding between the handler and the dog can help mitigate this, particularly if the dog's needs are placed before the handler's personal ambitions.

Perhaps not commonly viewed as equipment induced injuries, but inappropriate use of conditioning equipment, such as balance cushions, gym balls, pods, ladders, etc., can predispose to chronic overuse injuries. Correct engagement of certain muscle groups is not always easy to achieve, and this often results in widespread stiffening or splinting of the muscles of the body. It takes a reasonable amount of experience to use such equipment correctly – and this cannot be gained by watching the plethora of videos that are available on the internet. There is no quality control associated with these videos and many are posted by inexperienced people that are clearly demonstrating 'bad' techniques which are then be copied by thousands of viewers around the world.

Handlers often want to do more with their dog at the expense of the basics. Using balance equipment is very trendy at present and, as dogs are keen to please their owners or work for a reward, they can be trained to do all sorts of exercises – often to their own detriment. Canine fitness is becoming a competitive sport but with no regulation to safeguard the athlete. It takes a considerable amount of balance, proprioception and strength to use such equipment correctly; dogs should not be progressed on to them until they can achieve these skills on a stable, supportive surface.

Conditioning exercises should always be carried out under supervision.

IS MY DOG IS AT RISK OF INJURY?

There are many instances when a dog tries to tell us that all is not right, but we are particularly bad at reading the signs. Long before the dog starts to show stiffness or holds up a leg, there is almost certainly a variable period of time when their performance will have changed subtly due to pain or inflammation. An intuitive and observant handler will be aware of these changes and can take steps to prevent further serious tissue damage and injury.

Athletes are high drive and keen to perform; they rarely go sour unless they are training too hard or are in some form of discomfort. Therefore if a dog that previously went clear starts to knock poles, it should be a red flag that all is not well. Sometimes it may even be as subtle as slight stiffness after rest, a reluctance to jump into the car or out of it after training, or a change in desire to work. All these should be read as signs of potential pain and inflammation.

RED FLAGS THAT MAY INDICATE INJURY

- Knocking poles with forelimbs – front leg pain, neck pain.
- Knocking poles with hind legs – hindlimb pain or low back pain.
- Change of jumping style.
- Early or late take off.
- Going under jumps.
- Coming out of the weaves.
- Change of weaving style.
- Failure to hold contacts.
- Increased running times.
- Failure to turn or reluctance to turn.

All of the above should be taken seriously and should be a reason to have the dog checked out. Left unchecked, the tissue damage can become progressive, leading to stiffness, loss of balance and eventually to lameness. Often, such is the desire of the athlete to carry on performing, he will find ways of changing his movement pattern to reduce pain on certain structures which will allow him to carry on running. However, this inevitably affects both balance and speed.

Over a period of time, under-loading of certain areas causes the dog to stiffen further, and over-loading of other structures starts to cause tissue damage and inflammation in these structures. Often when the dog goes lame, it is the over-loaded tissues that break first, e.g. a dog with pain in the right hind will load the left fore. The pain in the right hind goes unnoticed, but the left fore eventually starts to show lameness. To fix the problem, both the left hind and right fore issues must be addressed. However, if the change in performance had been taken seriously, the lameness in the left fore might never have happened.

Always give your dog the benefit of the doubt and if his performance changes, he needs to be examined. Remember, he will be doing his best to please you, so pay attention to every small detail. Regular video analysis of performance can make identifying subtle changes much easier.

References

Kronfeld, D.S. et al ,1989, *Nutrition, anaerobic, aerobic exercise and stress*, in Burger, I.H., *Nutrition of the dog and cat*, Waltham symposium, New York, Cambridge University Press, 133-145

Martin Levy, M.D., Charles B. Hall, Ph.D., Natasha Trentacosta, and Monica Percival, *A Survey of Injuries Occurring in Dogs Participating in Agility*, Clean Run, (February 2007)

Chapter Nine:

COMMON INJURIES OF THE AGILITY DOG

Injuries in the canine athlete largely fall into two categories: acute trauma sustained during exercise, training or competition, and chronic repetitive strain injuries. Whilst the former are dramatic they are less common and generally, with a few exceptions, are mainly associated with bruising and mild (grade 1-2) muscle and tendon injuries or grade 1-2 ligament strain.

On rare occasions more severe traumatic injuries are encountered which require immediate veterinary attention. These include tearing of the cranial cruciate ligament, complete rupture of the muscle belly or tendon, fractures, dislocations and, even less commonly, neurological damage.

According to a 2007 survey in *Clean Run* magazine, shoulders and backs were most commonly injured (20 per cent and 18 per cent of all injuries). These traumatic injuries were primarily associated with equipment contact rather than ground contact or slippage.

Chronic injuries are, in general, performance related and develop slowly over a period of time. It is possible that a traumatic episode underlies them, but went un-noticed until the athlete was forced to alter his movement pattern. Whilst this can be a useful strategy on the part of the athlete to reduce pain and maintain performance in the short term, inevitably such compensatory movement patterns lead to overuse of certain structures which can lead to muscle stiffness, joint inflammation and eventually remodelling.

Some muscles increase in size (hypertrophy) due to increased use whilst others reduce in size (atrophy) due to decreased use. Extrinsic factors, such as the type of training surface, the intensity of training and the type of equipment, can all play a role in chronic injury. Intrinsic factors that predispose to injury include gait biomechanics, conformation, muscle imbalances, lack of flexibility, age, and body composition.

Chronic cases often initially present with very subtle signs, such as pole knocking, a reluctance to turn in a certain direction, missing weave entries, loss of drive or simply putting in a slower time. Over a period of time, these subtle signs of altered performance can progress to full blown lameness if not addressed at an early stage. Although rest and non-steroidal therapy can appear to help in the short term, performance issues and lameness generally re-manifest as soon as the dog returns to normal activity. Chronic injury can affect all tissues within the musculoskeletal system.

Telltale signs of injury may be as follows:

In the joint: Swelling, heat and pain on manipulation may be noted. Stiffness after rest or first thing in the morning can also be a characteristic. Often the lameness will disappear after a few strides in the early stages.

Ligament and Tendons: Soft swellings may be noticed in the tendon sheaths along with pain on stretching of these structures. Achilles tendon injuries are one of the more frequently encountered tendon injuries in the agility dog; they are relatively easy to detect as a swelling or distension just above the point of the hock.

Muscle: Overuse injuries are commonly encountered in the athlete. Such injuries are associated with bleeding into the muscle and tearing of a few fibres. Subsequently these areas tighten with the muscle fibre being replaced by inflexible connective tissue. The muscle may feel hard and stringy to the touch and be difficult to stretch. Palpation of the muscle may also cause significant pain. As a consequence of injury, the muscle often weakens and the individual becomes much stiffer when moving.

The Forequarters

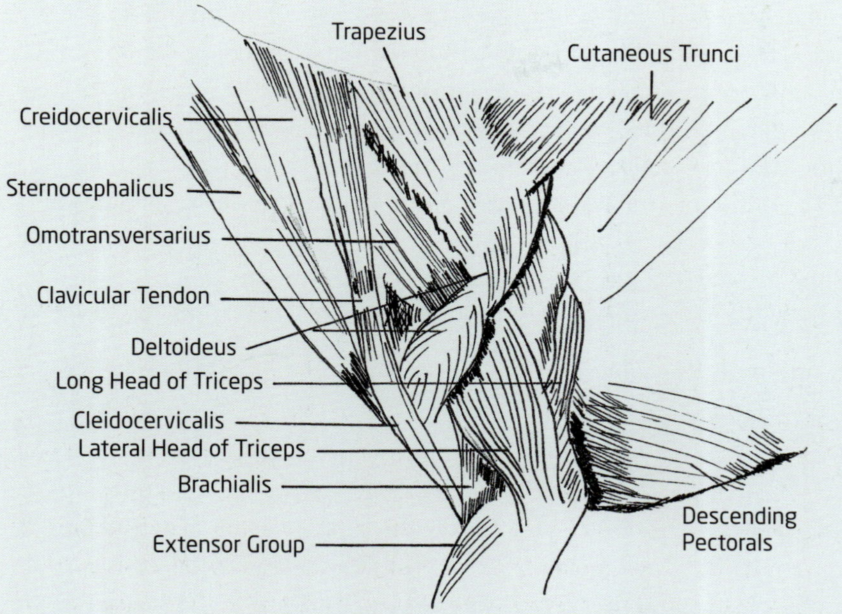

Muscles of the neck and front legs.

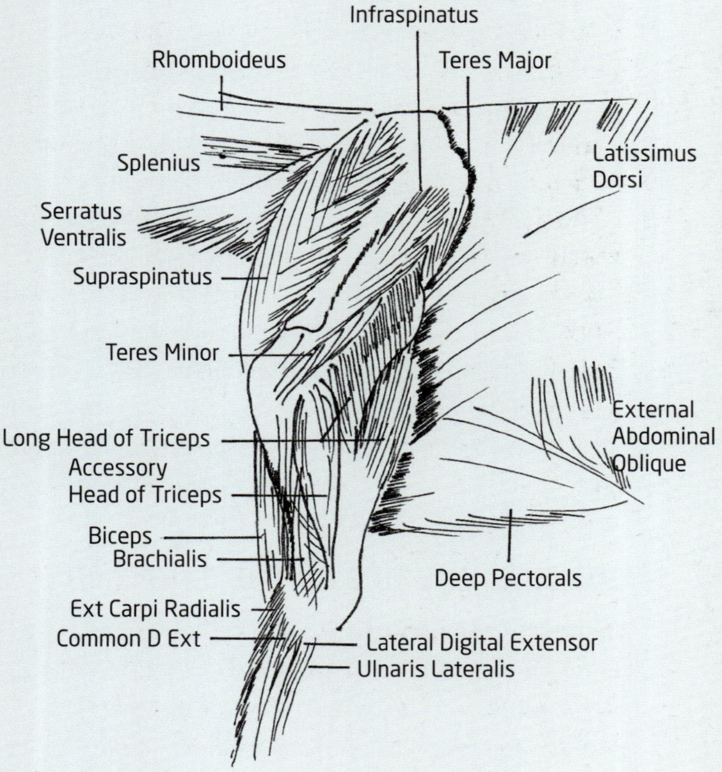

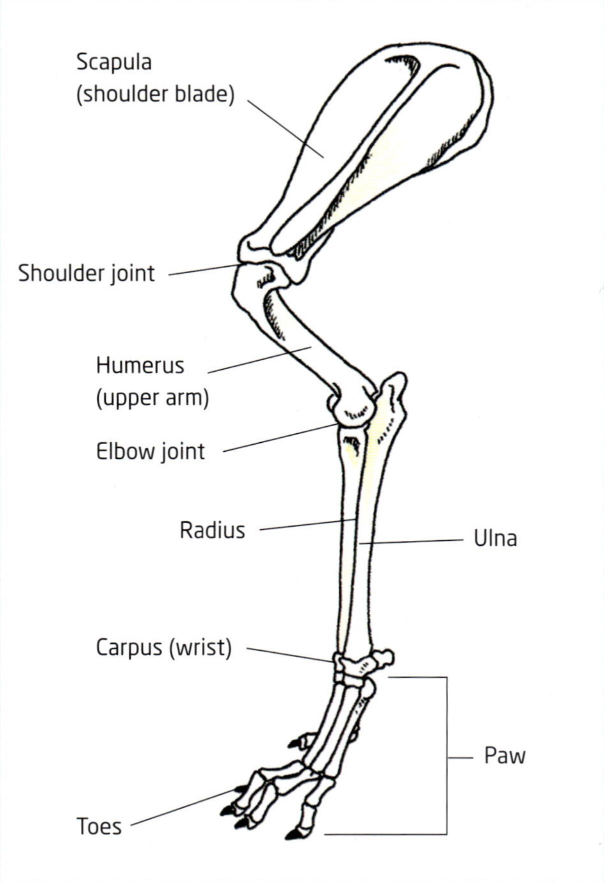

Forelimb skeleton.

MANAGEMENT OF ACUTE TRAUMA

The lines between treatment and rehabilitation are often blurred. The most important time in the treatment of acute soft tissue injuries is the first 24 hours. When soft tissues are damaged, blood vessels are also inevitably compromised leading to haemorrhage within the tissues and a rise in pressure locally. This further damages tissues, reduces their oxygen supply and leads to more inflammation. Pain is generated both from mechanical stretching of the tissues due to local swelling, and due to sensitisation of local nerve endings through the release of inflammatory chemicals such as histamine and prostaglandin.

Prompt and appropriate treatment at this stage can help reduce pain and promote healing. Every first aid box should be equipped with an ice pack which, primarily, has three beneficial effects:

- Shuts down blood vessels locally and reduces swelling.
- Reduces the release of inflammatory chemicals.
- Slows down nerve activity and helps with pain relief.

A short period of immobilisation (restriction of movement) has beneficial effects, but it should be limited to the first few days following injury only. The period of immobilisation allows healing tissues to stabilise and gain sufficient strength to withstand the forces of movement and gravity. This reaction is known as the inflammatory response – without inflammation, tissues would not heal at all. It is therefore important not to overuse anti-inflammatories; potentially they should only be considered for a short treatment period of up to 5 days. Often regular applications of an ice pack, coupled with immobilisation, will be sufficient pain relief on their own.

Once the acute inflammatory phase is over (approximately 5 days), the next stages of healing – the reparative and remodelling phase – can be influenced significantly by exercise. Allowing movement on a little but often basis is crucial for tissue recovery. If movement is too limited, excessive scar tissue can form which is stiff and inflexible and can permanently hinder movement. However, too much movement will cause the scar tissue to break down and healing will be delayed. Expert advice as to how to maximise healing should be sought at this stage.

Other aids to management include: therapeutic ultrasound, cold laser, acupuncture, passive or active movement of joints and nutritional manipulation.

COMMON INJURIES OF THE FORELIMB

Biceps tendon injury

The biceps muscle is the main muscle that extends the shoulder and flexes the elbow. It is often damaged when the shoulder joint flexes, and the elbow joint extends, such as can happen when landing from a jump. Two-on two-off contacts, and turning quickly, can also be risk factors in developing this injury. Poor balance, lack of control of the forelimb joints, inadequate muscle support, muscle shortening and stiffness can all lead to overuse of the tendon of the muscle, and damage where the tendon and muscle join. Since blood supply to the tendon of the biceps muscle is poor, it often fails to heal well *(Sharma and Mafulli, 2005)*.

Common signs associated with biceps tendon injuries include knocking poles with the forelimbs, due to difficulty in lifting and stretching the front legs, and turning wide. There may be lameness, generally in one front leg, which is often intermittent and subtle to start with, but becomes progressively worse, particularly after exercise. Pain is often generated on palpation of the tendon as it crosses over the point of the shoulder.

Pain can also be generated by simultaneously flexing the shoulder and extending the elbow. The lameness will often improve with rest but deteriorate as soon as exercise is re-introduced.

Occasionally, the tendon will tear away from the shoulder taking a fragment of bone with it.

Appropriate treatment methods include:

- Therapeutic ultrasound.
- Acupuncture.
- Massage.
- Cold therapy if the tendon is actively inflamed.
- Cold laser.
- Stem cell therapy.
- Controlled exercises to improve proprioception, endurance and strength in the affected limb.

Surgery to re-attach the tendon should be considered in cases where the tendon has pulled away from the bone, but cutting of the tendon should be avoided wherever possible.

Shoulder joint instability

Although shoulder joint instability appears to be frequently reported as a common injury of agility dogs, in my experience, incidence does not appear to be that high. This may reflect different running conditions to those encountered in other countries such as those in the USA.

The shoulder is designed to allow significant movement in 6 planes:

- Flexion and extension.
- Abduction and adduction (movement away from and towards the mid line).
- Internal and external rotation.

The shoulder has to support the weight of the dog against the forces of gravity whilst allowing all-round movement. In order to facilitate this, 25 muscles contribute to the shoulder girdle. Due to its role in supporting the body and countering the force of gravity, it is no wonder that the shoulder is susceptible to damage from repeatedly performing manoeuvres, such as jump-turn combinations and weaving, where the forelimb must slide away from the body, predisposing muscles, tendons and the shoulder joint capsule to injury.

The severity of the lameness varies from mild intermittent to an inability to place any weight through the limb *(Marcelline Little et al, 2007)*.

The biceps tendon.

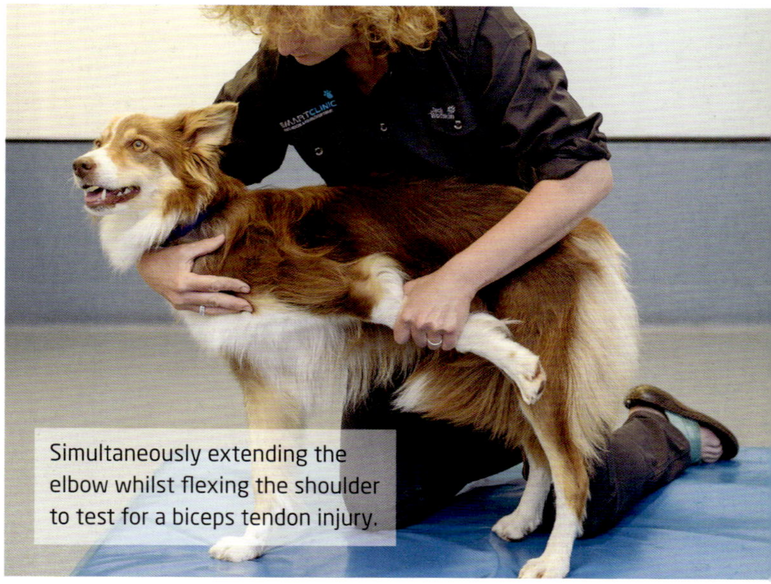

Testing for injury.

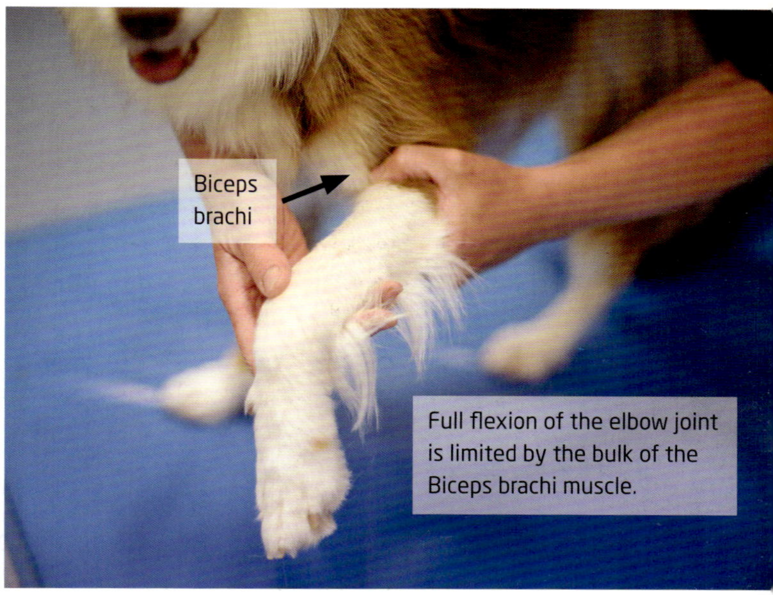

Full flexion of the elbow.

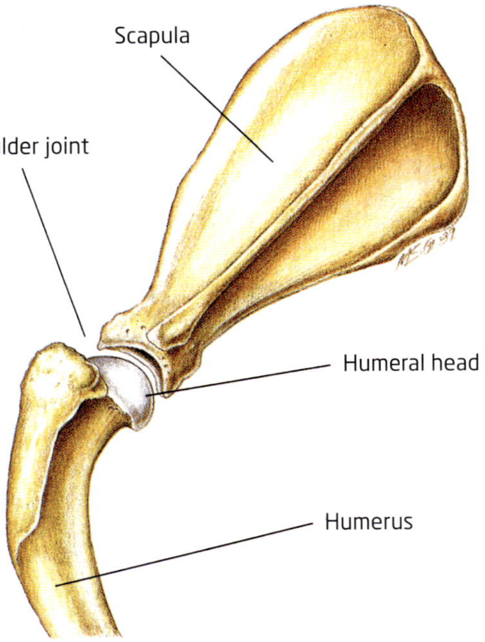

Shoulder joint.

Pain is often encountered on manipulation of the shoulder, particularly when the front leg is moved away from the body. The most commonly affected structures are the subscapular muscle, which lies below the shoulder blade, and the joint capsule itself. Diagnosis often involves shoulder arthroscopy coupled with radiography and ultrasound.

Many treatment options are available which depend on how severe the damage is. In all cases, the dog will need to be confined and lead exercised for up to 12 weeks. In the most severe cases, surgery will be required to repair the joint capsule and reconstruct the local ligaments. In all cases, a well-structured therapeutic exercise regime is essential to restore correct movement patterns to the local musculature which, in turn, serves to support the joint.

Some therapists prefer to place the dog in hobbles, which prevent the forelimbs from moving apart. Although in the short term this can protect the injury, it takes away from the work of the local musculature, which can deteriorate further in terms of both size and function. Personally, I feel that hobbling is best avoided, if possible. The better option is to use appropriate exercises to try and develop the local muscles to support the shoulder as quickly as possible.

Additional treatment options include:

- Acupuncture.
- Therapeutic ultrasound.
- Cold laser.
- Cold therapy during active inflammation.

Treatment through conservative management is largely rewarding *(Bruce, 2000)*.

Once inflammation has been reduced, reasonable range of motion has been restored and functional stability has improved, more strenuous exercises can be introduced. Figures of eight and weave poles enhance abduction and adduction of the shoulder joint, cavaletti poles and agility tunnels can promote shoulder flexion while theraball work, and walking down gradients can assist with shoulder extension. Jogging on lead can be introduced along with short periods of off-lead work.

Osteochondrosis dissecans (OCD)

OCD of the shoulder is a relatively common cause of forelimb lameness in young Border Collies, around 4-6 months of age. It frequently affects large, fast growing male dogs and is caused by abnormal development of the cartilage overlying

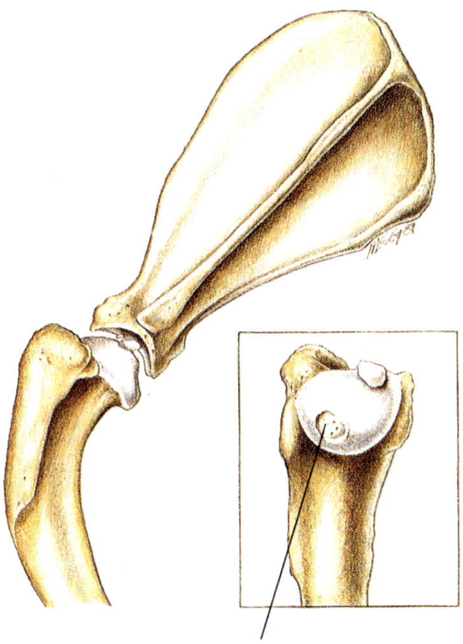

Osteochondritis dissecans.

Note the extension of the forelimbs as the dog lands from a jump.

the head of the humerus in the shoulder joint. Normally as the dog grows and develops, the soft cartilage that forms the end of the long bones becomes stiffer as mineral is laid down and the cartilage is slowly changed to bone.

Occasionally this fails to happen and the cartilage become thicker and thicker until eventually it detaches and forms a flap. This flap interferes with joint movement and causes pain and inflammation. Typically the lameness is worse with exercise, but often there is very little pain on manipulation of the shoulder joint.

The condition is generally diagnosed with imaging (contrast radiography or CT). Although some people advocate a conservative management approach whereby the dog is exercised in order to try and detach the flap, in my experience, early surgical intervention followed by rehabilitation provides the best outcome.

Carpal Injuries

The carpus functions as a shock absorber in the canine forelimb. During locomotion it often undergoes extreme motion and will even extend well beyond 200 degrees as the dog lands from a jump. Despite this, it is not often implicated as a cause of lameness. Common injuries include sprains (grade 1-3), dislocations, fractures and chronic osteoarthritis.

Treatment depends on the nature of the injury. Dislocations, fractures and severe (grade 3) ligament disruption often require surgery to stabilise the joint (pancarpal arthrodesis). Less severe strains (grade 1-2) will often resolve through controlled exercise, the use of carpal supports in conjunction with ice, non-steroidal therapy, and an appropriate exercise regime and physiotherapy.

COMMON CONDITIONS OF THE HINDLIMB

Cruciate ligament injury/disease

Damage to the cranial cruciate ligament is the most common cause of lameness in the dog. Agility dogs are also prone, though far less commonly, to damaging the caudal cruciate ligament, which results in mild hind leg lameness, generally resolved after 4-6 weeks.

In the case of injury to the cranial cruciate ligament, lameness is often severe with the dog reluctant to bear any weight on the limb. Injury can either happen very quickly, in the middle of an agility round for example, or manifests as a long-term low-grade lameness which suddenly becomes worse at exercise.

Cranial cruciate ligament injury is recognised as two distinct conditions. In the sporting dog, traumatic rupture of the ligament is a relatively common injury. This happens when large forces are brought to bear on the leg during extension and inward rotation. The dog will instantly go from

The Hindquarters

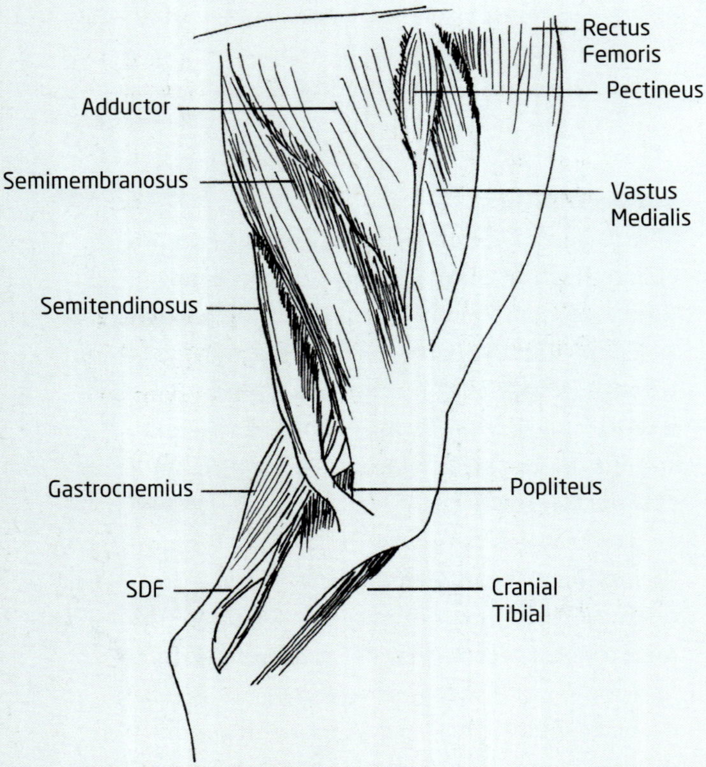

Muscles of the pelvic limb.

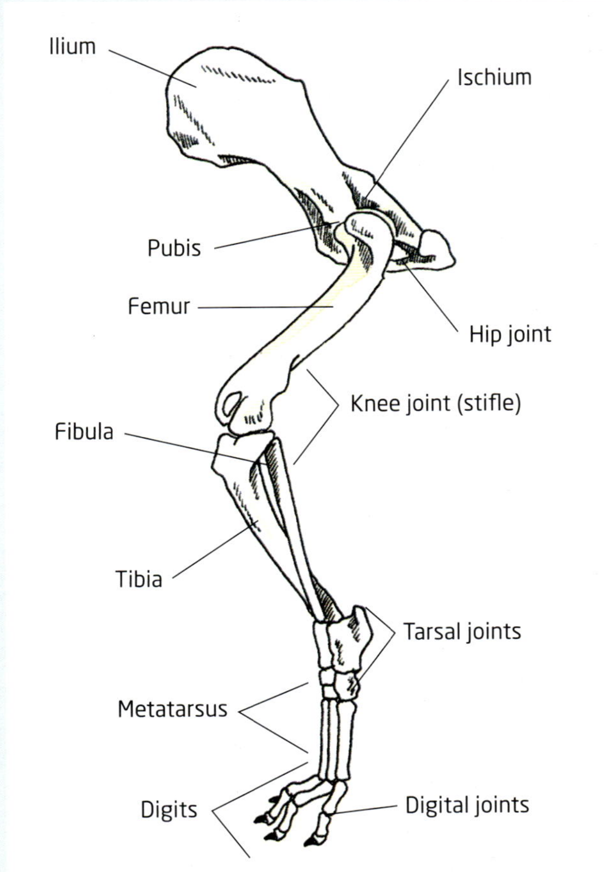

Hindlimb skeleton.

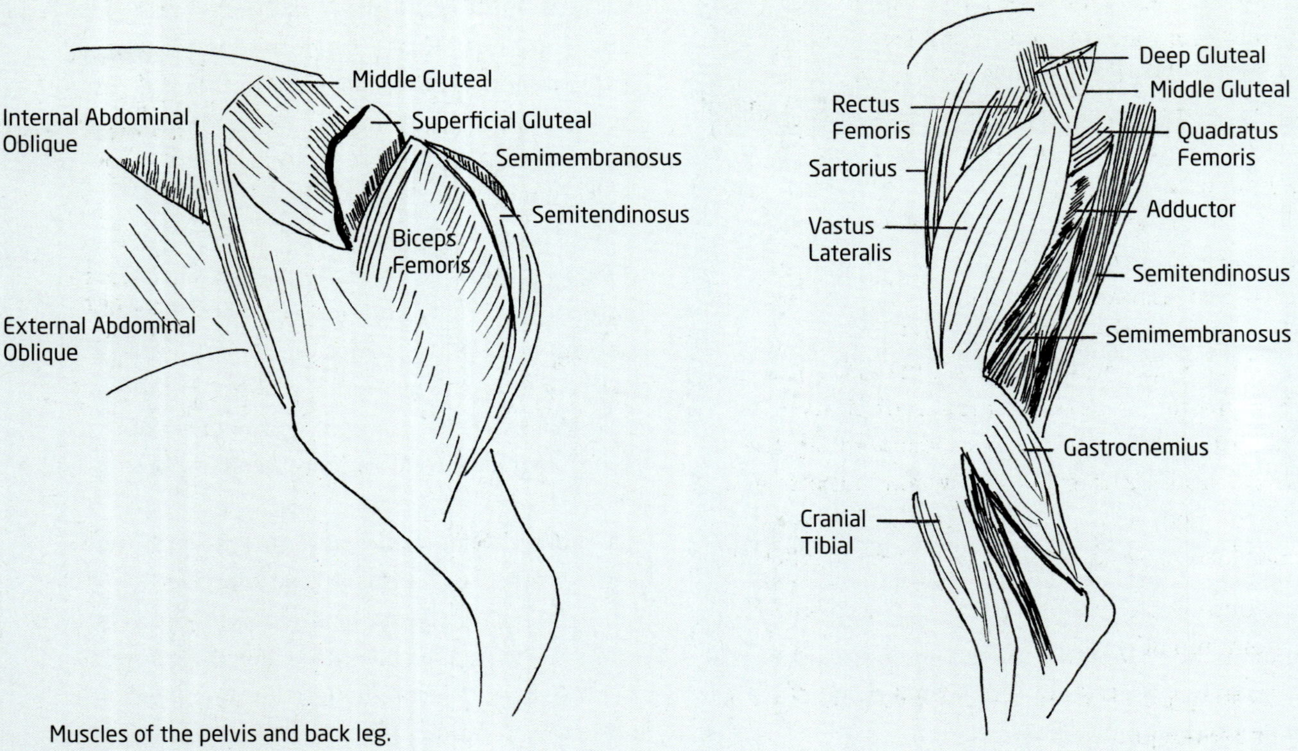

Muscles of the pelvis and back leg.

being sound to non-weight bearing on the limb. Swelling of the knee joint, along with local heat and pain, may also be noted but not in every case.

The second scenario is more commonly encountered amongst the non-athletic population where chronic wear and tear damages the ligament and causes chronic inflammation and lameness. In the latter, the condition will commonly affect both knees. The dog will exhibit a variable degree of lameness, but will often sit with the affected leg turned out. He will commonly move his weight forward over the front legs, and considerable atrophy of the hindlimb muscles may be present. Although in most cases diagnosis is relatively simple, the loss of stability within the knee joint may make it difficult to detect. This is particularly true in large dogs, where the joint is very painful, or where the condition is chronic and the joint is extremely thickened.

Clinical experience would suggest that following this injury, the best chance for the canine athlete to return to full athletic activity is provided by taking a surgical approach to the knee. Techniques that alter the biomechanics of the knee joint, such as tibial plateau leveling osteotomy (TPLO) or a tibial tuberosity advancement procedure (TTA), can result in a high level of function when coupled with appropriate rehabilitation.

There is very little research to support the most appropriate methods of rehabilitation in the canine. We, therefore, have to make use of studies in the human field along with some studies carried out on cats. Human athletes now employ techniques known as neuromuscular training, or 'motor learning', whereby they carry out very slow and precise movements to increase awareness of their knee joint and to fine tune the muscles which stabilise and move it *(Agberg, 2002)*.

This is in contrast to more traditional techniques where the focus was on restoration of muscle strength alone. Clinical experience suggests that such an approach works equally well in the canine athlete when used as part of a comprehensive rehabilitation protocol which addresses the following:

- Control of inflammation and maintenance of joint mobility.
- Restoring activity in muscles which stabilise and move the joint.

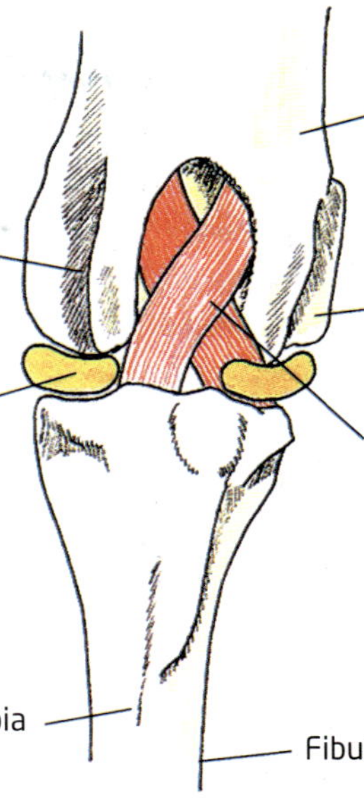

Cruciate ligament.

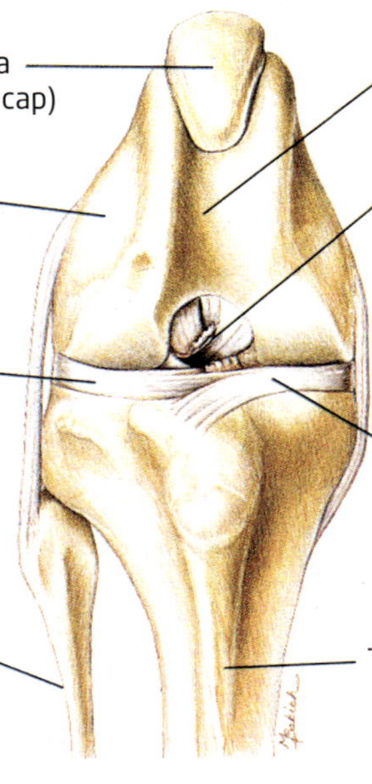

Ruptured cruciate ligament.

- Restoring muscle strength.
- Increasing muscle endurance.
- Restoring muscle power.
- Improving proprioception (spatial awareness).
- Restoring cardiovascular fitness.

Suitable techniques include:

- Topical cold therapy.
- Cold laser.
- Passive and active range of motion.
- Therapeutic exercises.
- Walking in a water treadmill.
- Acupuncture.

Illiopsoas muscle injury

Damage or strain of the illiopsoas muscle is a commonly encountered cause of hindlimb lameness in the agility dog. It often presents as an intermittent or low-grade hindlimb lameness which often gets worse with exercise. The handler may notice that the dog's jumping style has changed and he has started to tuck jump. Equally, he may often start to knock poles with his hindlegs, particularly as he gets tired towards the end of the round. When standing, he will frequently move his weight away from the injured leg and will often just rest on his toes.

The main action of the muscle is to extend and support the back and to flex the hip. Illiopsoas strain is often accompanied by pain through the lower back, in general, and may extend to pain in the abdominal muscles that make up the side-wall of the trunk. Diagnosis is often based on eliminating any other cause of lameness, pain on local palpation, and on hip extension coupled with internal rotation of the hip. Ultrasound scanning and MRI can be useful in demonstrating abnormalities within the muscle.

Acute, stretching-induced muscle injuries are estimated to account for over 30 per cent of injuries seen in a typical human sports medicine practice. Such injuries are far less frequently reported in canine sports medicine, but this may be a lack of reporting or inability to diagnose the condition rather than the fact that the problem does not exist.

Iliopsoas strains occur as a result of overload or excessive strain on the muscle. The muscle-tendon junction is the commonest site for injury as this represents the weakest part of the system. The muscle is most often damaged when it is stretching,

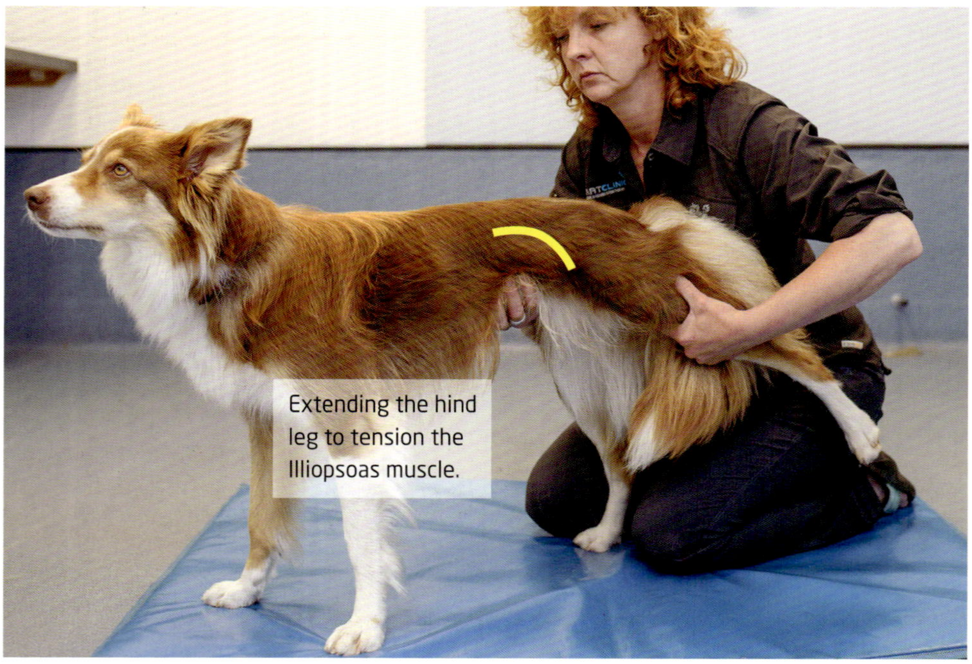

Tensioning the illiopsoas muscle.

for example, when the hind leg moves up and out to clear a jump. The injury is often seen in association with poor control through the back, which results in increased twisting of the low back and pelvis.

Treatment focuses on high-quality rehabilitation that reduces inflammation within the muscle-tendon unit and correctly activates and strengthens the muscle. It is equally important to work on the abdominal muscles, the back muscles and the pelvic.

It is equally important to work on the abdominal muscles, the back muscles and the muscles of the pelvic limb, which together form the dog's core musculature. These stabilise the trunk and back during movement, enabling the legs to move freely and to allow power to flow between the back legs and the body.

In the acute stage, inflammation can be managed by:

- Controlled rest.
- Topical ice therapy.
- Non-steroidal anti-inflammatory medication.
- Gentle neuromotor training exercises, such as weight shifting.
- Cold laser.
- Therapeutic ultrasound.
- Acupuncture.

Stretching should be avoided during the acute inflammatory stage as it is likely to contribute to the breakdown of the healing tissue.

In the chronic state, it may be necessary to re-start the inflammatory process to facilitate healing; non-steroidal therapy and ice should therefore be avoided. Appropriate treatment for chronic strain include:

- Topical heat.
- Acupuncture.
- Cross fibre massage.
- Stem cell therapy.
- Gentle stretching.

As function is restored, a progressive re-training programme should be embarked upon to address issues of proprioception, balance and flexibility, muscle strength and endurance and, finally, muscle power and all round cardiovascular fitness.

Coupled with these techniques it is essential to introduce exercises which assist with developing the core musculature. Once normal range of motion has been restored and the patient is pain free on hip extension and internal rotation, the intensity of the exercise regime can be increased. Walks can be extended, on-lead jogging can be introduced, walking on more challenging surfaces, such as sand dunes, can be added, progressing to the reintroduction of off-lead work. The final step is re-introduction of discipline specific training.

Gracillis muscle injury

This is one of the commonest muscle injuries in racing Greyhounds but is only infrequently encountered in agility dogs. It is associated with a severe lameness which comes on during exercise, and the development of large swellings down the inside of the hindleg. If the animal is to compete again, surgical re-attachment of the muscle, followed by intense rehabilitation and physical therapy, is the treatment of choice.

Achilles tendon injuries

The achilles tendon is easily palpated at the back of the hind leg just above the hock. It is made up of the tendons of the superficial flexor tendon – the gastrocnemius and the common calcaneal tendon. Tendon strain can be recognised as a soft swelling or thickening in the tendon, just above the point of the hock. Complete rupture results in the dog adopting a classic plantigrade stance, whereby the hock joint collapses down to the floor. Surgical correction of the injury is required, coupled with immobilisation of the hock joint for up to 6 weeks to protect the healing tendon. Subsequently aggressive rehabilitation is required to restore movement to the hock joint.

Lumbosacral disease

Forces generated in the hindlimbs during movement are transmitted directly to the sacrum and significant stress is generated at the lumbosacral junction. This, in turn, can lead to abnormal movement and instability at this site and remodelling of adjacent bone and soft tissue structures. The net result is a narrowing of the spinal canal and disruption of blood supply to the spinal nerves, as well as potential compression of the local nerve roots.

The main clinical sign in the early stages is acute pain along with loss of jumping ability, and an inability to carry out such activities as stair climbing. A shifting or intermittent hindlimb lameness is often seen, coupled with a characteristic arching of the low back and a backwards tilting of the pelvis. Later on in the disease process, neurological signs such as hindlimb weakness, loss of co-ordination and urinary and faecal incontinence may develop.

Non-surgical management through rehabilitation can be relatively successful. However, surgical decompression may be required in cases where neurological signs are deteriorating or inadequate pain management can otherwise be achieved.

References:

Levy I.M. et al, *Agility Injury Survey*, Clean Run, February 2007

Agberg E. et al, *Consequences of a ligament injury on neuromuscular function and relevance to rehabilitation*, Journal of Electromyography and Kinesiology, 2002; 12: 205-212

Bruce W.J. et al, *Bicipital tendonitis and tenosynovitis in the dog: a study of 15 cases*, NZ Vet Journal, 2000; 48: 44-52

Sharma P. et al, *Tendon Injury and tendinopathy: healing and repair*, J Bone and Joint Surgery Am, 2005 87, 187-202.

Marcellin-Little D. et al, *The Canine Shoulder-selected disorders and their management with physical therapy*, Clin Tech Small Animal Practice, 22, 171-182.

Chapter Ten:

PHYSIOTHERAPY TECHNIQUES

Numerous options are available that can assist with management of acute and chronic injuries in the agility dog. These include acupuncture, chiropractic, hydrotherapy, massage and soft tissue therapy, thermotherapy (hot and cold), electro-modalities, such as cold laser and therapeutic ultrasound and electro-stimulation. Therapeutic exercises are outlined separately in Chapter 11.

ACUPUNCTURE

The use of acupuncture to manage painful musculoskeletal conditions in the dog is becoming widely accepted. Its use in the management of both acute and chronic pain is well documented, however in the hands of a skilled practitioner it has far more to offer the canine athlete than just a means of managing pain. For the athlete in training, it can be used as an adjunct to support their general wellbeing through its effect on the immune system, the endocrine system and the gastro-intestinal system.

WHAT IS ACUPUNCTURE?

Acupuncture involves the placement of very fine, sterile needles into points located at specific locations around the body. The majority of these

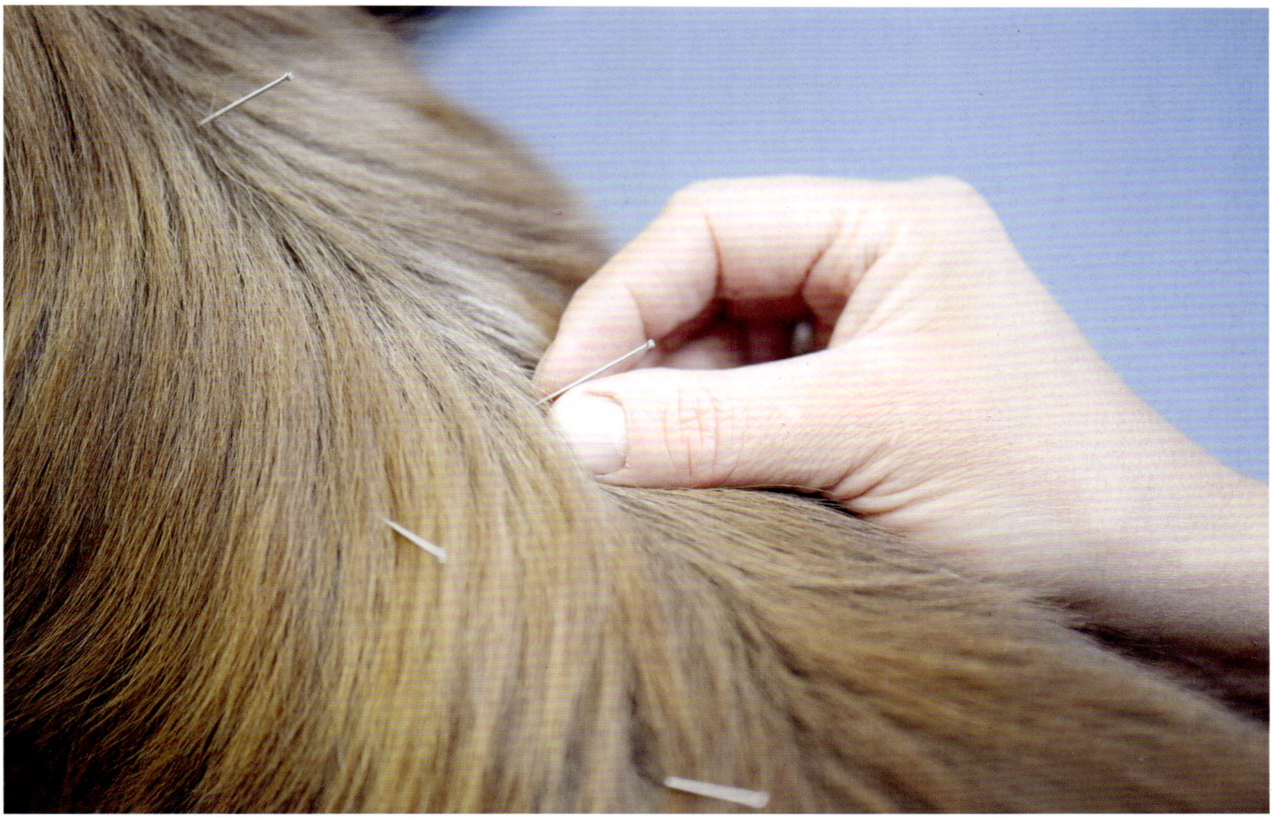

Needles are inserted at specific locations.

points lie close to where nerves branch, or where blood vessels are located.

To insert a needle safely, the practitioner must have an excellent understanding of the patient's anatomy. Acupuncture points can often be felt as small depressions in the tissues. They have different electrical properties to surrounding tissue and are much better at transmitting electrical currents due to their lower resistance. In the dog, there are over 600 recognised acupuncture points, all of which have specific functions.

In the UK, acupuncture is considered an act of veterinary surgery and as such can only be performed by a veterinary surgeon. The reason for this is that, in exactly the same way that the prescribing of drugs is dependent on evaluation of the patient, accurate history taking and palpation, the choice of acupuncture point is similarly determined. The needles are normally left in place for 10-20 minutes and are generally very well tolerated. Some common signs associated with acupuncture include:

- Sleepiness.
- Panting.
- Lifting of the hair around the needles.

Most needles can be placed without the patient showing any awareness of the needle at all. Some practitioners may twist the needle whilst, in other cases, a small electrical current can be run through the needles to increase the stimulation. At the site of needle insertion, local inflammation is generated. In people this can be clearly seen as a small circle of redness appearing around the needle. Hair coat and pigment often prevents us from seeing this in the dog, but occasionally it can be seen.

Two main branches of acupuncture are practised in the UK, namely traditional Chinese acupuncture and western dry needling. Both involve the placement of sterile acupuncture needles into specific points along the body, but whereas western dry needling is largely used to treat musculoskeletal disease, the scope of traditional Chinese acupuncture is much greater. Both work through stimulating the body's nervous system.

Western Medical Acupuncture

Western dry needling relies on palpation to find painful spots within the tissues of the body. These areas are commonly known as trigger points and are often compared to taut guitar strings within the body of the muscle. Trigger points have been mapped in humans and are often associated with pain far away from the trigger point itself. A good example of this is a headache caused by trigger points in the shoulder region. Trigger points are discrete, irritable foci within skeletal muscle or fascia, which are not caused by acute local trauma, inflammation, degeneration, infection or neoplasia.

There are similarities between western dry needling and acupuncture. Both involve the placement of solid needles within the muscle. Acupuncture points and trigger points overlap significantly in the treatment of pain.

Traditional Chinese Acupuncture

Traditional Chinese acupuncture originated in Asia some 5,000 years ago. Initially it was handed down from generation to generation as an oral tradition. In around 300 BC the first acupuncture text book was written, *The Yellow Emperor's Internal Classic* or the *Neijing*, and this has formed the basis of much of modern Chinese acupuncture up until the 20th century and the Cultural Revolution. Chinese acupuncture has continuously evolved from its birth, but its core its philosophy has remained the same. It takes a holistic approach to the patient and involves very detailed palpation/ examination and history taking.

When taking a holistic approach, the acupuncturist looks at all aspects of the dog's environment, physical and mental wellbeing, as all of these interact to cause disease or ill health. This falls in line with the World Health Organisation's definition of health:

> *"Health is a state of complete physical, mental and social well-being and not merely the absence of disease or infirmity."*

Within this model, working out the factors that led to the disease process in the first place is as important as treating the disease itself. Such disease causing factors include:

- Environmental conditions
- Dietary habits
- Emotions and stress

Poor nutrition including over-eating, or excesses in any of the other three factors, disturbs physiological wellbeing resulting in illness. Treatment is aimed at restoring balance in all aspects of life rather than just choosing a drug to block or mask the symptoms. This is why an acupuncture consultation involves a lot of questioning regarding the dog's sleep patterns, urination and defecation, eating habits and emotional balance. In traditional Chinese acupuncture, the aim of therapy is to restore balance between the mind, the body and the environment.

HOW DOES ACUPUNCTURE WORK?

Acupuncture works by changing neural responses within the body. Neural responses can be altered in many ways including:

- Changing the sensitivity of the nervous system to pain.
- Changing the sensitivity of the nervous system to various hormones, which, in turn, affects their pain sensitivity.

Other effects include:

- Changing the amount of hormone produced by various body organs.
- Improving blood flow locally.
- Preventing inflammation.
- Reducing muscle tension.
- Influencing the autonomic nervous system.

The painkilling effect of acupuncture is complicated in nature. The placement of acupuncture needles increases the amount of endogenous painkillers from within our own body that each of us produces. These are commonly known as endorphins and enkephalins. These are the same chemicals that give us a 'high' after exercise.

ACUPUNCTURE AND STRESS

In the sporting dog, a fine line exists between training for peak performance and over-training and descent into injury. Although athletes, in general, are much more tolerant of stress than the population at large, there is a limit beyond which the balance of stress and repair is lost in the body. The athlete will start to show symptoms of damage or injury to several body systems – not just their muscles, ligaments and tendons.

Stress and over-training can lead to changes within both white and red blood cell production within the body. The most common changes include anaemia, or lack of red blood cells, which affects the oxygen carrying capacity of blood and therefore reduces athletic ability. A drop in the total white blood cell count can also be commonly seen in athletes in training.

White blood cells are a crucial part of the body's defence system against disease; when they drop in number the individual is more susceptible to disease. These changes are easily identified by a simple blood test and any abnormalities should be immediately addressed. Acupuncture can have a strong effect on promoting both red and white blood cell production through its ability to stimulate the bone marrow.

ACUPUNCTURE TO SUPPORT THE GI SYSTEM

During exercise, blood is diverted away from the gastro-intestinal tract to the actively working muscles. This, in turn, affects the function of gastric tissue which results in:

- Reduced mucus secretion
- Reduced bicarbonate secretion
- Reduced ability to neutralise the acid produced in the stomach

Increased acidity, and loss of protective mucous barrier, results in damage to the gut lining which can lead to ulceration and blood loss. Stress makes the situation worse by increasing the production of a hormone, known as cortisol, which amplifies these changes. Normally when exercise stops, blood is shunted back to the gastro-intestinal tract, making sure that the changes are self-limiting

However, in heavy training or stressed individuals, this is not necessarily the case. Changes in blood flow to the gastro-intestinal tract also affect the body's ability to absorb food, which makes the timing and type of food fed to an athlete so critical. Acupuncture can assist with regulating gastric acidity, reducing cortisol levels and promoting bicarbonate secretion to buffer gastric acid secretion.

CHIROPRACTIC

Chiropractic technique is a gentle and precise form of manual therapy. In most cases, it is used to address spinal problems or musculoskeletal conditions. It works to improve an individual's biomechanics. It can also benefit overall health and promote normal function of internal organs.

Chiropractic treatment was first documented in the United States in 19th century. In 1895 the founding chiropractor was Daniel David Palmer; his son, Bartlett Joshua Palmer, developed the techniques and theories.

An important principle used in chiropractic treatment is that structure governs function. We are talking primarily about structure of the spine and function of the nervous system.

The practitioner examines the spine to check for limitations in movement. He/she works to address these restrictions as they can have an adverse effect on the patient's mobility, nervous system and general health. The mode of treatment is known as an adjustment. It is a high velocity, low amplitude thrust on to the restricted vertebra. It is a very precise action with a specific direction and point of contact with the patient.

The aims of chiropractic care are:

- Relief of pain.
- Return to function.
- Promotion of healing.
- Reduction of the likelihood, severity and frequency of recurrences of injury or pain.
- To prevent the development of joint degeneration.

WHAT CASES BENEFIT FROM CHIROPRACTIC?

Many sports dogs benefit from being checked chiropractically, even if they are not showing any impairment in their performance. Imbalances can be addressed in the very early stages, and this can start with puppies. Any dog with a mobility problem would most likely benefit from chiropractic assessment. Some examples of suitable candidates for assessment include:

- Acute back pain.
- Acute neck pain.
- Reluctance to move.
- Inability to jump into vehicle or traverse stairs.
- Signs of pain when doing certain movements or being lifted.
- Undefined lameness.
- Hypersensitivity to being touched.
- Repetitive licking of lower limbs.
- Altered posture in standing or sitting.
- Spondylosis.
- Compensations brought on by osteoarthritis in the limbs.
- Sciatic neuralgia.

In some cases the chiropractor will request that additional diagnostics take place with the primary care vet before starting treatment in order to ensure the best care possible.

THE NERVOUS SYSTEM AS A COMPUTER

One way of looking at the nervous system is with a somewhat electrical bias. Imagine that information from the body about its position in space, and information about the environment from the five senses functions as an input. Then imagine the brain as the processing station or factory. Output is the product, which manifests as movement and bodily functions.

In sport, we want quality output so that movement can be as efficient, coordinated and strong as possible. Good quality output is only possible with decent quality input. If there are restrictions in the spine caused by limitation to the range of movement between vertebrae, the quality of the input from the body to the brain will be inhibited.

THE VERTEBRAL SUBLUXATION COMPLEX (VSC)

This is the unit of abnormality being treated with a chiropractic adjustment. It is defined as 'the limited mobility of adjacent vertebrae'. This is occasionally associated with functional misalignment. To truly understand chiropractic, it is more useful to think in terms of addressing anomalies in function rather than an anatomical incorrect positioning of a bone or 'bone out of place'.

If a VSC is present, movement of the spine is impeded. This can have the knock-on effect of stiffness, muscle tension, pain and reduced performance. At the site of the subluxation complex, the nerves exiting the spine may be irritated. These nerves conduct information to the brain from the body, and from the brain to the muscles and organs. As you may imagine, even a mild interruption in this flow of information can affect limb function and function of the internal organs including digestive or lung function. If a peripheral nerve is severed or injured, or if there is marked pressure on a nerve within the spinal cord, the outcome can be dramatic and cause complete loss of function in one or more limbs. Disease processes causing such signs would not be classified as VSCs.

There is a wide variation from case to case in the number and severity of subluxation complexes present, leading to a wide range of signs of dysfunction. For the canine athlete, small restrictions in the spine can have dramatic effects on performance as they are being tested so much more than is the case with pet dogs. We are asking for much more in the way of flexibility and strength.

HOW DO SUBLUXATIONS OCCUR?

Trauma is one cause of a VSC. In many cases, significant trauma will lead to a rapid onset of dramatic signs. Repetitive strain in a particular area may also lead to VSCs. In these cases, signs generally appear gradually. Long-term postural adaptations to a lameness, instability, or pain elsewhere in the spine, may also lead to the development of VSCs. The rough and tumble of everyday life can also contribute to restrictions in spinal movement.

In many cases the practitioner will need to work on muscular and spinal compensations that have developed in the medium-term before being able to address the original chiropractic lesion. This way a clinical improvement is more likely to be achieved and then sustained.

THE CHIROPRACTIC EXAMINATION

The chiropractor watches the dog move and observes him when standing before starting a hands-on exam. As well as examining the spine, the limbs and muscles will be evaluated. The chiropractic practitioner will enquire about any medical history that may be significant. Skin temperature may also be palpated.

The specific examination technique used in chiropractic is called motion palpation and involves assessing the range of motion that any given joint is able to move through. When referring to joints in the spine, we are focusing on the facet joints between adjacent vertebrae. The orientation of these joints determines the axis and potential range of movement between two vertebrae. If a restriction is detected during this examination then it is treated chiropracticly with an adjustment.

The practitioner may also perform soft tissue techniques on muscles and fascia to facilitate the treatment and relax muscles prior to treatment. In some cases, the adjustment technique may be modified at the discretion of the chiropractor. For example, a more gentle thrust than normal is often applied in the case of an elderly dog with spondylosis.

THE MOTION UNIT

When an adjustment is made, the chiropractor is working on a motion unit. A motion unit is described as a functional unit made up of two adjacent articulating surfaces, the connecting tissues binding them and all the structures in between.

THE INTERVERTEBRAL FORAMEN

The intervertebral foramen is the space between adjacent vertebrae. It allows passage of spinal nerves from the spinal cord to the rest of the body, and from the rest of the body to the spinal cord. These nerves therefore gain information from

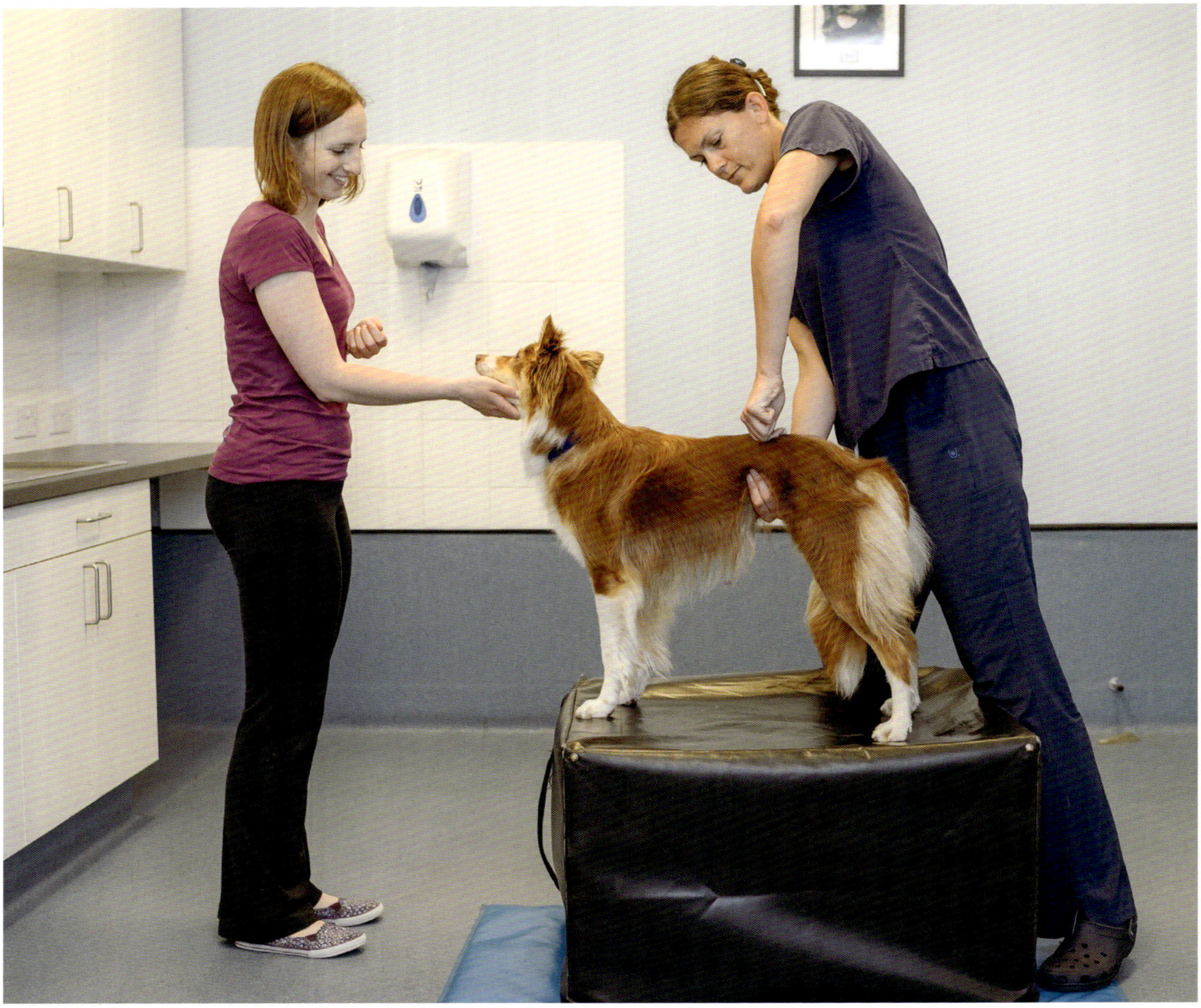

The practitioner examines the spine for limitations of movement.

the body about its location in space and external surroundings, which is supplied to the brain. In turn, the same nerves provide impulses to muscles for movement, and to internal organs for maintenance of normal function.

Looking at the anatomy of the intervertebral foramen, it becomes apparent that if two vertebrae are not moving normally in relation to each other, the intervertebral space may be narrowed. This could cause disruption to normal movement and organ function. As well as allowing the passage of nerves, there are many other vital structures found within the intervertebral foramen.

They include:

- Spinal nerve.
- Part of the dura, which is the outer membrane protecting the spinal cord.
- Cerebrospinal fluid, which protects the central nervous system.
- Veins.
- Arteries.
- Lymph vessels.
- Connective tissue.
- Sensory nerve bundles (dorsal root ganglia).

This list gives an idea of how a change in the way that the spine is moving can affect the body and overall health. The intervertebral foramen could be seen as the portal between having a mental life and a physical life.

INTEGRATED CARE

Chiropractic is an extremely useful tool. It is most effective when used in conjunction with physiotherapy so that functional changes can be maintained by improved posture and more appropriate global biomechanics. It also works well with acupuncture.

Chiropractic should be carried out as an adjunct to traditional veterinary medicine. Ethically, chiropractic treatment should take place as the result of a referral from the primary care veterinarian – all quality animal chiropractors require this. Referring vets carry responsibility for their choice of chiropractor.

FINDING A QUALITY ANIMAL CHIROPRACTOR

Unfortunately, there is a wide range of spinal manipulators with varying degrees of expertise. To ensure the highest quality of training and an appropriate level of clinical knowledge in chiropractors, contact the International Veterinary Chiropractic Association (www.ivca.de) or the British Veterinary Chiropractic Association (bvca-uk.org). Members of either organisation are either vets (registered with the Royal College of Veterinary Surgeons) or human chiropractors (registered with the General Chiropractic Council).

HOW MANY SESSIONS WILL BE NEEDED?

There is usually an improvement after 2-3 treatments. Acute problems will respond more quickly, whereas chronic problems are more likely to require on-going treatment. Some chronic patients, e.g. the elderly arthritic, may benefit from top-up treatments which could be monthly to yearly. A chiropractor aims to see the animal as often as needed and as little as possible.

STRESS AND THE IMMUNE SYSTEM

The existence of a VSC causes a degree of stress to the body. There is increasing evidence to show that stress inhibits function of the immune system. Therefore, chiropractic adjustments improve the coordinated responses of the nervous system and the immune system. The autonomic nervous system, which is responsible for regulating function of the internal organs, has an influence on immune tissues and organs including the spleen, lymph nodes, thymus gland and bone marrow. On-going research is showing that the sympathetic branch of the autonomic nervous system has a level of influence on immune function.

INNATE INTELLIGENCE

A significant idea in chiropractic philosophy is the existence of innate intelligence; a term first used by D.D. Palmer. It is known as the force which organises, maintains and heals the body. It is the chiropractic belief that, through performing a chiropractic treatment and allowing the nervous system to function unhindered, it can help the body to heal itself. This ties in with the recent work on stress and the immune system, but also holds more esoteric meaning for many.

CHIROPRACTIC TREATMENT AND OSTEOPATHY

There are as many similarities as there are differences between chiropractic and osteopathy. They are both manual techniques used to address mobility problems, and both also have positive effects on general health. If you watched a range of chiropractors and osteopaths at work, there would be a significant amount of overlap.

Both disciplines work with the body's own ability to heal itself. The osteopathic texts highlight the importance of the body working as an integrated whole, which is a theme also adopted by chiropractic practitioners. Benefits in general well-being are often a result of both techniques.

The main differences are:

- Osteopathy was founded 21 years before chiropractic, although both started in the 19th century in the USA.
- In chiropractic the focus is on correcting abnormalities in the nervous system, while osteopathy works to improve the overall structure of the body.
- The treatment technique used by osteopaths includes soft tissue stretching, deep tactile pressure and mobilisation and manipulation

of joints and vertebrae. The key chiropractic treatment mode is the high velocity, low amplitude adjustment. However as mentioned above, many chiropractors will use adjunctive soft tissue work.

References

International Veterinary Chiropractic Association, public information leaflet

Kandel E.R., Schwartz J.H. and Jessell T.M., *Principles of Neural Science*, 4th Edition, 2000 (ISBN 978-007-139011-8)

International Academy of Veterinary Chiropractic and Options for Animals, Basic Animal Chiropractic Course notes, 2012 and 2013

ELECTOTHERAPIES

Several forms of electrotherapy are used in rehabilitation of the injured athlete.

These include:

- Therapeutic ultrasound
- Laser
- Neuromuscular electro-stimulation
- TENS
- Shock wave

They are generally used as part of a comprehensive programme combining therapeutic exercises, thermotherapy, soft tissue techniques and, possibly, acupuncture and chiropractic manipulation. Laser therapy, in particular, is gaining popularity in veterinary practice and is often prescribed as a standalone therapy. When used in this way, it can be of assistance in wound healing, but in terms of managing the injured athlete it should form part of a comprehensive rehabilitation programme.

THERAPEUTIC ULTRASOUND

In therapeutic ultrasound, high frequency sound waves (greater than 20,000Hz) are applied to damaged tissues through a transducer. The energy from these sound waves is absorbed to a varying degree by different body tissues and converted to kinetic energy. Tissues, such as muscle, ligaments and tendons that have a high protein content, are the best at absorbing sound energy.

Therapeutic ultrasound has the potential to heat tissues and, if used inappropriately, can cause burning. However, the thermal effect can improve blood flow through tissues, increase the elasticity or compliance of tissues, increase tissue metabolic rate and raise the pain threshold. It is particularly useful in treating muscle pain and spasm, and in stimulating ligament and tendon healing.

Since ultrasound waves are attenuated in air, the animal's coat has to be clipped in order to achieve transfer of energy between the ultrasound transducer and the body. A water-soluble gel is also applied to the skin to act as a coupling agent and help the transfer of sound waves.

Therapeutic ultrasound is particularly effective in reducing muscle spasm and assisting with the healing process in ligaments, tendons and muscles. When used in a heating mode, it can also be extremely useful in helping with stretching scar tissue and breaking down adhesions.

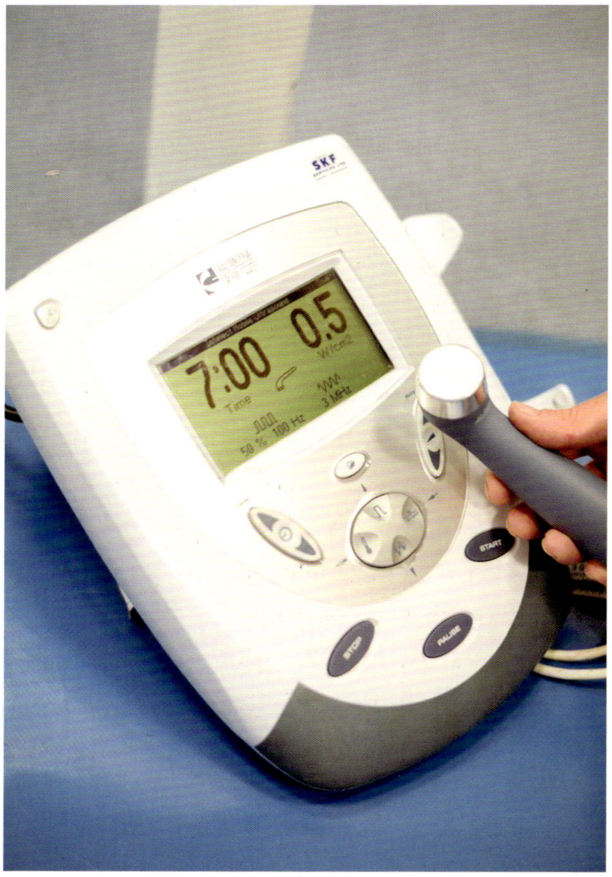

High frequency sound waves are applied through a transducer.

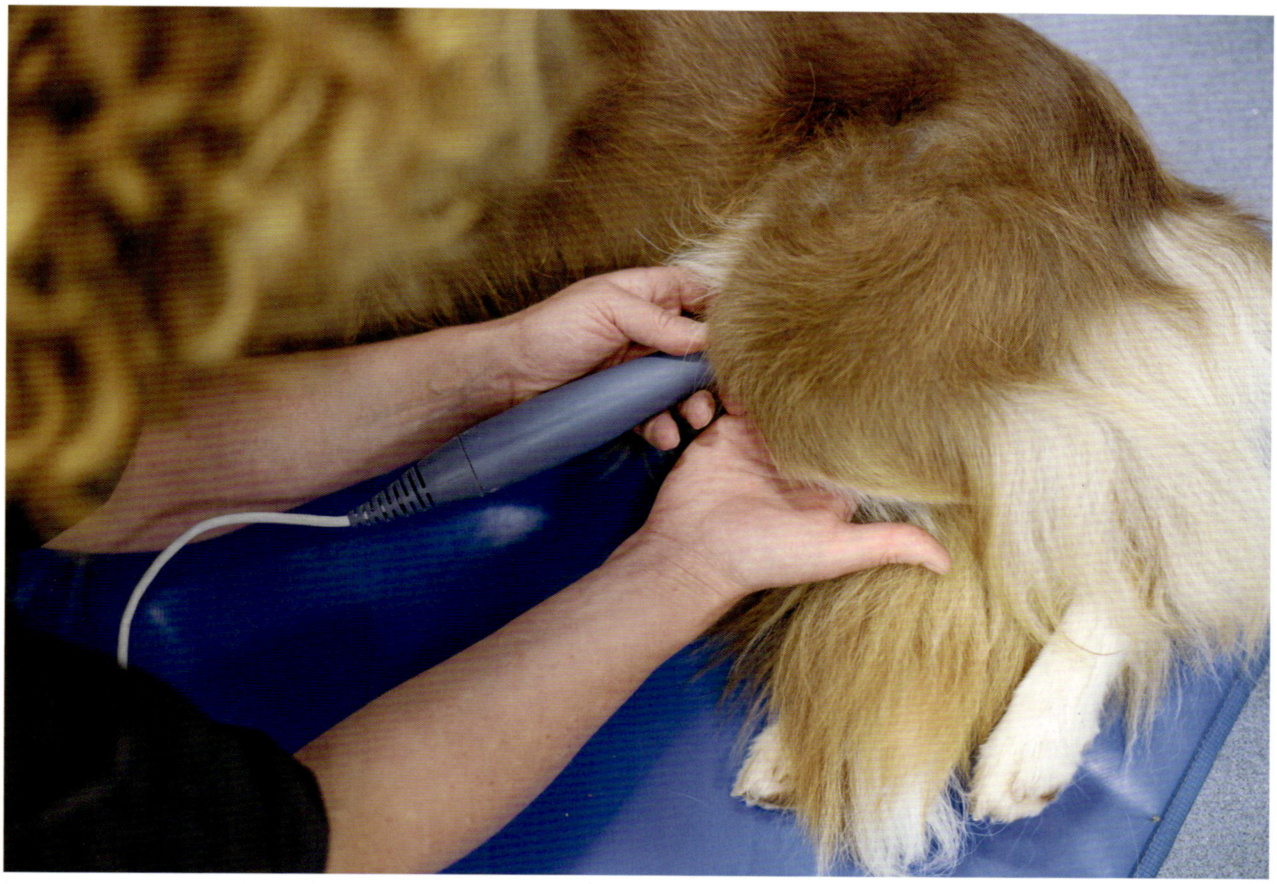

The thermal effect improves blow flow through the tissues.

LASER THERAPY

Laser stands for: light amplification by stimulated emission of radiation. It is associated with the production of monochromatic electromagnetic radiation, which is collimated. Several types of lasers exist and all are classified by the amount of power they produce and the wavelength they emit:

Class 1: Very low in energy, e.g. a CD player

Class 2: Slightly more powerful, e.g. a laser pointer.

Class 3: Generally has a power setting of 1-500mW. Used in rehabilitation and potentially can cause damage to the eye.

Class 4: Very powerful and becoming progressively more widespread in rehabilitation. These are potentially very harmful to the eye and protective glasses must be worn when using them.

Lasers work on the principle of using light energy to kick-start or speed up biological processes within the body. Light energy is absorbed by pigmented particles, known as chromophobes, which are generally found within cell mitochondria.

Laser treatment enables:

- Improved collagen synthesis, which is important for wound healing.
- Increased growth factor release, again, critical for tissue healing
- Blood vessel proliferation.
- Potential nerve growth.
- Pain reduction.

It is used to assist with wound healing, for musculoskeletal injuries, resolving inflammation and assisting with pain management from osteoarthritis.

Clipping of the hair coat is again recommended prior to laser application. Dark skin absorbs more light energy and is more likely to burn.

NEUROMUSCULAR ELECTRO-STIMULATION (NMES)

NMES is generally used to increase muscle mass and strength. It involves the application of a small electrical current to a muscle through a stimulator to induce muscle contraction. It is most often used in rehabilitation where the patient cannot actively contract the muscle, e.g. following spinal injury.

TENS

This is another form of electro-stimulation, but the function is associated with pain relief rather than improving muscle mass. Whereas NMES stimulates the motor nerves, TENS stimulates the sensory nerves and is associated with the release of endorphins and enkephalins in the dorsal horn of the spinal cord. TENS is particularly useful mode of therapy when the patient cannot tolerate drugs such as non-steroidal anti inflammatories.

SHOCK WAVE

Shock wave involves the use of high-energy focused sound waves to treat musculoskeletal conditions, such as tendonitis and osteoarthritis. It can also be used to stimulate bone healing in fracture cases. The main disadvantage of shock wave therapy is that it is generally poorly tolerated and requires sedation or anaesthesia of the patient.

ERGOGENIC AIDS

Ergogenic aids are nutritional, physical, psychological or pharmacological products which potentially improve performance. In the human field, this includes: painkillers, alcohol, amphetamines, hormones, carbohydrates, amino acids, fatty acids, extra red blood cells, and stimulants such as caffeine and creatinine phosphate, to name but a few. Some of these products are also used in the animal field and each country has different laws regarding what is acceptable and what is not. Some confer no benefit over and above the placebo, some are genuinely performance enhancing, whilst others have extremely harmful side-effects, particularly if taken long term.

There follows a review of some products which are available and legal and, anecdotally, have performance enhancing properties. It must be remembered that these products are not subject to clinical trials or rigorous controls that pharmacological agents have to undergo. Therefore, they do not always conform to what they say on the label, both in terms of expected response in the recipient or to their ingredient list.

Romans used to eat raw meat before competing whilst athletes in the 1908 Olympics drank brandy to improve performance. Today the focus is on the correct balance of fat, protein and carbohydrate to decrease muscle fatigue. As yet, there is no anti-doping legislation within the agility field in the UK. To ensure the welfare of the athletes, so that they are not forced to compete whilst on painkillers or sedatives, I, personally, would welcome the introduction of drug testing at competitions.

MODIFICATION OF CARBOHYDRATE INTAKE

Whilst of considerable benefit to human athletes, controversy exists as to whether there is a benefit of preloading dog with carbohydrates. It may have some rationale in anaerobic sprinters, such as the racing Greyhound. But in other athletes that are expected to compete for longer, combining both aerobic and anaerobic activity, such loading can impair the use of fat as an energy source and lead to more rapid fatigue and reduced aerobic performance.

However, the use of small amounts of high-energy, quick release carbohydrates during prolonged periods of exercise can enhance performance and help prevent the use of protein as an energy source. This strategy also provides glucose to act as a primer for fat metabolism, helping to conserve muscle glycogen and making sure that fat is burnt as efficiently as possible. This can prevent the dog from 'hitting a wall'.

Post-exercise glucose supplementation helps restore muscle glycogen and helps reduce muscle protein breakdown. The manufacturer, Purina introduced a performance nutrition line in the US in January 2016 but, at the time of writing, it is not yet available in the UK.

Purina has also produced two nutritional supplement bars that are designed to optimise performance nutrition before and after exercise. The prime bar is a pre-exercise, protein-rich (whey and hydrolyzed soy) supplement to be fed 30 minutes prior to activity. This allows key protein building blocks to be digested and absorbed into the blood to enhance muscle activity during exercise, and to minimise muscle damage. These protein sources contribute to enriched levels of the amino acid leucine, which is the primary amino acid to activate protein synthesis and offset the protein and muscle fibre breakdown that occurs with exercise.

The refuel bar is a post-exercise nutritional supplement bar that helps replenish muscle energy stores and promotes muscle rebuilding. It should be fed within 30 minutes of exercise, which is important because of the brief window of time after exercise when muscles are maximised for nutrient uptake. It also contains key nutrients to help reinvigorate tired muscles, and is formulated with rapidly digested ingredients to help deliver these nutrients within the optimum time following exercise. The bar contains a targeted blend and proportion of carbohydrates, anchored by maltodextrin. This, is the 'optimal' carbohydrate source, as it is rapidly digested and absorbed, yet avoids the immediate insulin spikes that can occur when ingesting simple sugars.

METHYLSULFONYLMETHANE MSM

This has an anti-inflammatory effect:

L CARNITINE

Aids aerobic metabolism through improving fatty acid transport into mitochondria.

L-TRYPTOPHAN

A calming agent that reduces anxiety and pain response.

ARGININE

Produces creatinine, enhances performance and recovery.

CREATININE

A high-energy source that increases creatinine within muscle and enhances performance. It can also improve recovery though facilitating muscle relaxation. Meat, fish and poultry are good sources of creatinine. It can also be purchased as a supplement and fed at a rate of 2-3g daily. A quantity of 100g of raw meat contains 0.5gm of creatinine. In humans, creatinine absorption can be increased by combining it with a soluble carbohydrate.

HYDROTHERAPY

In recent years, canine hydrotherapy has become increasingly popular with a range of centres offering swimming or walking in an underwater treadmill. The majority of owners are under the misguided impression that swimming is an easy and entirely safe form of exercise for their dogs. This misconception is fostered by the hydrotherapy centres and can result in inappropriate training or may result in permanent damage to the dog. When used correctly as part of an integrated training regime, hydrotherapy can assist with rehabilitation and conditioning of the canine athlete. However, it should never be the mainstay of treatment and should never be regarded as an easy form of exercise.

Research in the human field has demonstrated that both cardiovascular fitness and muscle fitness is very specific. Individuals who trained in the pool failed to demonstrate a crossover in cardiovascular fitness to running on land. Similarly, swimming is very forelimb or arm dependent and, whilst it can be excellent for building muscle at the front end, it often does nothing for the back end. Racehorse trainers have moved away from exercising in water for this very reason. They found that horses that were swam regularly ended up performing worse due to an over-development of forelimb muscles which restricted their ability to expand their chest and deliver oxygen to their lungs. At the same time, no improvement was seen in the ability of their hindlegs in terms of muscle strength and power.

Whilst walking in an underwater treadmill can target the same muscle groups that a dog needs to move over land, care must again be taken to condition appropriately. In general, where the focus is on resistance training, dogs are required to walk against a large volume of water. Whilst this approach can increase muscle mass in the long term, it can be self-defeating as too much muscle can actually restrict joint range of motion, reduce stride length and impair the athletic performance of the dog. In addition, walking against a lot of resistance does not help movement in terms of balance, co-ordination and development of skilled movement patterns. The water functions as a crutch, supporting the dog and taking away the need to control his own movement. Therefore if the dog is moving badly on land, he will also move badly in the water. The only difference is that there is less weight or load on his joints.

Walking or swimming against the resistance of the water is very demanding in terms of energy utilisation. If the dog is not fit, he will quickly run out of oxygen and start to work anaerobically. This, in turn, can lead to significant build-up of lactate and, if continued, to severe muscle damage and post exercise soreness.

WHY EXERCISE IN WATER?

When exercising in water, the body is affected by the properties of water itself, namely:

- Buoyancy.
- Hydrostatic pressure.
- Viscosity, cohesion and turbulence.

Buoyancy

Buoyancy is the upward thrust of water acting on a body that creates an apparent reduction in bodyweight when immersed.

Archimedes principle states:

> *"The body when immersed experiences an upward thrust equal to the volume of water displaced."*

Buoyancy reduces the load placed on the limbs and slows movement of the limbs. Whilst it unloads the joints, it actually increases the workload of muscles, which is why it is such a demanding exercise. The more adipose tissue (fat) an animal has, the more buoyant he is. In paretic and paralyzed animals, buoyancy plays an important role in facilitating affected limbs.

Hydrostatic pressure

Hydrostatic pressure is the pressure exerted by water on a body.

Pascals law states:

> *"Fluid exerts an equal pressure on all surfaces at a given depth. Fluid pressure is directly proportional to both depth and density of fluid."*

If the dog that is walking in water, the feet are at greater pressure than the shoulder. This, in turn, assists in pushing fluid back towards the heart. This can help with the management of swollen joints or tissues. Hydrostatic pressure prevents blood and fluid from pooling in the extremities and can therefore assist with reducing swelling.

Viscosity, cohesion and resistance

It is much more difficult to move through water than through air. This is due to the attraction or cohesion between the water molecules and it is greatest at the surface. The greater the cohesive force, the greater the viscosity and the more difficult it is to move through the fluid. In this way cohesion and viscosity provide resistance to movement.

The velocity of water, at any one point, will vary in magnitude and direction. As a body moves through water it generates turbulence, and turbulence also contributes to a resistance to movement. The less coordinated and controlled the movement, the more turbulence it generates and, therefore, the greater the resistance to the movement through water. An increase in velocity of movement, or an increase in surface area, will also lead to an increase in resistance to movement through water.

EFFECTS OF HYDROTHERAPY

Exercising in water should improve both muscle strength and muscle endurance. It should also contribute to improved cardiovascular performance, though less efficiently than walking or running on land; Underwater treadmill is preferable to swimming in this respect.

Training in water with continuous exercise results in an increase in heart rate and the potential to improve aerobic performance in the moderately fit animal. The increased resistance to movement that occurs when exercising in water leads to an increase in tissue demand for oxygen by between 25-35 per cent. Training in water therefore helps increase the number of blood vessels within the muscle. This, in turn, improves oxygen delivery to the muscle and removal of heat and waste products. Electron microscopy demonstrates that the total number of capillaries per muscle

Exercising in water

Exercising on a water treadmill increases cardiovascular and muscle fitness.

averages 40 per cent higher in endurance-trained athletes compared with untrained counterparts.

Potentially, exercising in water can have wide-ranging effects on cardiac output. Studies show that arm exercises on land produce an increase in resting heart rate from 77bpm to 92bpm in men. Exactly the same exercise in water produces an increase in heart rate from 60bpm to 99bpm. The hydrostatic pressure effect increases blood flow back to the heart from the tissues. This, in turn, means that the heart can move a greater volume of blood with each beat. This then allows the heart rate to fall to maintain the same cardiac output, which reduces the workload on the heart.

HYDROTHERAPY EQUIPMENT

Water treadmill

The water treadmill, when used correctly, allows the dog to use the same muscle groups and roughly the same movement patterns as it would do when walking or running on land. In this way it provides a functional method of training and can increase cardiovascular and muscle fitness in a useful way. It is closed chain in nature, which means that the limbs are subject to a ground reaction force (at each step the foot pushes off and lands on the ground which controls the movement). This is safer and is more closely related to everyday activities than open chain exercises (where the foot never contacts the ground, such as when we swim) because it recruits muscles in a more functional manner.

Swimming

Swimming is an open chain exercise and therefore less controlled than walking in water. Because it relies mainly on the forelimbs, it can place the dog's body in an abnormal position with the head and neck stretched upwards. This can potentially increase the pressure on the shoulders and the neck, and is likely to cause pain and inflammation in these areas if overdone. Equally, it places increased pressure on the lower back and can lead to inflammation in the tissues surrounding the nerves of the hindlimbs. In severe cases, it can lead to a dropped or swimmer's tail, loss of bladder control and severe pain. Swimming against jets increases the work done by the heart, lungs and muscles and can increase the chance of damage.

WHEN NOT TO SWIM

It is essential to ensure that the dog is comfortable in the environment; if he is in anyway stressed, he should be removed from the water. A resistance to swimming can be a sign of pain and/or fatigue, so if this is apparent the dog should be taken out of the water. Many inexperienced therapists misread this as the dog behaving badly and persist with the exercise causing severe damage. Remember that even if a dog is fit, moving in water is a challenge and, initially, sessions should be very short. Dogs should not be allowed to swim in the following circumstances:

- Pool water is too hot.
- The dog has heart problems.
- The dog has chest problems.
- The dog is unwell.

WHY DO THINGS GO WRONG?

Hydrotherapy can be a useful adjunct in the management of a wide range of orthopaedic and neurological conditions. With an increasing population of overweight and elderly dogs, it can be an excellent aid to increasing mobility and assisting with weight loss in osteoarthritic patients.

Many patients start off with a very low base line of fitness and are over-challenged in the early sessions. Poor cardiovascular and musculoskeletal function will predispose to overheating, muscle membrane breakdown and lactic acid generation on top of potentially exacerbating any existing orthopaedic condition. Therefore, it is essential that initial sessions be of short duration and low intensity. As fitness increases, the sessions can be lengthened.

Exercising in water which is too warm can also lead to poor performance and will increase the demand placed on the cardiovascular and respiratory system. Although it is desirable to provide warm water (30-32 degrees centigrade) to increase tissue elasticity and improve circulation, in reality animals work better at cooler temperatures (26-28 degrees centigrade).

THE BENEFITS

Used correctly, water treadmill therapy can be a useful aid to recovery in the following conditions:

- Osteoarthritis.
- Fractures.
- Hip and elbow dysplasia.
- Degenerative disc disease.
- Obesity management.
- Fitness training.

To minimise risk and increase benefits, use a centre that is managed by veterinary surgeons and nurses working with a qualified physiotherapist.

SOFT TISSUE TECHNIQUES: MASSAGE AND STRETCHING

Peak performance depends on being able to move in a balanced and coordinated way whilst conserving as much energy as possible during the movement. Numerous factors interact to facilitate this including:

- Conformation.
- Joint range of motion.
- Flexibility.
- Training and nutrition.
- Proprioception.
- Muscle strength, endurance and power.
- Movement biomechanics.

Whilst some factors such as conformation and muscle fibre type are difficult if not impossible to manipulate, joint range of motion, muscle extensibility, flexibility and proprioception can all be influenced for better or worse by factors which include:

- Warming up.
- Cooling down.
- Stretching.
- Massage.
- Therapeutic exercises specifically targeting balance, co-ordination, proprioception and flexibility.

Handlers can improve performance through adopting a simple routine of regular stretching and soft tissue manipulation. However, it is important to remember that no technique is completely safe – carrying out a stretch badly or at the inappropriate time is worse than doing nothing at all.

This section will review the difference between static and active stretching, when to stretch and when not to stretch, along with reviewing basic massage techniques.

RANGE OF MOTION

The total movement available to a joint is known as its range of motion. It describes movement from full flexion (when the two bones on either side of the joint are moved towards each other) to full extension (when the two bones on either side of the joint are moved as far away from each other as possible). Reduced range of motion results in the athlete having to take more strides to cover the same amount of ground which, in turn, increases the energy demand of exercise and makes them less efficient athletes.

Total range of motion is dependent on numerous factors including:

- The bony configuration of the joint.
- The muscles surrounding the joint.
- Other joints in line.
- Abnormal changes within the joint.

How much movement a joint is capable of is often determined by the bony architecture of the proximal (top) and distal (bottom) bones. If we consider the elbow joint, extension (straightening) of the joint is limited by the olecranon of the ulna locking into the olecranon fossa of the humerus. In comparison, full flexion (bending) of the joint is limited by the biceps brachi muscle. The biceps brachi muscle can influence the joint in several ways. In cases of over-training, where the muscle becomes over-developed or hypertrophic, joint movement can be limited.

If we compare a weightlifter to a gymnast, a weightlifter has traded power for flexibility. The excessive over-development of muscle mass through resistance training might confer an advantage in static weight lifting, but would be counter-productive in any activity that requires flexibility, skill and balance. In contrast, a gymnast remains strong and powerful but without over-developing their musculature to a point when it becomes stiff and inflexible and restricts their movement. The same is true for agility dogs; they must be strong and powerful whilst retaining flexibility. Therefore, excessive muscle bulk is undesirable and will impair their performance and should not be part of a training programme.

Muscles can also be restrictive on joint motion if they are tight and inflexible. This can happen due to over-training where pain can lead to spasm and shortening of the muscle. Chronic low-grade injury, and replacement of muscle tissue with connective or fibrous tissue, can also reduce the compliance of muscles. Muscles that cross more than one joint, such as some of the hamstring muscles, are more likely to demonstrate insufficient stretch to allow each joint that they cross to fully extend.

Lack of movement in one joint can also affect movement in adjacent joints. For example if the stifle joint cannot fully flex, it will limit movement in the hock joint. Scar tissue, osteoarthritic changes and pain can all lead to disuse and replacement of muscle tissue with fibrous tissue which, in turn, will further restrict movement and potentially cause more pain.

STRETCHING

The ability to move a joint smoothly through full range of motion is essential to sustained, injury-free, athletic activity. There is an hereditary component to good flexibility and certain joints may become stiff through injury, over-use, or under-use. The aim of stretching is to take tissues beyond their normal range of motion whilst remaining within their elastic limit. If they are pushed beyond this, tissue damage will occur resulting in pain, inflammation and further restriction of movement.

Stretches can be broadly divided into two types: passive and active. In a passive stretch, the handler physically moves the body part for the dog, without active muscle contraction on the part of the dog. In an active stretch, the dog moves the body part himself, generally in response to a toy or treat. These are also referred to as baited stretches. In general, active stretches are easier to carry out as the dog is unlikely to move himself into a painful position, whereas with a passive stretch it is possible to over-stretch a muscle or joint.

Tissues such as skin, muscle, tendon and ligament are known as viscoelastic materials. In simple terms this means that they will behave differently at different temperatures, and at different states of hydration. They will also yield or give a little with time – a phenomenon which can be described as relaxing into the stretch. The nervous system will also have a strong input into the degree of relaxation that is achieved.

Dehydration reduces the water content in skin, muscles, tendons and ligaments. This, in turn, makes the tissues less elastic and more sticky. Not only does it limit the ability of different tissues to slide past each other, but it also reduces the elasticity of individual tissues. As little as a 2 per cent drop in body water content can have an adverse affect on performance; therefore it is essential that, prior to stretching, the dog is properly hydrated.

Tissue temperature also affects the compliance of collagen within the body. At colder temperatures, tissues are stiffer and less compliant whilst at warmer temperatures, the reverse is true. Therefore prior to stretching, it is essential that tissues are properly warmed up. This is most efficiently achieved by allowing the dog to run, but can be assisted through the use of a coat and heat-packs or pre-stretching massage.

Resting muscle tone can also be influenced by the body's state of alertness which, in turn, is under the control of the autonomic nervous system. This is the same system that influences and co-ordinates all body systems and interactions: heart rate, blood pressure, gastro-intestinal motility, endocrine function and sleep, to name but a few. When we are in danger, the sympathetic nervous system becomes dominant; this is the system responsible for our flight and fight reflex. It brings about such changes as:

- Increased heart rate.
- Increased blood flow to the muscles.
- Mobilisation of energy stores.
- Increased alertness.
- Increased resting muscle tone.

Active stretch: The dog does the stretch himself.

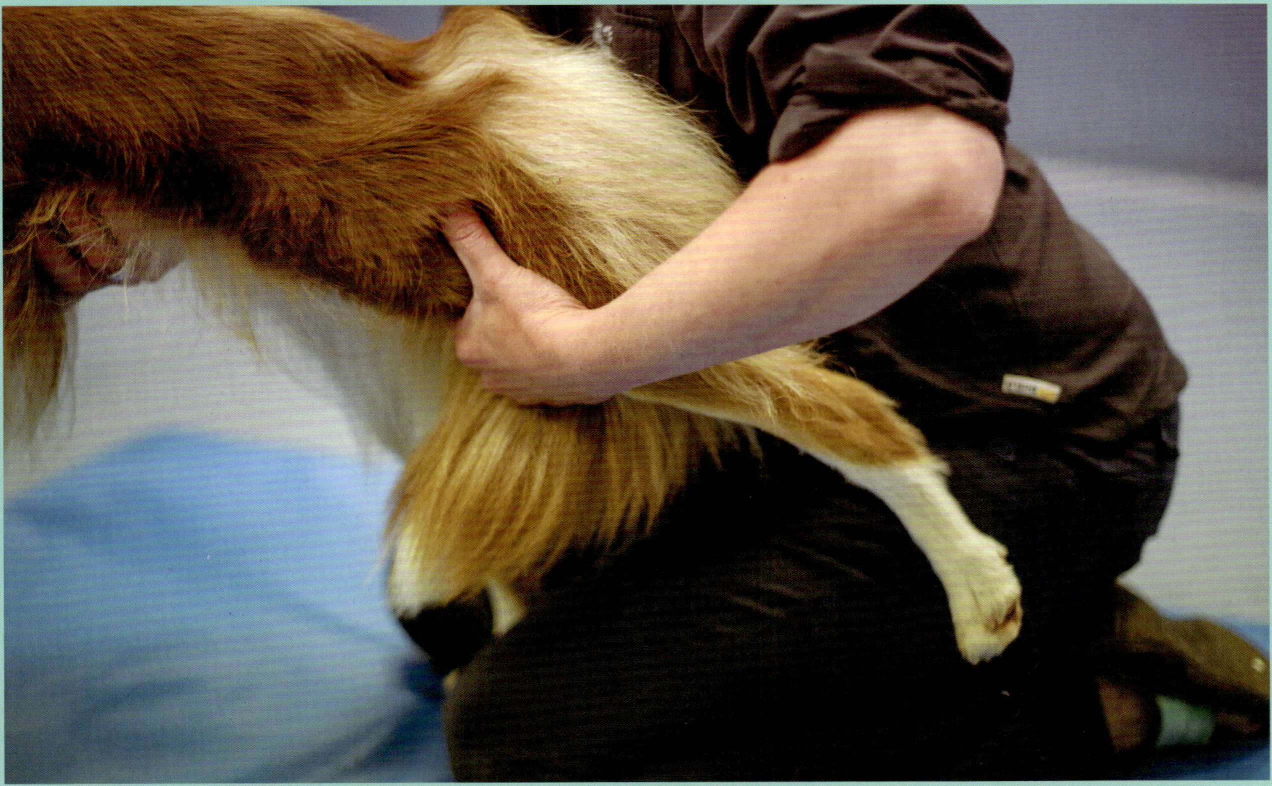

Passive stretch: The owner does the work.

Essentially it is designed to take the body away from danger. Rest and repair can only occur when the parasympathetic nervous system takes over. Under parasympathetic control, tissues repair and sleep can occur and resting muscle tone reduces. It is important that prior to stretching that the dog is not in fight and flight mode as this will increase muscle tone and make it difficult to stretch the tissues.

WHEN AND HOW TO STRETCH

Pre-exercise stretching in isolation does not decrease overall injury rates – in fact, the converse is true. Recent studies with human athletes have demonstrated an increased risk of injury associated with stretching immediately before exercise. It is thought that this is due to changes in how we control our joints – specifically our ability to fine tune their movement through a specific control system known as the proprioceptive system. Proprioception is what fine-tunes all body movement and stops joints from being overstretched. Therefore whilst regular stretching is beneficial, it should not be undertaken immediately prior to exercise.

The main aims of stretching exercises are to improve flexibility, relieve pain, prevent injury and enhance performance. They also improve balance, body awareness and proprioception. By increasing tissue compliance and reducing the viscoelasticity of resting muscle, stretching can enhance range of motion (ROM) in a single or a system of joints. Compliance represents the ability of tissues to lengthen under minimal force and poor compliance during active muscle contraction is a significant factor in tissue injury.

Principles of stretching
Warm up prior to stretching
Work gently and slowly
Stretch to the point of tension but not pain
Make sure the dog and therapist are relaxed
Do not stretch immediately before exercise
Stretch in the cool down period

Stretching post exercise is an important component of preventing muscle stiffness and soreness and should be incorporated as part of a regular cool down regime.

PASSIVE STRETCHING

In a passive stretch, the owner does the work. The dog should be placed on a comfortable conforming surface and should be as relaxed as possible. For all passive stretches, a firm but relaxed hold should be used on the body-part which is to be moved whilst the other hand is placed in a stabilising fashion on the adjacent body segment. Slowly, the moving segment should be advanced towards the outer range of motion. It is important that the muscles adjacent to the joint are at their most relaxed. For example, in order to move the elbow into flexion, the shoulder should be flexed as well. This passive movement should be repeated 3-5 times and held for 10-20 seconds. The movements should not cause the dog any discomfort.

There is no consensus of opinion as to what is the most effective stretching technique. When starting a stretching programme, it is important to make an easy start and increase the intensity of the stretch as the tissues warm and adapt. The point of stretching is not to see how far you can bend to pull the leg, but rather to slowly lengthen the tissues

STATIC STRETCHING

With a static stretch, the joint is moved into a position and then held in that position for the duration of the stretch. The position is assumed slowly and held for up to 30 seconds. The stretch should not cause discomfort, and tension from the stretch should not cause the dog to pull away. Before releasing, the muscle can be stretched a little further. This second stretch should be held for 30 seconds.

BALLISTIC STRETCHING/DYNAMIC STRETCHING

In a dynamic stretch, the muscle is stretched to near the limit, then stretched further with gentle, bouncing motion. The quick bounce causes a reflex muscle contraction; it may heighten the chance of injury as the tension generated within the muscle can be up to twice that achieved in a static stretch. Inexperienced handlers should not attempt these stretches.

ACTIVE STRETCHING

During an active stretch, the dog is in control of the stretch with a varying degree of guidance from the handler. Active stretches generally use less of the available joint movement and muscle stretch and are, therefore, safer. They involve persuading the dog to flex and bend by using a treat or toy. Once in position, the stretch should be held for up to 20 seconds and repeated 3-5 times.

DANGERS OF STRETCHING

All stretches have the potential of causing injury; the risk of injury increasing with the intensity, repetition and duration of the stretch. Stretching would be contraindicated in cases of ligament laxity, e.g. stretching the stifle after cruciate ligament damage or the hock after achilles tendon injury.

MASSAGE

Regular soft tissue therapy helps with soft tissue recovery. Intense training causes prolonged elevation of muscle tone, both during exercise and rest. This is often felt as muscle 'tightness' and is most prevalent during periods of adaptation to higher intensity or overload training.

Small changes in resting muscle tone can actually squeeze shut the small capillaries that normally deliver oxygen and nutrients to the muscle, remove waste products, and restore normal electrolyte balance. Not only does this reduce the muscle's capacity for work, which is seen as reduced performance or fatigue, but it will also impair the muscle's ability to adapt to training and its ability to heal. Increased tone will also limit the extensibility and shock absorbing capacity of the muscle and increase the predisposition to strain.

Fatigue associated with hard training also impairs proprioceptive mechanisms and may trigger a pain response. During hard training, there might be insufficient time for the muscle to recover between training sessions, and this can lead to muscle soreness and increase the risk of injury. Massage can, potentially, improve muscle recovery and reduce fatigue.

Muscle soreness can develop as a result of strenuous exercise, particularly where the athlete has undergone inadequate training and the muscles are poorly adapted to the demands of performance. Well-conditioned muscles are generally less likely to exhibit post-exercise soreness. The onset of this soreness is often delayed by 24 hours and this is why new exercises should not be added on a daily basis at the start of training. A gap of 48 hours should be left in order to assess the effect on the body and to allow time for post-exercise muscle soreness to develop. The problem can be avoided through appropriate training. This results in well-conditioned muscles which are perfused with capillary beds, and have an appropriate energy store in the form of muscle glycogen.

HOW DOES MASSAGE WORK?

Soft tissue therapy is thought to work by reducing excessive post-exercise muscle tone, increasing muscle range of motion and increasing circulation to damaged tissue and promoting lymphatic drainage. It may also serve to deactivate trigger points. Techniques to release fascial planes can significantly enhance limb mobility, assist with pain management and the restoration of motor function.

CIRCULATORY EFFECTS OF MASSAGE

The term 'massage' is derived from the Arabic word 'mass' which means to press. Massage increases pressure within the body tissues and assists in moving fluid from the tissue spaces back into the circulation down a pressure gradient. Massage often involves a combination of kneading, squeezing, pulling and pressing tissues, working in several different directions and at different tissue depths. Not only does massage help drain fluid back into the circulation, but it also replenishes fluid within tissue spaces, ensuring a continuous supply of oxygen and nutrients to the cells.

It is postulated that massage also helps remove inflammatory chemicals, such as prostaglandins, from the tissues which potentially contribute to post-exercise pain and cell damage. Massage also stimulates the flow of lymph through lymphatics in the body.

MASSAGE AND MUSCLE PAIN

Some practitioners have advocated the use of massage to reduce muscle pain post-exercise due to its role in breaking the cycle of pain and spasm within the muscle. It can also assist with reducing resting muscle tone. In humans, massage has also been shown to increase the pain threshold.

Following low-grade muscle damage, such as often happens in the early stages of training before the muscle adapts to work, low-grade inflammation occurs in the muscle post-exercise. This increases the permeability of local blood vessels, i.e. they become leaky and a product called fibrin is released between the muscle fibres. Whilst it is critical in preventing haemorrhage, it also serve to trap the muscle fibres together and reduce the extensibility or stretchiness of the muscle. Massage can overcome these adhesions and help maintain muscle elasticity. Massage can also stretch the repeating units of actin and myosin that make up skeletal muscle, helping the fibres slide over each other as the muscle contracts.

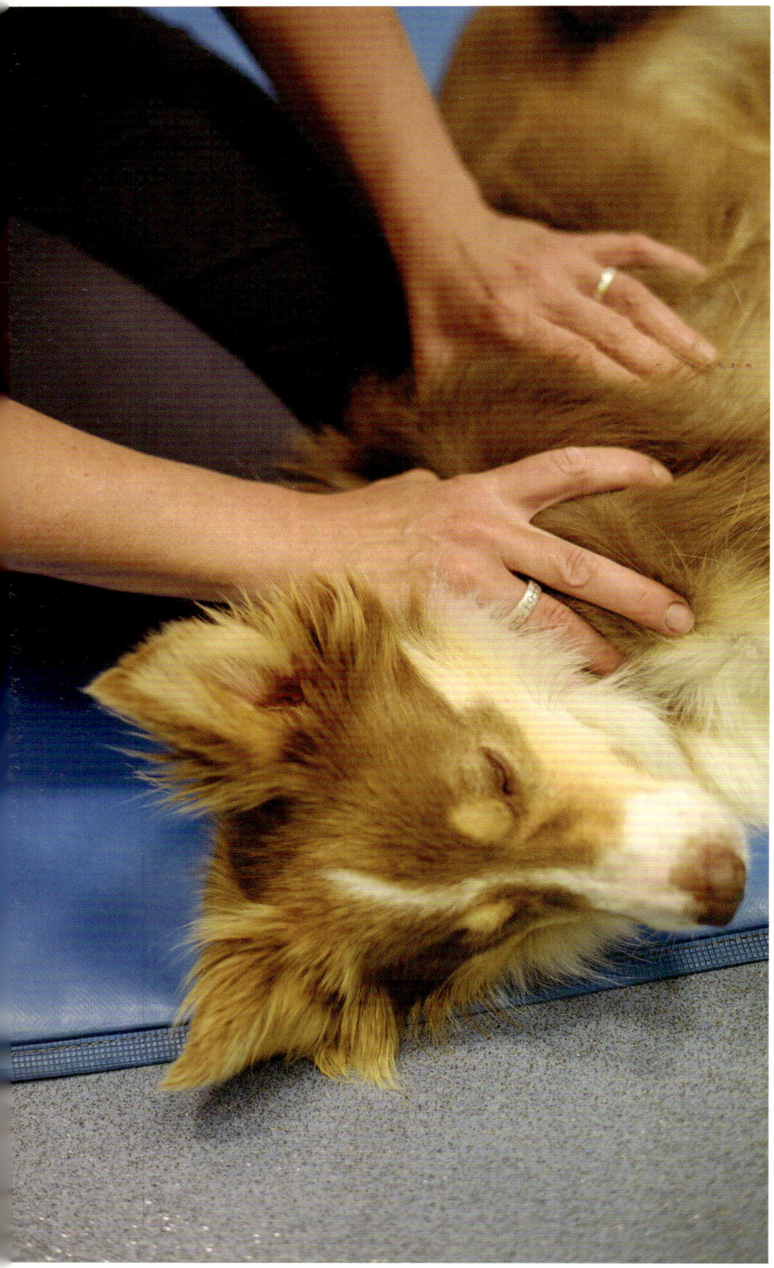

Massage helps to increase circulation to damaged tissues.

STROKING

Stroking is an effective and gentle introduction into massage which helps relax the patient and the therapist. It also allows the therapist to evaluate muscle tone and identify swellings, temperature differences and areas of pain. The flat of the hand is used and should be kept in contact with the dog at all times. Stroking helps relax the tension in the muscle.

EFFLURAGE

This is the most common massage technique used in dogs and involves long, slow strokes of light pressure parallel to the fibre direction. This is a useful technique to improve the circulation and reduce swelling and also to promote lymphatic drainage and reduce muscle tone. Effluráge can also assist with increasing soft tissue extensibility and with the removal of waste products.

The therapist should work from the extremities of the digits, up the limb towards the heart. The whole hand should be in contact with the dog, but with pressure applied through the heel of the hand. In small dogs, or over the limbs, the thumb and forefinger alone can be used. Overlapping strokes can also be utilised.

PETRISSAGE

This technique targets the deeper tissues. It uses short, brisk strokes with moderate to deep pressure parallel or perpendicular to the fibres. It can include kneading and rolling, and picking up and squeezing the tissues. This technique will improve the circulation, improve soft tissue extensibility and reduce muscle spasm. It also assists with removing waste products from the tissues. The back of the hand can be used to push in to the tissues, or the pads of the fingers can be used to push the tissues towards the palm. Pressure is applied to the deeper tissues.

PERCUSSION

This involves rhythmic tapping or cupping, often with the tips of the fingers. It improves circulation and can also assist with releasing secretions in the respiratory tract and facilitating drainage. It also increases muscle tone in tired, flaccid muscle. The hand is positioned in a cup shape, the elbows should be flexed and the arms relaxed as the hand is 'clapped' over the treatment site.

CROSS FIBRE

This technique stimulates local blood flow, assists with tissue healing, reduces adhesions, increases scar mobility and increase soft tissue extensibility. It also assists with removing waste products. It is carried out with the tips of the fingers, applied in a circular motion, over the treatment site. The fingers should not slip over the skin, rather they should press down over the target tissue.

ISCHEMIC COMPRESSION

This involves sustained moderate or deep pressure to an area of localised hyperactivity. Resurgence of blood flow occurs on release of pressure. It is used to promote healing and reduce pain. It will also reduce muscle spasm and helps to eliminate trigger points.

TRIGGER POINT RELEASE

A trigger point is a reactive band, often described as a guitar string within the muscle. The dog will often show clear discomfort when the area is palpated. The tips of the fingers are used to gently push down on the trigger point; the position is held for 20 seconds and then released before being repeated three times.

POSITIONAL RELEASE

The patient is positioned so the origin and insertion of the affected muscle are brought together. The position is held for 90 seconds and then the patient is slowly returned to neutral.

MYOFASCIAL RELEASE

This involves plastic deformation of connective tissue which is achieved through applying a slow, low, load. The load is applied in three planes of motion.

PROS AND CONS

Massage may have immediate benefits in terms of improved circulation and pain relief. However, regular treatment is required to assist with tissue healing and to maintain the tissues in their optimum state of health long term.

Massage should not be carried out if the dog has a fever or is overheating post-exercise. It should also be avoided over:

- Areas of acute inflammation.
- Areas of acute haemorrhage.
- Open wounds.

THERMOTHERAPY: SUPERFICIAL HOT AND COLD

Superficial heat and cold have been used for centuries to manage soft tissue and joint injuries. The three major treatment aims include:

- Reducing pain and inflammation.
- Increasing tissue compliance.
- Facilitating healing and a return to function.

Thermotherapy applications fall in the infra-red portion of the electro-magnetic spectrum, just beyond the wavelength and frequency ranges for visible light – the shorter the wavelength, the greater the frequency and depth of penetration. Electro-magnetic energy, and its transmission through the body, is governed by several physical laws.

In essence, the body tissue must absorb the energy from the thermal agent to stimulate normal function. If insufficient energy is absorbed, there will be no change within the tissue. If a tissue does not absorb energy, it is transmitted to deeper tissue layers. However, if the energy is absorbed more superficially, less will penetrate the deeper structures.

In general, superficial hot and cold therapy, administered through hot and cold packs, can potentially penetrate tissues to a depth of only 1-2 cm. Penetration will be affected by the hair coat and body fat. Electro-magnetic energy may also be reflected at the body surface or refracted where different tissues meet, e.g. at the dermis/subcutaneous fat interface.

CRYOTHERAPY

Cryotherapy, or ice therapy, is extremely beneficial during the acute stage of tissue damage. Simply, if the tissue is red, hot and swollen, it is likely to benefit from the application of ice.

The primary effects of cryotherapy are:

- Vaso-constriction (shutting down of blood vessels) thus reducing haemorrhage and swelling.
- Reduced tissue metabolism and oxygen requirements, thus increasing the survival rate of cells.
- Reduced sensory and motor nerve conduction velocity, thus reducing pain and muscle spasm.
- Reduced odema (swelling), thus reducing stretch in the tissues which is associated with pain.

There are many methods of applying cold therapy, including cryokinetic devices, vapocoolant sprays and ice baths. Practically, two methods are commonly used: ice packs and ice lollipops which are used in a massaging technique around the distal limbs.

HEAT THERAPY

As a rule, if the affected area is red and hot, do not apply heat due to its potential to increase inflammation. Heat should be applied to cold, stiff joints and muscles to improve their blood supply and increase the elasticity of the tissues.

The application of heat should result in:

- Local vasodilation and increased blood flow to an area. This improves the delivery of oxygen and nutrients to tissues and facilitates healing.
- An increase in nerve conduction velocity, promoting a relaxation of the muscle fibres, again helping with pain relief.
- An increased compliance of tissues, making it easier to stretch muscles, tendons and ligaments as well as scar tissue.

Superficial heat can be applied through heat packs, directly to the skin. Alternatively infra-red heat sources can be used.

Muscle pain and spasm

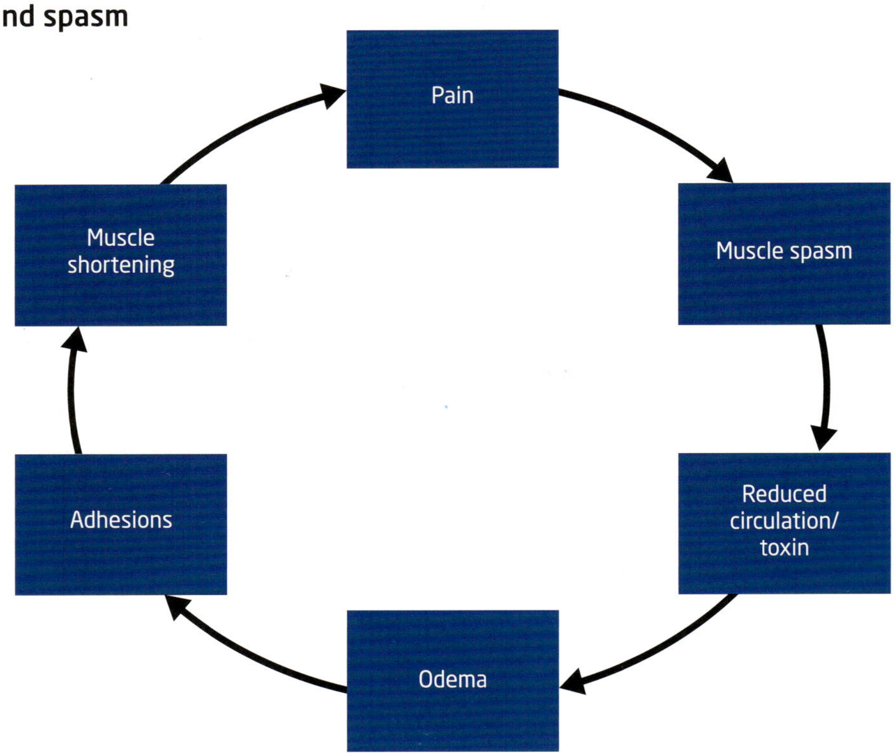

Tips for applying ice
Never apply directly to the skin – always wrap in a thin towel to prevent burning
Apply for 7-10 minutes
Make sure the pack and towel are wet to improve heat transfer
Reapply 4-6 times a day
Continue as long as redness and swelling persist

Tips for applying heat
If its comfortable on your skin it should not burn the dog
Apply for 15-20 minutes
Make sure the pack and towel are moist to improve heat transfer
Reapply 2-3 times a day
When applied before exercises, movement of stiff and painful joints can be facilitated

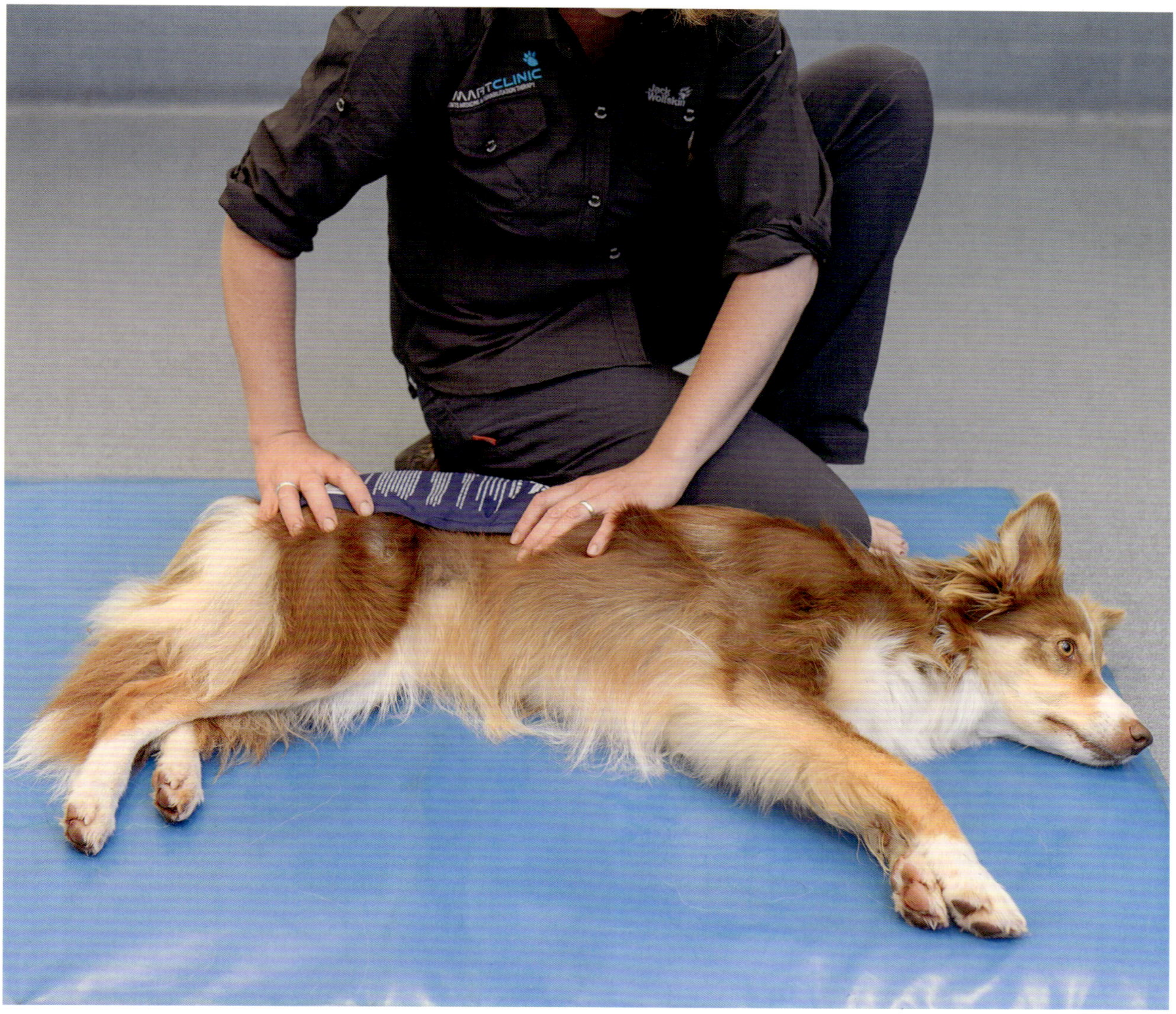

The application of heat improves blood supply.

CHAPTER 11: THERAPEUTIC EXERCISES

Therapeutic exercises, whilst an integral part of any rehabilitation programme, can also have a role to play in the correct development of movement patterns and core muscle function in all dogs. As with any exercise, practice does not make perfect, but it can make permanent changes. It is therefore essential that the right exercise is chosen for the right reason and – most importantly – it must be carried out correctly.

With the rising popularity of balance trainers such as cushions, balls and boards, many owners inadvertently make their dogs stiff through the overuse and incorrect use of such equipment. If the challenge is too great, then the dog's natural instinct is to stiffen. So whilst it may be appealing to use novel training aids, it is essential that the dog or puppy is first allowed to develop reasonable balance and stability on unchallenging surfaces. Do not be tempted to place your athlete on a balance cushion unless he is first able to carry out a weight shift on the floor. This trains proper balance and co-ordination of limbs during the stance or weight-bearing phase of the stride.

Weight shifting is often thought of as a simple exercise and is thus undervalued. However, carrying out a weight shift correctly can be difficult, even in sound dogs. It is essential that the dog stands with a leg at each corner and with toes pointing as near to 12 o'clock as possible. Postural symmetry is a fundamental component for each standing exercise, whether it is working on the floor on one or more balance cushions, or when walking and trotting in a controlled manner.

Training the young or adult dog to walk correctly is as fundamental as training him to stand symmetrically. Any dog that pulls on the lead will not be able to engage their hindquarters correctly and will tend to rely on their back, shoulders and even the head and neck to pull themselves forward. This, in turn, is not only inefficient in terms of energy production but is also damaging to those structures that are being inappropriately used. In the worst example it can lead to chronic forelimb, neck and back pain.

The dog must learn to walk in a balanced manner at the handler's side. Various devices, such as the balance harness or the figure of 8 lead, can be used to assist with this. To prevent one side becoming dominant, particularly if the dog has a tendency to look up at the owner, it is critical that dogs are walked in both the left and right hand.

It must also be remembered that walking slowly at the handler's side, whilst relatively undemanding in terms of cardiovascular function, is extremely challenging in terms of accurate control of movement. The dog will tire just as quickly, if not more quickly, than when running around freely. For this reason, sessions of very slow walking, which is used as a rehabilitation exercise, should be of limited duration.

Whilst learning to walk on the lead is a critical skill as it assists with the correct recruitment of muscles and develops the dog's spatial awareness, it is equally important that he is allowed to run off lead, over all terrain, to help not only with cardiovascular and muscle fitness but also to develop good balance skills under challenge. Achieving a good mixture of slow and fast work is vital, but repeating maneuveres over and over again should be avoided. No exercise, however simple, should be underestimated. A fit dog that has been recently injured may well struggle to stand correctly for just 30 seconds or walk correctly for more than 5 minutes at a time. Exercise does not have to be fast and explosive to be challenging.

The following is a selection of useful exercises

that can be used to assist with developing a dog's balance and co-ordination as well as core muscle function and flexibility.

CONTROLLED LEAD WALKING

This is a fundamental exercise from which all other gait patterns develop. A dog must be able to walk correctly in a balanced and coordinated fashion before progressing to other gaits.

GOOD FOR

- Basic conditioning.
- Physical and mental control.
- As a progression monitor – if a pup or a dog cannot walk for 30 minutes continuously then he is not capable of undertaking more sports specific training.
- Coordination.
- Tissue adaptation, i.e. helps condition and strengthen bones, tendons, ligaments and muscle.

SUITABLE FOR

- Puppies at all stages of development.
- Bitches after whelping.
- Geriatric dogs.
- Early conditioning.
- Tapering.
- Rehabilitation.

HOW TO DO IT CORRECTLY

- Straight nose to tail alignment.
- Neutral head position – not lowered, lifted or turned to the side.
- Carry out on both sides of the handler.
- The dog should be moving freely and not pulling.
- Build variation in terrain into the walk.

PITFALLS

- The dog must be walking, not trotting.
- Avoid pulling.
- Avoid walking on one surface only, e.g. tarmac.

Nose and tail must be in straight alignment.

You can build your own proprioceptive road, as well as making use of the outside environment.

PROPRIOCEPTIVE ROAD

This is a fundamental exercise for developing body awareness and joint control.

GOOD FOR

- Co-ordinating front and back and left and right.
- Helps mature the gait in readiness for balanced trot work and any other future proprioceptive challenges, such as surface variation.
- Basic conditioning – viewed as an essential element.
- Physical and mental control.
- Development of Type 1 muscle fibre (postural fibres).
- Resetting joint and muscle receptors following injury or surgery.

SUITABLE FOR

- Puppies at all stages of development.
- Bitches after whelping.
- Geriatric dogs.
- Early conditioning.
- Tapering.
- Rehabilitation.
- Warming up.

HOW TO DO IT CORRECTLY

- Walk slowly from one surface to the other in quick succession, i.e. 1m runs before surface change.
- Use lots of novel surfaces and change regularly.
- Avoid over-challenging in the early stages.
- The dog should be moving freely and not pulling.
- Build variation in terrain into the walk.

PITFALLS

- The dog must be walking not trotting.
- Pulling must be avoided.
- Slippery surfaces and very unstable surfaces must be avoided initially.
- This is very challenging for injured dogs, both in terms of mental and physical challenge, therefore keep sessions short.

SQUARE STANDING

It is important that dogs learn to stand in a relaxed but centered manner, and not always expect to perform a task and seek a reward. Getting into the correct position, and then maintaining a square stand, is a reasonable challenge for any dog.

GOOD FOR

- Focuses and calms the mind.
- Symmetrically recruits appropriate muscle groups throughout the body.

SUITABLE FOR

- Puppies at all stages of training.

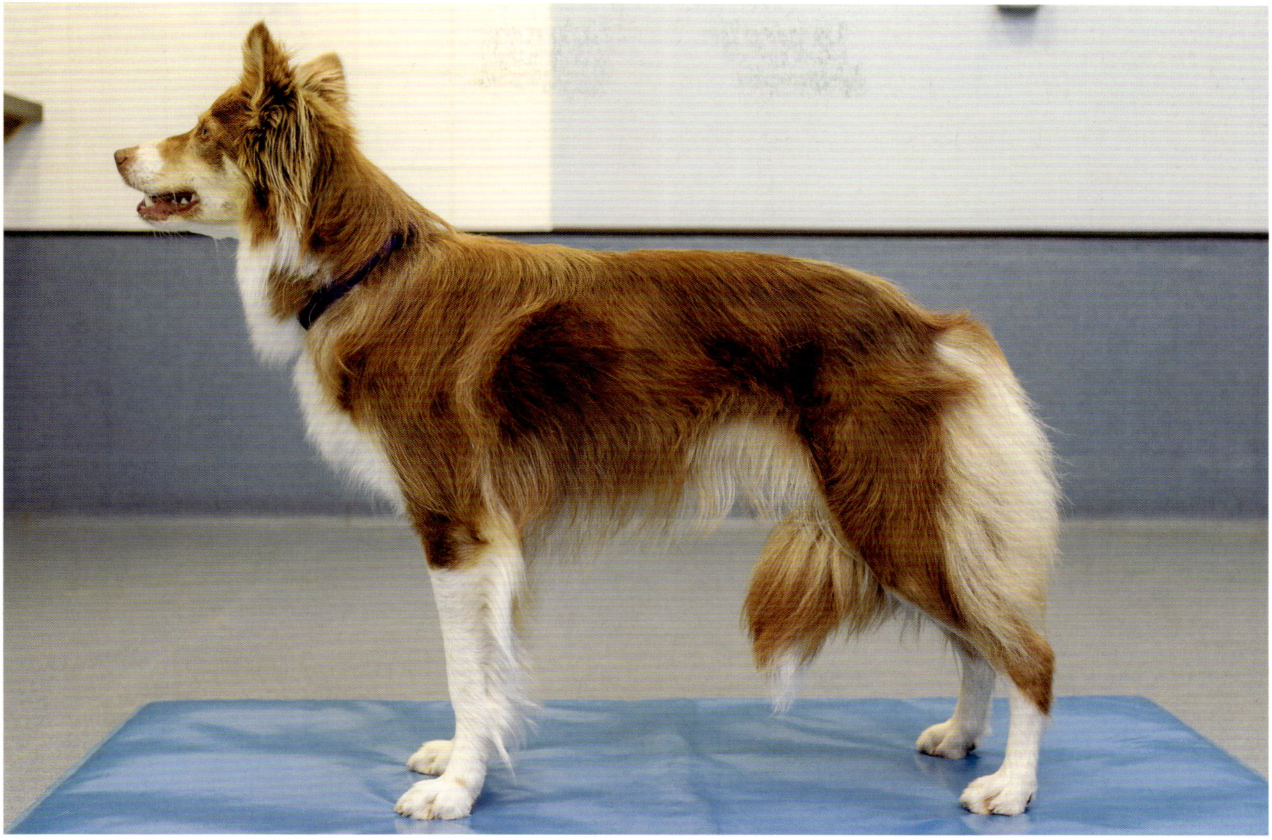

A dog should work on a straight stand before attempting to work with a balance cushion.

- Bitches after whelping.
- Geriatric dogs.
- Rehabilitation.
- Warming up.

HOW TO DO IT CORRECTLY

- Place the dog in a square stand with the forelimbs directly under the shoulder and the hindlimbs angled straight down.
- A straight line should be drawn between the head and the tail.
- The top of the back should be parallel to the floor.

VARIANTS

- The dog can be taught to stand on a small, square plank with a bamboo cane placed underneath the plank to create very slight instability which starts to aclimatise the young agility dog to the seesaw.

PITFALLS

- Pushing the dog to stand with all four legs too close together or in a box.

STANDING WEIGHT SHIFT

This is a fundamental exercise for the recruitment of correct muscle groups which underlie core stability, strength, power and speed.

GOOD FOR

- Development of stabilising Type 1 muscle fibre.
- Development of abdominal and back muscles.
- Development of symmetry between the left and right side of the body.
- Promoting weight bearing in a limb after injury.
- Development of proprioception.
- Tissue adaptation, i.e. strong bones, tendons, ligaments and muscle.

SUITABLE FOR

- Puppies after 6 months.
- Bitches after whelping.
- Geriatric dogs.
- Early conditioning.
- Tapering.
- Rehabilitation.

HOW TO DO IT CORRECTLY

- Put the dog standing square (see page 130).
- Carry out very, very small adjustments to the limbs in a slow, rhythmical manner, either from side to side or forwards and backwards.

VARIANTS

- For forelimb motion, place hands on the outside of the shoulders.
- For hindlimb motion, place hands on the thighs (this can be in front or behind depending on the dog).
- Gentle trunk taps can be introduced to increase the challenge as the dog improves.

PITFALLS

- The dog must be standing square, not rotated.
- The dog must not be bracing against you.
- The dog is weight bearing through all four limbs.
- Head to tail must be positioned in a straight line.
- Avoid moving too fast or too vigorously.
- Must be built up gradually.
- Only use under the guidance of a qualified practitioner (vet/physio) if the dog has been injured.

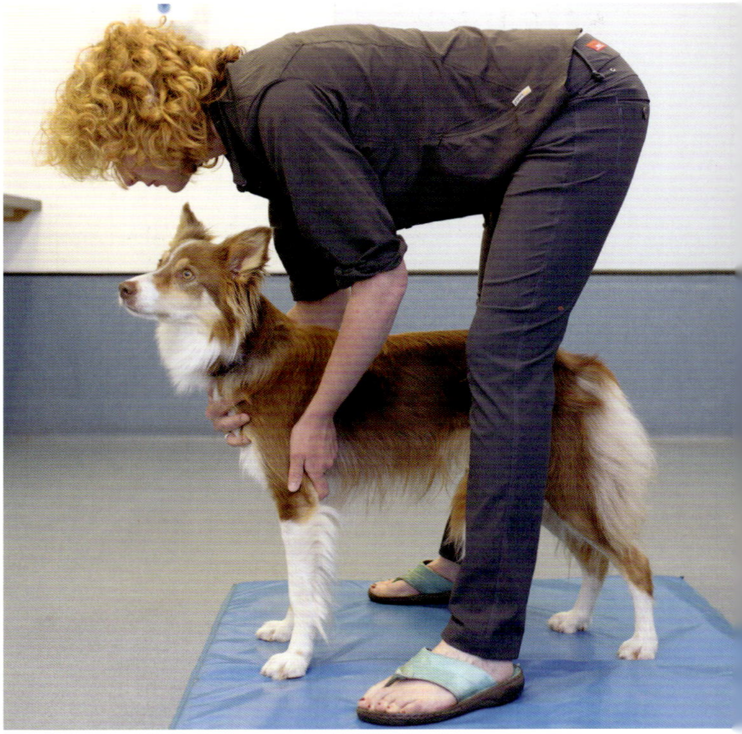

A standing weight shift helps to develop symmetry between the two sides of the body.

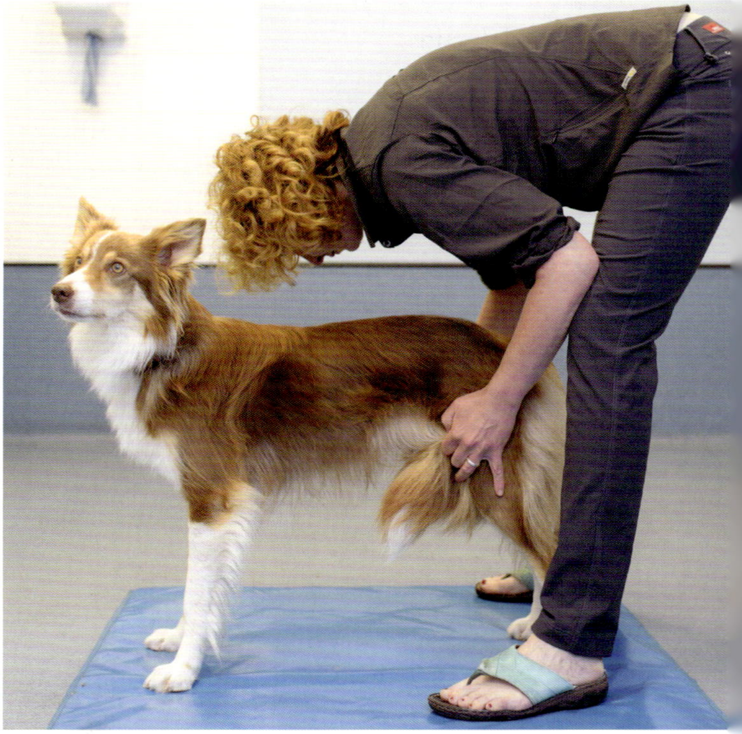

Hands should be placed on the thighs for hindlimb motion.

HEAD TURNS

This is a fundamental exercise for balance, co-ordination and flexibility.

GOOD FOR

- Strengthening the core – abdominal and back muscles.
- Proprioceptive training.
- Suppleness.
- Development of slow, controlled movement patterns.

SUITABLE FOR

- Puppies at all stages of development.
- Bitches after whelping.
- Geriatric dogs.
- Early conditioning.
- Tapering.
- Warming up and cooling down.
- Rehabilitation.

HOW TO DO IT CORRECTLY

- The dog must be standing square.
- Movements should be slow and controlled.
- No physical contact is required – the dog should follow a treat or a toy.
- All parts of the body should bend.
- Feet should be stationary during the exercise.
- The bottom of the jaw should be parallel to the ground.
- Work to both sides.
- There should be no evidence of pain or discomfort.

VARIANTS

- Stretching to the ground.

PITFALLS

- The dog is constantly shuffling his feet.
- The dog rotates rather than stretches.
- The dog arches up through the back when dropping his head.
- The dog drops through the elbows.

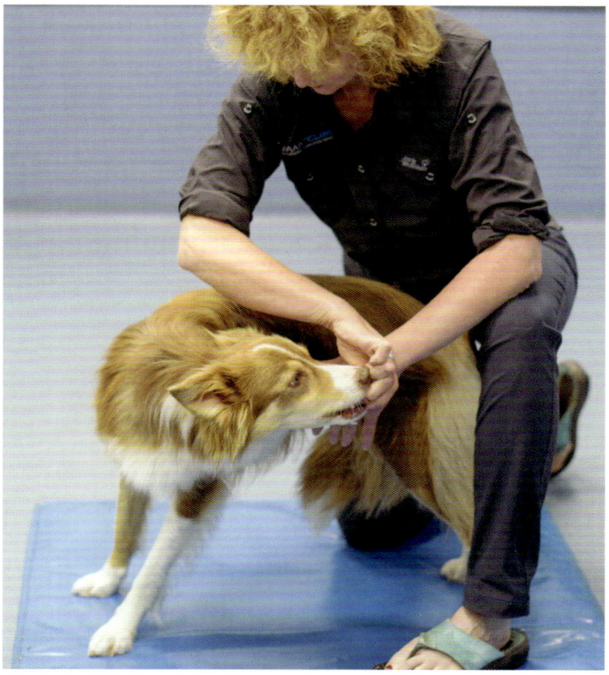

Head turns exercise the core and increase suppleness.

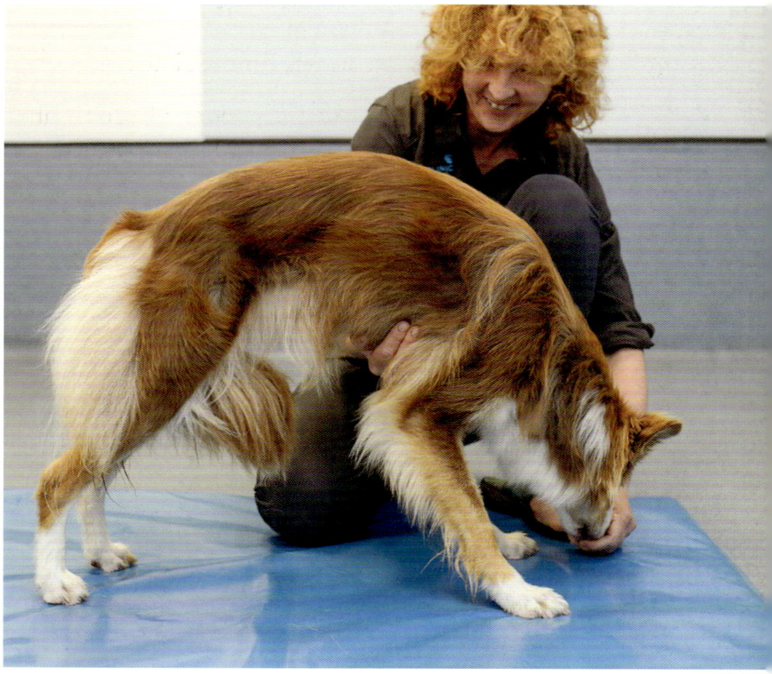

You can also lure your dog so he bends to touch the floor.

FIGURE OF EIGHT

This is a fundamental exercise for developing body awareness and joint control.

GOOD FOR

- Encouraging and maintaining spinal flexibility, coordination and balance between left and right sides of the body.

SUITABLE FOR

- Puppies in all stages of development.
- Bitches after whelping.
- Geriatric dogs.
- Tapering.
- Warming up and cooling down.
- Rehabilitation.

HOW TO DO IT CORRECTLY

- Use an upright pole, cone or marker to show the centre of the two circles making up your figure of eight.
- Space your markers appropriate for your individual dog (3 metres between markers is a good starting point).
- Walk your dog slowly on lead in a figure of eight formation using the markers as a guide, paying attention to control and symmetry.
- Repeat in the opposite direction.

VARIANTS

- Trotting in a large figure of eight.

PITFALLS

- Immature dogs are more flexible than mature dogs so be careful not to overstretch youngsters by keeping the figure of eight large.
- If the figure of eight is too small then this may lead to excessive splinting through the back muscles.
- Only use under the guidance of a qualified practitioner (vet/physio) if the dog has been injured.

Walking in a figure of eight encourages spinal flexibility, balance and coordination.

LABYRINTH AND TRAM-LINES

These exercises are useful to teach hindlimb awareness and flexibility.

GOOD FOR

- An introduction to the seesaw and dog-walk.
- The labyrinth assists with tight turns.
- Tram-lines are a way of safely and easily teaching dogs to keep straight in their movement, and get them used to a narrow base for footfall.

SUITABLE FOR

- Puppies in all stages of development.
- Bitches after whelping.
- Some geriatric dogs.
- Rehabilitation.

HOW TO DO IT CORRECTLY

Labyrinth

- Poles are placed in two tightly interlocking Us and the dog is walked in both directions through the labyrinth.
- The dog will need to step his inside leg under his body to negotiate the tight corners.

Variants

- The dog can be taught to side step over the poles.

Tram-lines

- Poles are laid on the ground in two parallel rows, roughly as wide apart as the broadest part of the dog's body. The dog is then walked slowly up and down between the poles.

PITFALLS

- The dog habituates.
- The dog pulls through the exercise.

POLE-STEPPING

This is a fundamental exercise for developing body awareness, joint control, coordination and balance.

GOOD FOR

- Encouraging flexion in the forelimbs and hindlimbs.

Your dog needs to maintain a slow pace as he steps over the poles.

SUITABLE FOR

- Puppies in all stages of development.
- Bitches after whelping.
- Geriatric dogs.
- Tapering.
- Rehabilitation.

HOW TO DO IT CORRECTLY

- Create a series of 3-6 poles at an appropriate spacing and height for your dog.
- Walk with your dog slowly, on a lead, over the poles with his head in a neutral position.
- Ensure that you maintain a four beat walking pattern so that each limb flexes individually over each pole.

VARIANTS

- Place poles in a fan formation.

PITFALLS

- Avoid bunny hopping or trotting over the poles.
- Do not over-challenge by having the poles too high or too tightly packed.
- Avoid in dogs with joint pain.

When the poles are in fan formation, the dog has to turn as well as step over the poles.

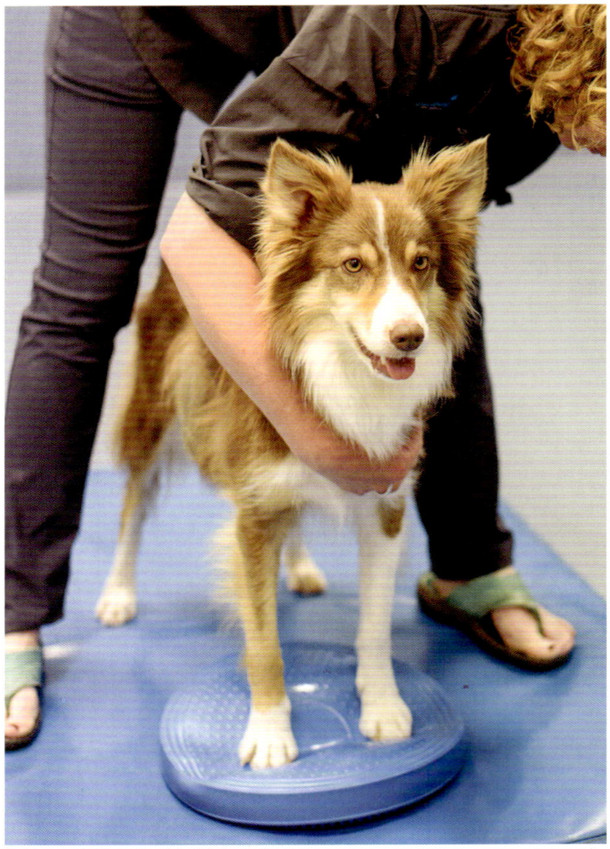

It is important to maintain a square stand when using a balance cushion.

- Only use under the guidance of a qualified practitioner (vet/physio) if the dog has been injured.

BALANCE CUSHION

This is a fundamental exercise for the recruitment of correct muscle groups which underlie core stability, strength, power and speed.

GOOD FOR

- Development of balance.
- Development of stabilising Type 1 muscle fibre.
- Development of abdominal and back muscle.
- Development of symmetry between the left and right side of the body.
- Promoting weight bearing in a limb after injury.
- Development of proprioception.
- Tissue adaptation, i.e. strong bones, tendons, ligaments and muscle.

SUITABLE FOR

- Puppies after 6 months (once basic standing exercises have been achieved and can be maintained).
- Bitches after whelping.
- Geriatric dogs.
- Early conditioning.
- Tapering.
- Rehabilitation.

HOW TO DO IT CORRECTLY

- Best results are achieved when the surface of the balance cushion is flat rather than convex or concave.
- Place the dog's front feet on the balance cushion so that they create equal indentation.
- Ensure that a square stand is maintained throughout this exercise.
- Use a slight movement to slowly rock the dog's centre of gravity backwards, hold this position for 2 seconds, and then release.
- Repeat, this time moving the dog from side to side.
- Backwards and side to side movements can be repeated, but using the balance cushion for the hind feet only.
- The dog can eventually progress to having one balance cushion under the front feet and one under the back.

PITFALLS

- The dog must be standing square, and not rotated.
- The dog is not bracing against you.
- The dog must be weight bearing through all four limbs.
- Head to tail is in a straight line.
- Avoid moving too fast or too vigorously.
- Must be built up gradually.
- The more textured side of the balance cushion may be uncomfortable for dogs with normal foot sensation.
- Many dogs are over-challenged by use of concurrent hind and front balance cushions.
- Only use under the guidance of a qualified practitioner (vet/physio) if the dog has been injured.

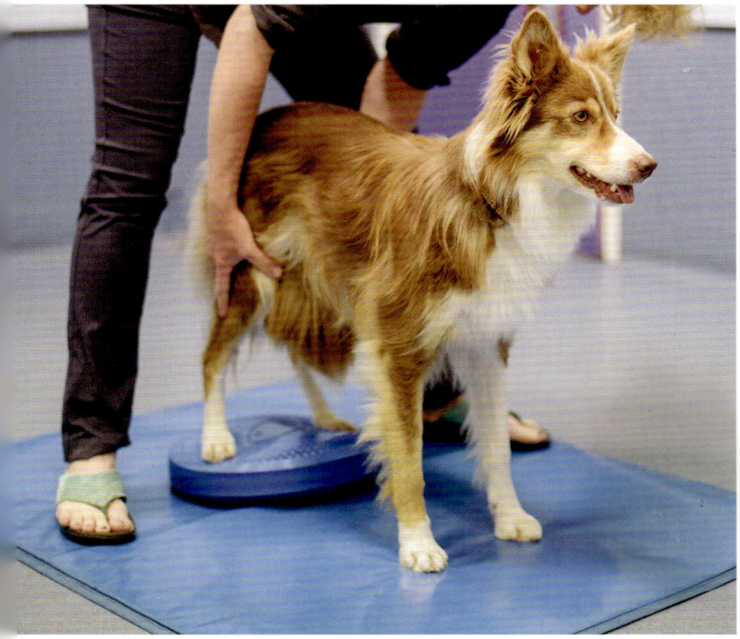

Work on backwards and side to side movement when the hind feet are positioned on the balance cushion.

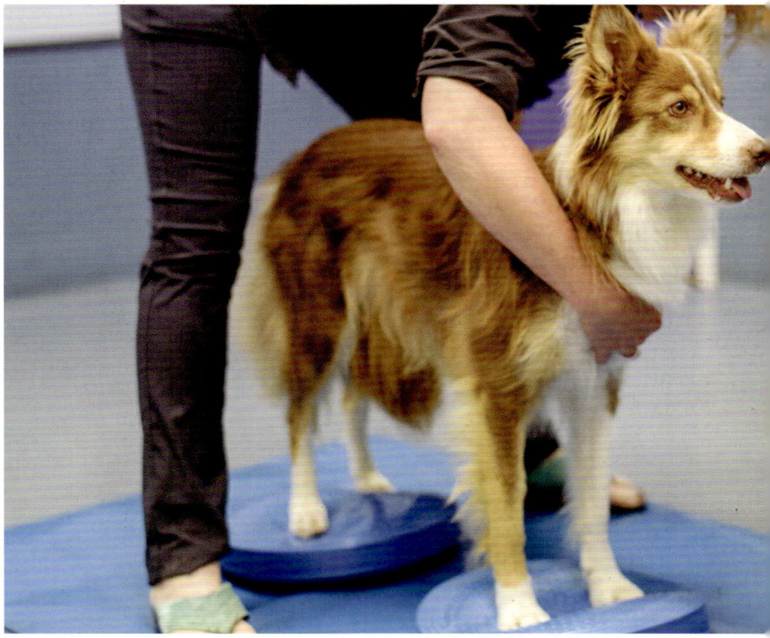

Progress to using balance cushions for both the front and hind feet.

When the dog is standing square, gently rock the balance board from side to side.

BALANCE BOARD

Assists with the recruitment of correct muscle groups which underlie core stability, strength, power and speed.

GOOD FOR

- Development of balance.
- Development of stabilising Type 1 muscle fibre.
- Development of abdominal and back muscles.
- Development of symmetry between the left and right side of the body.
- Development of proprioception.
- Tissue adaptation, i.e. strong bones, tendons, ligaments and muscle.

SUITABLE FOR

- Puppies after 6 months (once basic standing exercises have been achieved and can be maintained).
- Bitches after whelping (subsequent to 3-4 weeks of basic conditioning).
- Tapering.
- Later stage of rehabilitation.

HOW TO DO IT CORRECTLY

- Place the dog square in the centre of the board. Gently rock the board from side to side.
- Then turn the dog through 90 degrees and repeat.

PITFALLS

The dog must be standing square, and not rotated.

Head to tail in a straight line.

- The dog must be weight bearing through all 4 limbs.
- Do not move too fast or too vigorously.
- Must be build up gradually – it is easy to over-challenge with this exercise.
- Only use under the guidance of a qualified practitioner (vet/physio) if the dog has been injured.

GYM BALL

The correct use of a gym ball can be difficult to achieve. Often dogs are taught to balance with all four feet on a ball which, for all but the most balanced of dogs, is extremely challenging and often causes the dog to stiffen inappropriately.

GOOD FOR

- Depends on how the gym ball is used (see below).

SUITABLE FOR

- Dogs later on in training.
- End stage rehabilitation.

HOW TO CARRY IT OUT CORRECTLY

The ball can be used in a number of ways:

- To strengthen the back, trunk and hind limbs, the dog's front paws can be placed on the ball, initially when stationary and later they can be taught to walk around in this fashion. This also helps extend the hip and stifle.
- In reverse, the dog's hindlegs can be placed up on the ball which increases the load on the forelimbs. In this manner it serves to increase shoulder flexion and elbow extension and to strengthen the forelimbs.
- The very fit dog can be trained to stand with all four limbs on the ball for enhanced core strengthening work and balance training.

PITFALLS

- The dog's core is too weak and the back and stomach fall down into an upside down arch.
- The dog stiffens rather than becoming dynamically stable with the net result of a loss of balance and flexibility.

To begin with, the dog should be stationary – he can then progress to walking around the gym ball.

This position strengthens the forelimbs.

SUSTAINED TROTTING

This is the most efficient canine gait. It can be used therapeutically, in a controlled way, as when the dog is trotting correctly both sides of the body are working equally and symmetrically.

GOOD FOR

- Weight bearing and developing symmetry.
- Co-ordination and balance.
- Physical and mental control.
- Progressing fitness/endurance.
- Warming up and cooling down.

SUITABLE FOR

- Dogs over 12 months.
- Conditioning.
- Overweight dogs (with care).
- Rehabilitation progression.

HOW TO DO IT CORRECTLY

- Start with small sessions of trotting interspersed with walking.
- Build up the length of time spent trotting, eventually attaining 20 minutes of sustained trotting 3 times per week. The speed and rhythm of the trot needs to be steady and sustained so the handler may need to run or cycle to keep up with the dog.

VARIANTS

- Trotting over poles – good for developing the gait patter

PITFALLS

- The dog paces instead of trots.
- The dog has not adequately mastered controlled lead walking before progressing to trotting work.

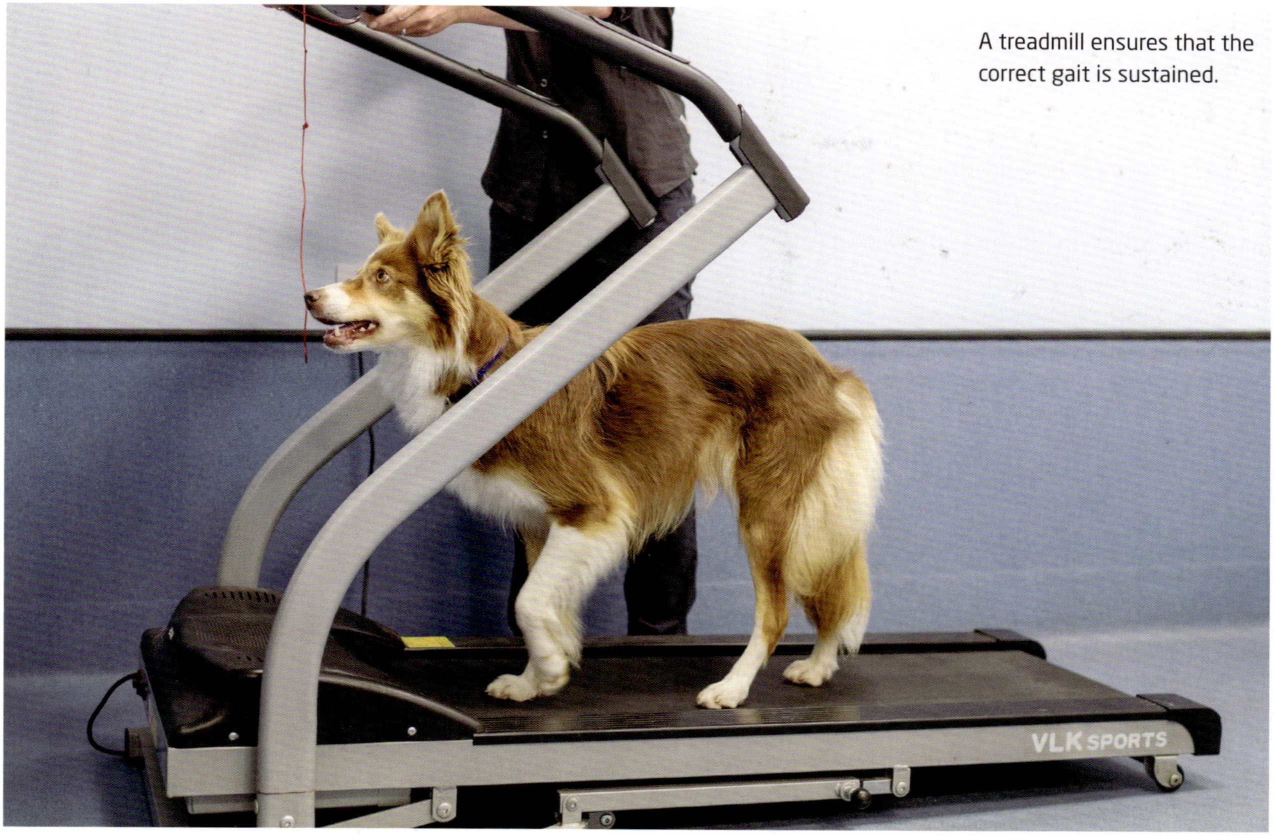

A treadmill ensures that the correct gait is sustained.

FRONT LEG LIFTS

A more advanced exercise recruiting the muscle groups underlying core stability and requiring strength and balance.

GOOD FOR

- Core stability and development of postural muscle strength.
- Promotion of Type I muscle fibres.
- Balance.
- Proprioception.
- Joint stability.

SUITABLE FOR

- Healthy, uninjured athletic dogs.
- Bitches after whelping (subsequent to 3-4 weeks of basic conditioning).
- Later stages of rehabilitation.

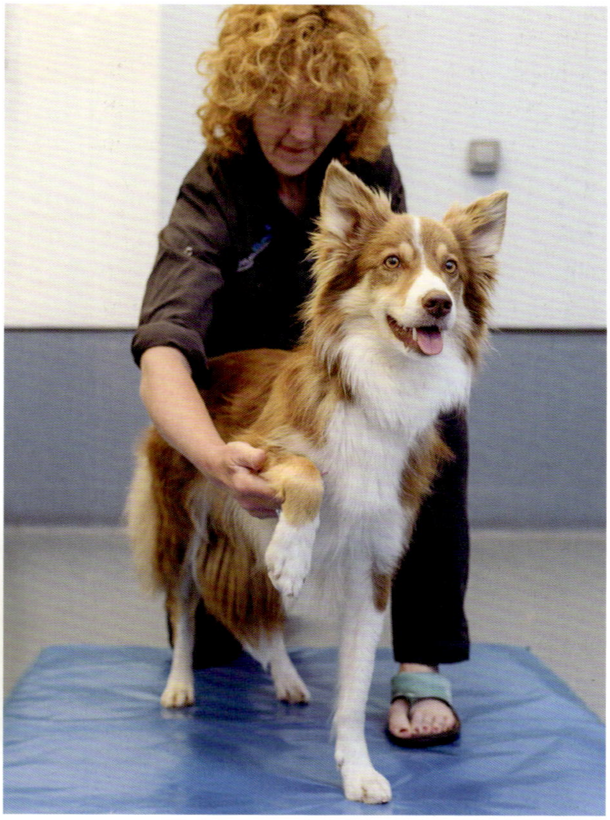

This exercise requires balance and strength.

HOW TO DO IT CORRECTLY

- Position the dog so he is standing square, and with straight nose to tail alignment.
- Lift one front paw off the ground and hold for up to 1 minute as the dog is able. Correct any changes in paw position, spinal alignment or posture throughout.
- Repeat with the other leg.

VARIANTS

- Diagonal standing with front limb and diagonal hindlimb raised.
- Front leg raise with standing limbs on a balance cushion.

PITFALLS

- Lifting the forelimb too high, or at an angle causing twisting of the trunk.
- Holding the position for longer than the dog is able to effectively maintain.
- Poor limb position and spinal alignment.
- The dog leans or braces.

STAIRS

Ascending and descending stairs are challenging exercises for the musculoskeletal and cardiovascular systems. They are also particularly challenging to injured joints. Ascending stairs may help to show up problems in the hindlegs whilst descending stairs is much more of a challenge in dogs with underlying shoulder and elbow pain, and any neck and back pain.

GOOD FOR

- Strength.
- Co-ordination.
- Stamina and endurance.
- Active range of joint movement.

SUITABLE FOR

- Dogs over 12 months.
- Conditioning.
- Dogs with no orthopaedic conditions.
- Healthy, uninjured athletic dogs.

HOW TO DO IT CORRECTLY

- The dog should start by slowly climbing the stairs, on-lead, in a controlled way, ensuring a reciprocal stepping gait.
- The stairs should have a low rise to start but, once mastered, the dog can progress to steeper stairs.

PITFALLS

- The dog bunny hops up or down stairs.
- The dog rushes, avoiding correct gait pattern.
- Injured dogs should have limited access to stairs whilst rehabilitating.

PLANK WALKING

Walking on a narrow plank challenges both balance and proprioception, and can assist with developing correct movement.

GOOD FOR

- Balance.
- Co-ordination.

SUITABLE FOR

- Young dogs.
- Later stage of rehabilitation.
- Bitches after whelping.

HOW TO DO IT CORRECTLY

- Place a plank, approximately 30 cm wide, on the ground and walk the dog slowly up and down.
- Once he has mastered the ability to walk over the plank on the ground, it can be raised slightly to further challenge balance.

PITFALLS

- Plank too narrow.
- Plank raised too quickly.

LADDER WALKING

Place a standard ladder flat on the ground and walk the dog up and down.

GOOD FOR

- Co-ordination.
- Proprioception.
- Improving co-ordination between all four legs.
- Improving flexion in the front and back legs.

SUITABLE FOR

- Young dogs.
- Later stage of rehabilitation.
- Bitches after whelping (2-3 weeks in to conditioning programme).

HOW TO DO IT CORRECTLY

- Place a standard ladder flat on the ground and then slowly lead the dog along.
- Repeat in both directions.

PITFALLS

- Rungs too close together for very large dogs.
- An inability to flex joint(s) sufficiently to clear the rungs.
- The dog tries to rush along.

SITTING AND GIVING PAW

This works for the core musculature, including the pelvic floor.

GOOD FOR

- Core control.
- Strengthening the pelvic floor.
- Strengthening the forelimb flexors.

SUITABLE FOR

- Young dogs.
- Dogs in training.
- Bitches after whelping.
- Rehabilitation.
- Geriatric dogs.

HOW TO DO IT CORRECTLY

- Place the dog in a square sit. This sounds easy but it can be difficult to achieve in young and injured dogs.
- Once the dog is comfortable in this position, gently lift a front paw and hold for a count of 10. A well-balanced dog with a strong core should place very little weight though the limb and it should be very light in your hand.
- Repeat with the other leg.

VARIANTS

- Once the dog is able to do this well, the forelimb can be lifted higher and stretched out further into a high 5 position. The dog should be able to give the limb freely rather than the handler pulling it into position.

PITFALLS

- The dog fails to sit square.
- The dog sits square but cannot maintain the position when his forelimb is lifted.

SIT TO STAND, STAND TO DOWN TRANSITIONS

This exercise teaches control through the core musculature and distal limbs.

GOOD FOR

- Strengthens the limbs.
- Improves joint range of motion.

SUITABLE FOR

- Young dogs.
- Bitches after whelping.
- Training.
- Later stages of rehabilitation.

HOW TO DO IT CORRECTLY

- Start with the dog in a square stand and ask him to move down into a sit.
- From a sit, ask him to push up (without stepping forward) into a standing position.
- Repeat with the stand to down manoeuvre.

PITFALLS

- The dog collapses into the down or sit position rather than controlling the movement.
- The dog preferentially uses one side more than the other.

PROGRESSION EXERCISES FOR THE YOUNG AGILITY DOG

Side stepping

- Ask the dog to step sideways with the hindlegs whilst the front legs remain relatively stationary.
- The dog should eventually be able to side step a full circle in either direction.

Pole work

- The distance between poles can be varied.
- The poles can be set at different angles or placed on different surfaces such as sand or grass.
- A toy can be placed at the end of the run of poles and the dog can be moved over them on a lead whist accelerating and decelerating.
- The dog can be taught to scope forward either into or out of the trotting poles.

These techniques are all fundamental skills required for jumping and speed changes later on in an agility dog's career.

Figure of eight

- This exercise can be progressed by increasing the tightness of the turn, and the speed at which it is carried out, with rapid changes of direction and size which provides the ground work for good flatwork handling.

Stops to start

- This teaches balance and body awareness at the difficult point in the gait, i.e. the transition. The dog should not slam to a stop and overshoot itself.
- Start slowly and build into a sprint.
- Eventually incorporate into flatwork and use to build on handling skills.

Backwards walking

- Improves body awareness and proprioception. The dog can also be taught to give a hind paw.

Poles can be placed at different angles.